DETERIORATION, THEY SAID—A Text for Cory Arcangel, Jessica Ciocci & Jacob Ciocci/Paper Rad, Shana Moutlon, Ryan Trecartin & Lizzie Fitch in the Form of an Alphabetic System which Got Hijacked for the Structure of this Book

Raphael Gygax[*]

The exhibition catalogue, entitled *DETERIORATION, THEY SAID*, unites the American artists Cory Arcangel, Jessica Ciocci & Jacob Ciocci/Paper Rad, Shana Moulton, and Ryan Trecartin & Lizzie Fitch. Each is presenting an individual project as part of the exhibition under the same title at the migros museum für gegenwartskunst. What these artists have in common is that they are members of a generation that grew up with the innovations in communications technology of the 1990s, such as the Internet, and this fact plays a significant role in their work. Yet they also represent a generation that came of age surrounded by the consequences of a largely globalized world: a sometimes frightening frenzy of commodity consumption and a flood of media images. If this situation can be summed up in the neo-liberal consumption maxim *MTV MADE US HARDCORE*, the positions presented by these artists would counter this maxim under the heading DETERIORATION. Their works realize an exaggerated and garishly colorful aesthetic, whose excessive density of signification reacts to this consumerism in Western society and, as it were, can take shape only by emerging out of this state of affairs. In the visual spaces they create, these four positions engage a culture of superabundance, framing their critique in a form of appropriation, and simultaneously unleashing a veritable flood of images. In the tradition of experimental film—and possibly drawing on the video aesthetics of the late 1980s and early 1990s—they examine unconventional patterns of possible narrative and the dissolution of images of identity. Shana Moulton and Ryan Trecartin frequently appear in their own video works. The overflow of visual material in these films also raises questions about the truth-content of such imagery or its deconstruction, and about the normalization of the viewer's taste and how to examine it. Many of the video works are shown in sculptural settings that amalgamate splinters of pop culture with handmade forms to create an "inter-media" work of art.

The following text will attempt to trace additional connections linking these four positions to one another without denying their autonomy. It is an "accident," reflecting in its holes and gaps the impossibility of stringent linear textual interrelations. It was appropriated by the graphic designer of the catalogue, Marie Lusa, and used as a structural element.[1] It aims to offer a meta-commentary, and simultaneously seeks to impart basic knowledge. It imitates methods of sampling of the sort employed in the works the exhibition presents.

* Studied art history, film and drama studies at the universities of Berne and Zurich and has been assistant curator of the migros museum für gegenwartskunst in Zurich since 2003. Ph. D. candidate. Previously curated exhibitions include Dawn Mellor (2008), Christoph Schlingensief (2007), Spartacus Chetwynd (2007), Gabriela Fridriksdóttir (2006) and Cory Arcangel (2005). He writes regularly for several art magazines.
1—Unless otherwise stated all the texts in the following pages are by Raphael Gygax.

Der Ausstellungskatalog bringt unter dem Titel DETERIORATION, THEY SAID die amerikanischen Künstler Cory Arcangel, Jessica Ciocci & Jacob Ciocci / Paper Rad, Shana Moulton sowie Ryan Trecartin & Lizzie Fitch zusammen, die in der gleichnamigen Ausstellung im migros museum für gegenwartskunst je ein Einzelprojekt präsentieren. Gemeinsam ist allen Kunstschaffenden, dass sie einer Generation angehören, die mit den kommunikationstechnologischen Errungenschaften der 1990er Jahre – wie beispielsweise dem Internet – aufwuchsen, was in ihren Arbeiten eine signifikante Rolle spielt. Die Künstler repräsentieren jedoch auch eine Generation, die im Zuge einer weitgehend globalisierten Welt mit einem ins Unheimliche kippenden Konsumrausch von Waren, aber ebenso mit einer Bilderflut der Medien gross wurden. Wenn dieser Sachverhalt unter der neoliberalen Konsummaxime MTV MADE US HARDCORE zusammengefasst werden könnte, dann würde diese Maxime den gezeigten Positionen mit dem Wort DETERIORATION[2] entgegentreten. In ihren Arbeiten kreieren diese Künstler allesamt eine übersteigerte, farbgeladene Ästhetik, die mit ihrer exzessiven Zeichendichte auf diesen Konsumzustand der westlichen Gesellschaft reagiert und sich gleichsam aus ihm heraus erst formulieren kann. Die vier Positionen befassen sich in ihren Bildräumen mit einer Kultur des Überschusses, formulieren ihre Kritik durch eine Form der Aneignung und lösen gleichzeitig eine wahre Bilderflut aus. In der Tradition des Experimentalfilms – in einer potenziellen Anknüpfung an die Videoästhetik der späten 1980er und frühen 1990er Jahre – werden mögliche, unkonventionelle Erzählmuster sowie die Auflösung von Identitätsbildern untersucht. In Shana Moultons und Ryan Trecartins Videoarbeiten treten die Künstler oftmals selber auf. Dabei stellen sich angesichts der überbordenden Bildwelt auch immer Fragen nach dem Wahrheitsgehalt heutiger Bildproduktion bzw. dessen Dekonstruktion sowie nach dem normierten Geschmack des Betrachters und dessen Überprüfung. Die Videoarbeiten werden dabei oftmals in skulpturalen Settings gezeigt, in welchen populärkulturelle Splitter mit handgefertigten Formen zu einem «intermedialen Gesamtkunstwerk» amalgamiert werden.

Der folgende Text versucht, diese vier Positionen weiter miteinander zu verbinden, ohne deren Autonomie aufzuheben. Der folgende Text ist ein «Unfall», er widerspiegelt die Unfähigkeit, stringent lineare Textzusammenhänge zu schaffen; er ist lückenhaft. Die Grafikerin des Katalogs, Marie Lusa, hat ihn sich angeeignet und als Struktur benutzt.[3] Er ist als Metakommentar und Basiswissen zugleich zu verstehen. Er imitiert Sampling-Methoden, die in den vorgestellten Arbeiten verwendet werden.

2—Zu Deutsch etwa: «Verderben», «Wertminderung», «Zerstörung», «Entartung», «Schädigung», «Verschleiss».
3—Sofern die Texte nicht anders gezeichnet sind, stammen sie von Raphael Gygax.

A — FOR ARCANGEL, CORY

Cory Arcangel works with what is allegedly obsolete. The resulting works know no media boundaries—whether they are video installations using antiquated personal computer game systems, videos in a low tech aesthetic, performances, homemade silkscreen prints, counterfeit websites, or computer software. (→ LOW TECH) (→ EXPERIMENTAL FILM / VIDEO) Looking at the body of works he has created over the past few years, we also notice that he likes to collaborate with musicians, programmers, and artists. Hence the programming ensemble Beige, which he founded with his former fellow students Paul B. Davis, Joe Beuckman, and Joe Bonn; or with Jessica Ciocci, Jacob Ciocci, and Ben Jones of Paper Rad. (→ PAPER RAD) (→ OUR OWN COMMUNITY) Beige's record *The 8-Bit Construction Set* (2000), which is composed using 8-bit computer and video game systems, was an international sensation. Arcangel built his reputation as a solo artist with his works based on the so-called 8-bit game systems, which revolutionized the entertainment market in the early 1980s. (→ JUNK-STORE AESTHETICS) For these works, he hacked into game modules and then modified and disfigured them, short-circuiting their narratives.

For his video installation *a couple thousand short films about Glenn Gould* (2007), the artist began from two opposing points of departure, which he correlated. On the one hand is Johann Sebastian Bach's *Goldberg Variations* (1741), a technically demanding work for the piano that is nowadays part of any concert pianist's standard repertoire; on the other hand, innumerable YouTube videos show amateur musicians performing on their instruments. (→ YOUTUBE) Arcangel rearranged the first variation of the *Goldberg Variations*, (audio)visualizing the composition on the basis of YouTube videos he re-cut. Arcangel's version employs one video for every note. (→ D(O)I(T) Y(OURSELF) AND BRICOLAGE) The double projection—representing the violin and bass clef—thus becomes a hysterical kaleidoscope of the most diverse musical instruments and practices, inundating the viewer's brain with visual stimuli in the tradition of the Flicker experimental film. The title's reference to the Canadian pianist Glenn Gould (1932–1982) is a double-entendre: Gould is one of the best-known and also one of the most controversial interpreters of the *Goldberg Variations*, because he sometimes hummed along in a low voice while recording. Yet Gould is also controversial because he always used the most up-to-date technology, such as tape editing, and later on digital recording technology, calling the classical idea of the musical performance into question. In the world of classical music, playing a piece straight through with perfect technique is still considered the gold standard. Arcangel takes up the Gouldian tradition, reflecting on the one hand on the history of digitalization and the use of technology in phonic production, and on the other about the conditions and possibilities of contemporary music.

Cory Arcangel arbeitet mit dem vermeintlich Obsoleten. Seine daraus entstandenen Werke kennen keine medialen Grenzen: seien es Videoinstallationen mit veralteten Heimcomputer-Spielsystemen, Videos mit einer Low-Tech-Ästhetik, Performances, selbst hergestellte Siebdrucke, gefälschte Internetseiten oder Computer-programme. (→ LOW TECH) (→ EXPERIMENTAL FILM / VIDEO) Bei Betrachtung des Werkkörpers, der sich in den letzten Jahren gebildet hat, lässt sich auch seine Bereitschaft zur Kooperation mit Musikern, Programmierern und Künstlern feststellen. Beispielsweise mit seinem Label Beige, welches er mit seinen ehemaligen Studienkollegen Paul B. Davis, Joe Beuckman und Joe Bonn gründete, oder auch mit Jessica Ciocci, Jacob Ciocci und Ben Jones von Paper Rad. (→ PAPER RAD) (→ OUR OWN COMMUNITY) Beige erregte mit ihrer Platte *The 8-Bit Construction Set* (2000), die nur aus Samples von 8-Bit-Computern und -Spielkonsolen besteht, international Aufsehen. Als Einzelkünstler wurde Arcangel durch seine Arbeiten mit sogenannten 8-Bit-Spielsystemen bekannt, die zu Beginn der 1980er Jahre den Unterhaltungsmarkt revolutionierten. (→ JUNK-STORE AESTHETICS) Für diese hackte er jeweils Spielmodule, um sie anschliessend zu modifizieren, zu verfremden und sie narrativ kurzzuschliessen.

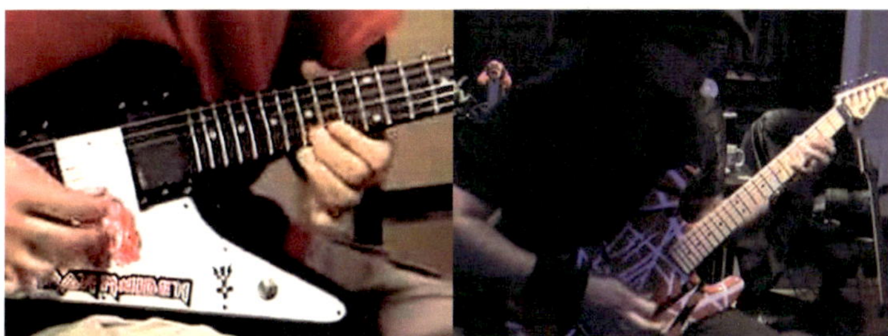

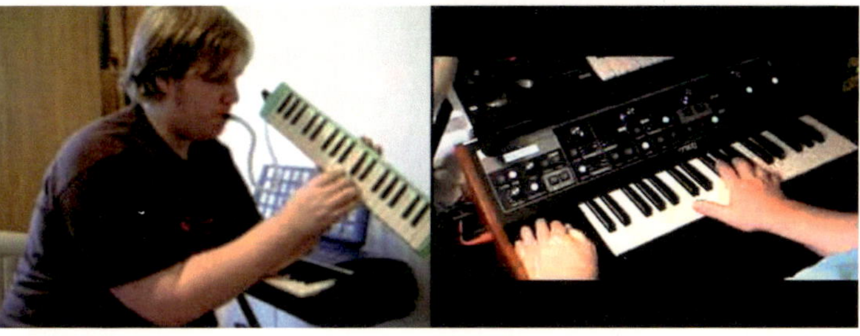

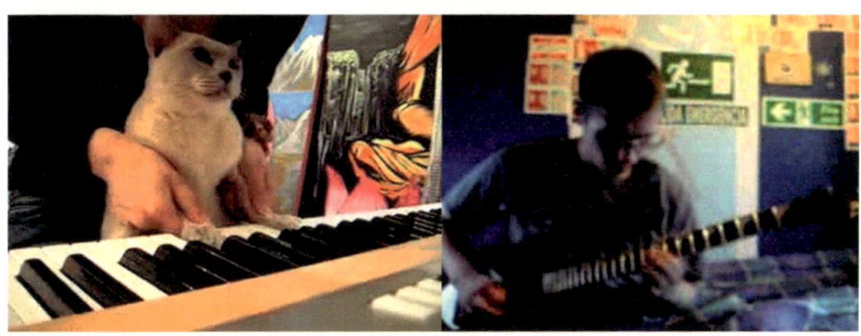

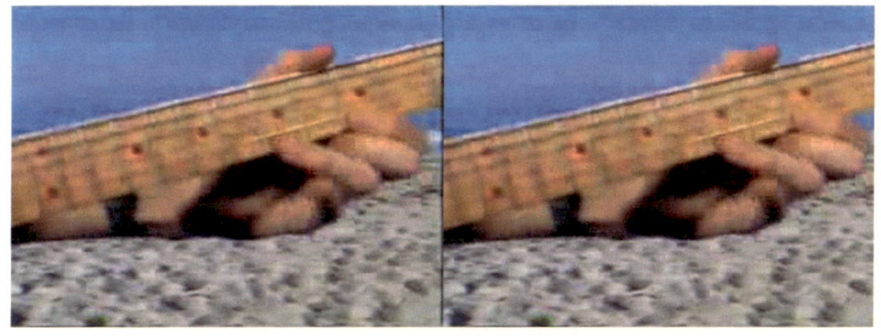

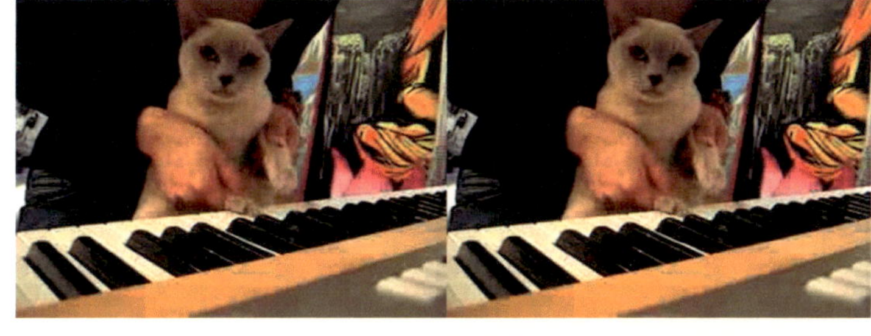

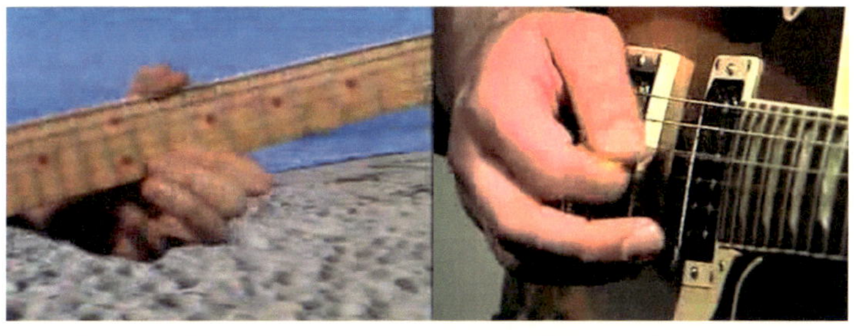

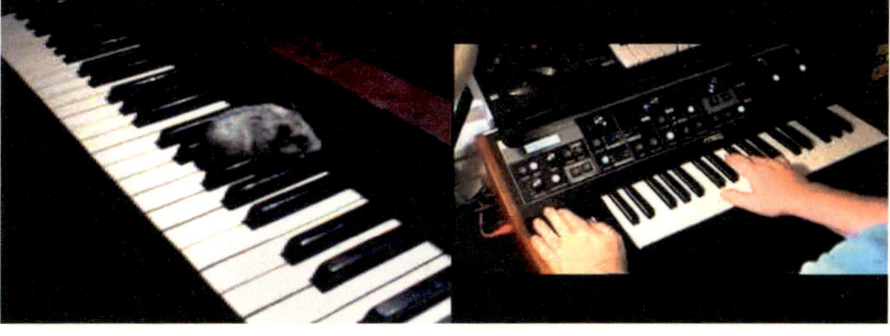

Für die Videoinstallation *a couple thousand short films about Glenn Gould* (2007) benutzte der Künstler zwei sich konträr verhaltende Ausgangspunkte, die er miteinander korrelieren liess. Einerseits handelt es sich um die *Goldberg-Variationen* von Johann Sebastian Bach aus dem Jahr 1741 – ein technisch anspruchsvolles Klavierwerk, welches heute zum Standardrepertoire eines jeden Konzertpianisten zählt –, andererseits das Phänomen der unzähligen YouTube-Videos, die Amateurmusiker beim Spielen zeigen. (→ YOUTUBE) Arcangel arrangierte den ersten Satz der *Goldberg-Variationen* neu und (audio)visualisierte die Komposition anhand von YouTube-Videos, die er neu schnitt. In Arcangels Version wird pro Note jeweils ein Video eingesetzt. (→ D(O)I(T)Y(OURSELF) AND BRICOLAGE) Die Doppelprojektion – stellvertretend für die Akkolade beim Klavier – wird so zu einem hysterischen Kaleidoskop verschiedenster Musikinstrumente und -praktiken, die in der Tradition eines Flicker-Experimentalfilms das Hirn einer visuellen Reizüberflutung aussetzen. Die Titelreferenz zum kanadischen Pianisten Glenn Gould (1932–1982) trägt eine Doppeldeutigkeit in sich: Einerseits gilt Gould als einer der bekanntesten und gleichzeitig umstrittensten Interpreten der *Goldberg-Variationen*, da er stellenweise bei den Aufnahmen leise, aber hörbar mitsummte. Umstritten ist Gould auch, weil er sich immer der aktuellsten Technologien wie des Zusammenschneidens bediente, später auch digitale Aufnahmetechniken nutzte und somit die klassische Bedeutung der musikalischen Performance in Frage stellte. Gerade das handwerklich perfekte Durchspielen eines Stücks gilt auch heute in der klassischen Musikszene noch immer als unantastbares Gebot. Arcangel stellt sich mit dieser Arbeit in die Tradition Goulds und reflektiert einerseits die Geschichte der Digitalisierung und den Einsatz von Technologie für die Tonproduktion – andererseits die Bedingungen und Möglichkeiten zeitgenössischer Musik.

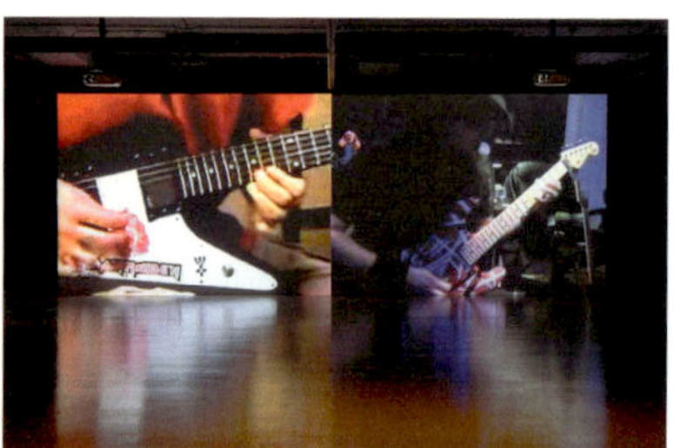

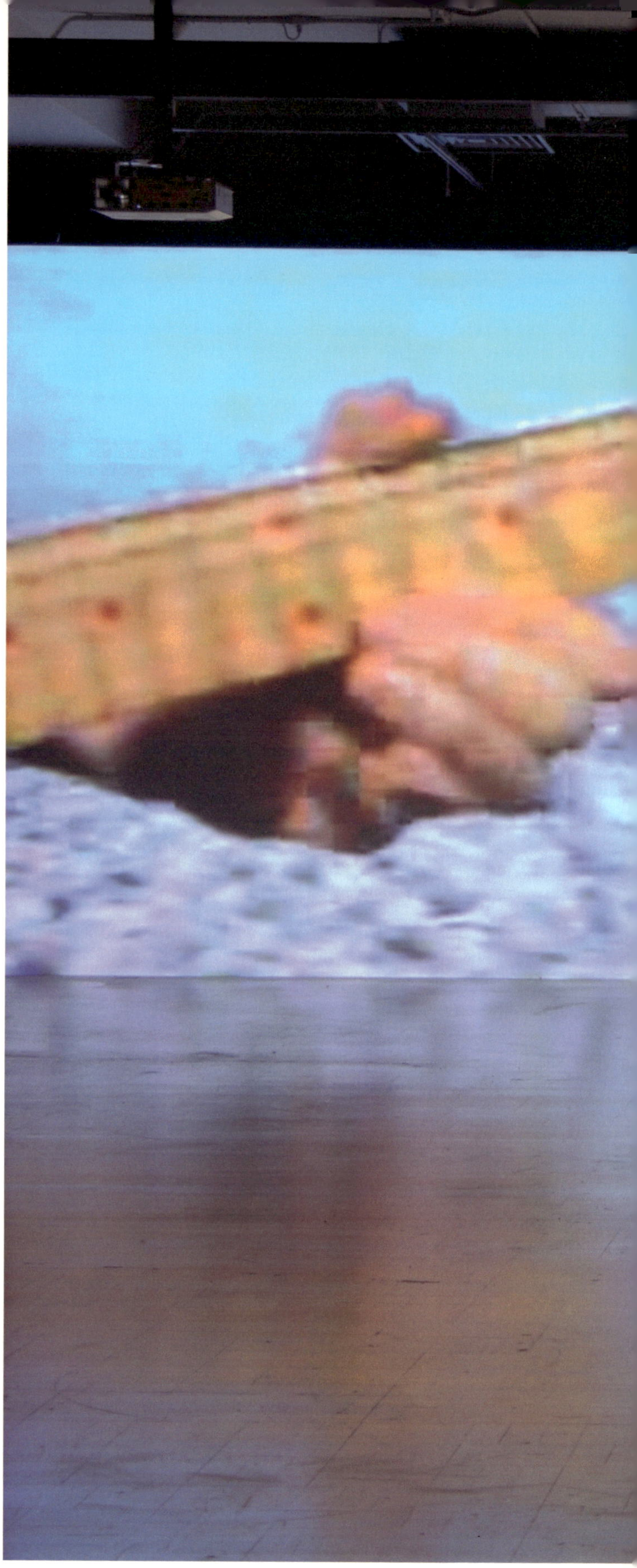

CORY ARCANGEL Born 1978 in Buffalo, New York; Lives and works in New York EDUCATION 2000 Bachelor of Music, Oberlin Conservatory, Oberlin SOLO EXHIBITIONS (SELECTION SINCE 2004) — 2010 Museum of Contemporary Art, Miami — 2009 University of Michigan Museum of Art; Montevideo – The Netherlands Institute for Media Art, Amsterdam — 2008 Adult Contemporary, Team Gallery, New York; Galerie Thaddaeus Ropac, Salzburg — 2007 Northern Gallery for Contemporary Art, Sunderland/Spacex, Exeter/Castlefield Gallery, Manchester; *Request for Comments*, Max Wigram Gallery, London; *Get back to me in a couple of years*, Brändström & Stene, Stockholm; Galerie Guy Bärtschi, Geneva — 2006 *subtractions, modifications, addenda, and other recent; contributions to participatory culture*, Team Gallery, New York; *contributions to participatory culture*, Galerie Thaddaeus Ropac, Paris, France, Don't Touch My Computer — 2005 *Nerdzone Version 1*, migros museum für gegenwartskunst, Zürich; *disassembling 48k*, Gallery Brändström & Stene, Stockholm; *Super Mario Movie*, Deitch Projects (in collaboration with Paper Rad); *welcome to my homepage artshow!!!*, Team Gallery, New York — 2004 *Fact*, Liverpool GROUP EXHIBITIONS (SELECTION SINCE 2001) — 2009 *Art and Pop Music*, Kunsthaus Graz; *Younger than Jesus*, New Museum, New York; *First Stop*, Nam June Paik Art Center, Yongin/Seoul — 2008 *The Possibility of An Island*, Museum of Contemporary Art, Miami; *Close Encounters– Facing the Future*, American University Museum, Washington D.C.; *Sound of Art*, Museum der Moderne, Salzburg; *Color Chart*, Museum of Modern Art, New York; *Peer to Peer*, Casino Luxembourg — 2007 *Automatic Update*, Museum of Modern Art, New York; *Speed 3*, Instituto Valenciano de Arte Moderno — 2006 *Experiments in Pop*, Zentrum Paul Klee, Berne; *Time Frame*, P.S. 1, New York; *Action*, FRAC PACA, Marseille; *Outside the Box: New Cinematic Experiences*, University of Akron — 2005 *Moving Pictures*, Dallas Center for Contemporary Art; *Greater New York*, P.S.1, New York — 2004 *Expander*, Royal Academy of Art, London; Liverpool Biennial; *Pattern Playback*, Moore Space, Miami; *Whitney Biennial*, Whitney Museum of American Art, New York; *Seeing Double: Emulation in Theory and Practice*, Guggenheim Museum, New York — 2003 *Killer Instinct*, New Museum of Contemporary Art, New York; *Blinky*, Foxy Productions, Brooklyn — 2002 <ALT> Digital Media, American Museum of the Moving Image, New York; *Unknown Pleasures*, Daniel Reich Gallery, New York — 2001 *Interface: Exploring Possibilities*, Fassbender Gallery, Chicago; Numerous screenings, performances and lectures worldwide.

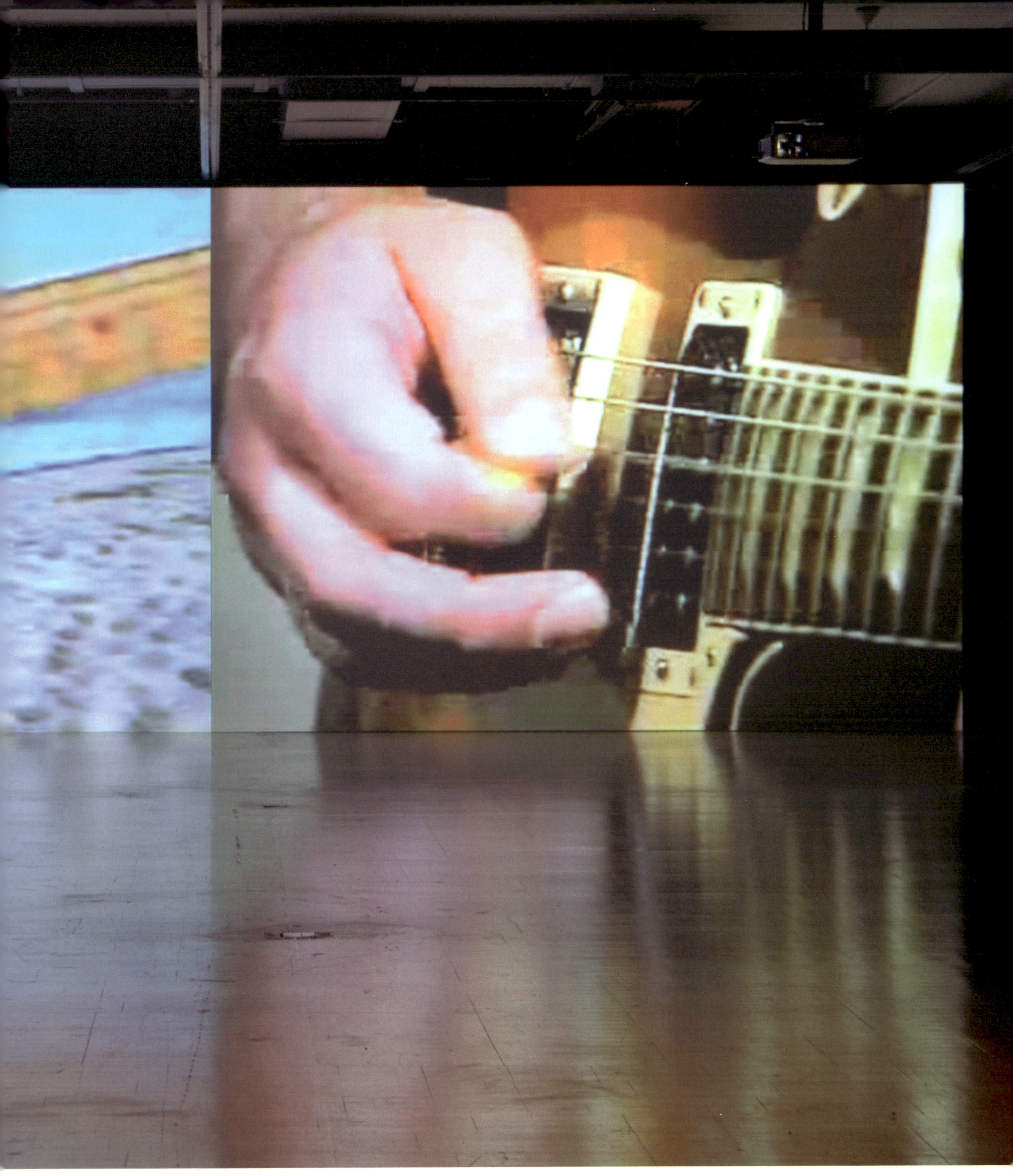

Cory Arcangel
*a couple thousand short films
about Glenn Gould*
2007

On C is a short PDf that explains why JPEGs look the way they do. These kinda documents are quite common around the Internet (its seems many CS departments require students to make them) so this was really an exercise in understanding it myself. *On C* is reprinted here exactly as it appeared originally in *a couple thousand short films by Glenn Gould* a Film and Video Umbrella commissioned book based on a text by Paul Morley, written in relation to a project of the same name by Cory Arcangel, edited by Steven Bode, and arranged by Dexter Sinister.

¬ Cory Arcangel

ON COMPRESSION

Cory Arcangel
2k7 – 2k8

ABSTRACT: JPEGs look the way they do because of quantization and their use of the Discrete Cosine Transform (DCT). The DCT is a technique for converting a signal into elementary frequency components. It is widely used in image compression. Here we will go through some examples to explain how the DCT works. The text is kind of a summary, and if you want to bring the noise, all the math is in the end notes.

1. LOSSY VS. LOSSLESS

The whole point of digital image compression is to be able to reconstruct an image without having to send all the data. This is because data, especially in large amounts, is expensive and slow to transport. Either over cable lines, phone lines, or wirelessly, it is all slow. To this day, the most efficient and cheapest way to transport large amounts of data is by mailing a hard-drive to the destination, and I don't mean emailing, I mean the kind of mailing that involves the post office. So compression is valuable because the less we need to send the cheaper and faster it is. There are two kinds of compression. One is called Lossy, and the other is called Lossless. Lossless compression does not lose any information from the original source. How can this be? Well, let's say we wanted to send this: 'a a a a a a a a a b a' and we were going to send it over the phone by voice. As opposed to having to send all the information by reading out each letter one at a time, we could just tell someone '9a's, one b, and one a' and they would know we meant 'a a a a a a a a a b a' and we have saved ourselves a bit of breath. In computer language it means we have stored all the information using less space. To generalize a bit, if you have ever opened a 'zip' file, your computer has seen '9a's, one b, and one a' and translated it to 'a a a a a a a a a b a'. This is Lossless compression. On the other hand, Lossy compression actually loses data. Lossy compression, therefore, can not be used for text, or any application where all the information must remain intact. It is used for images, music, and video. This is because, believe it or not, our eyes and ears are pretty crap, and we don't usually notice missing bits here and there. Lossy compression works by getting rid of the information which isn't so important to us. To generalize a bit again, if we tried to send 'a a a a a a a a a b a' using Lossy compression over the phone, we would just get lazy and say '11a's'. In this article, we are going to focus on the Discrete Cosine Transform, aka the DCT, a math formula used in Lossy compression. The reason I'm interested in this Transform is because, when used with quantization, it is what gives JPEGs that 'JPEG look'. By 'JPEG look' I mean those crappy compressed blocky images you need to squint your eyes to understand that are all over the internet. And in case you haven't noticed, this look is everywhere else as well (ads, digital cameras, digital video, etc.) If the '80s gave us 'hot' colors and 'rad' graphics, and the '90s gave us slick vector design, then

the 00's are giving us compressed blocky images.

JPEGs are everywhere today because they have become a standard, or a universally agreed upon set of rules. Today JPEG is a nickname for a file type, but JPEG originated as a shorthand for the group that proposed the standard, the Joint Photographic Experts Group. This standard was created in Geneva in 1992 when members of the CCITT and the ISO/IEC (now together known as JPEG) got together in Geneva and released the technical document ISO/IEC IS 10918-1 / ITU-T Recommendation T.81. This paper recommended 'REQUIREMENTS AND GUIDELINES' of the 'DIGITAL COMPRESSION AND CODING OF CONTINUOUS-TONE STILL IMAGES'. These guidelines, through third party development, eventually became known as JPEG files.

2. THE GUY BEHIND THE GUY BEHIND THE GUY

As mentioned earlier, the heart of JPEG is the DCT formula, and the DCT relies on cosines. The easiest way to think of cosines is to imagine yourself walking counterclockwise around a circle. This circle is centered on the X and Y axis, and has a radius of 1. Radius is the length from the center of the circle to the edge. A cosine of the angle in respect to the positive horizontal axis (aka, the length in our case because we are on a unit circle (radius = 1)) is our position on the x axis as we walk around the circle if we started at X = 1. We must also remember that the length around a circle with a radius of 1 is 2pi. So, cos(0) is 1, because we haven't gone anywhere; we are still standing at the beginning, at X = 1, cos(pi) is -1, because we have travelled halfway around the circle to X = -1, and cos(2pi) is 1, because since we have travelled all the way around our circle, we have ended up back at the beginning (Figure 1). It is this cyclical pattern which is useful in compression (Figure 2). To see the DCT in action we will start with the 1D DCT (Figure 3) formula and use it to compress the input 3,2,1 (Figure 4). DCT-based compression has four steps. First the DCT formula creates basis functions, then it compares the input data to those basis functions, creating what are called DCT coefficients, then those coefficients are quantized, and the last step is decompression, where all this is done in reverse to recreate our data. The first step of our process can be seen in Figure 5.[1] These are the basis functions for our input, which

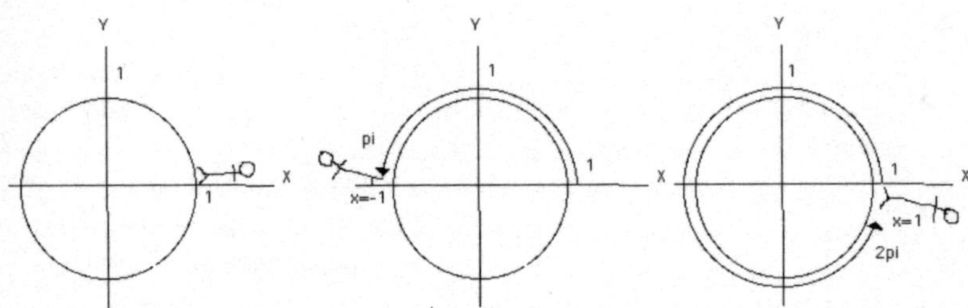

Figure 1: cosine of 0, pi, and 2pi

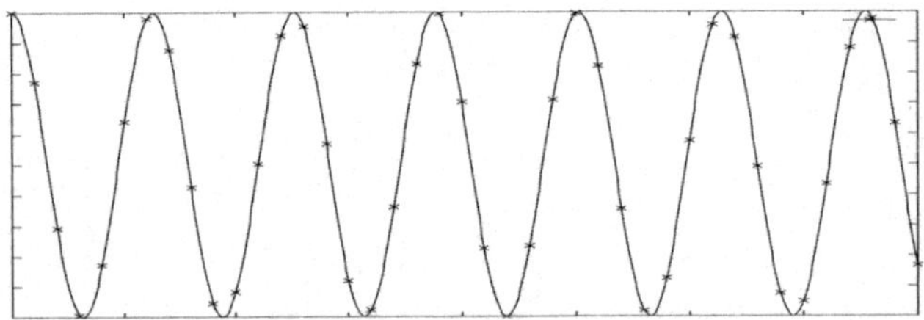

Figure 2: Cosine curve of x = 0 to 40

consist of cosine curves of increasing frequency. They can be thought
of as building blocks. Every combination of 3 digits can be recreated
by adding these blocks together in different proportions. The second
step in the process is comparing our input to our three basis functions
to generate three DCT coefficients. Our DCT coefficients represent how
much of each basis function is present in our input. In our example, our
three DCT coefficients generated by the 1D DTC are 3.46410, 1.41421,

$$F(u) = \sum_{x=0}^{N-1} w(i)f[x]\cos\frac{(2x+1)u\pi}{2N}$$

if i = 0, $w = \sqrt{1/N}$, and if i ≠ 0, w = $\sqrt{2/N}$

Figure 3: 1D DCT formula. w(i) is a weighting factor fyi

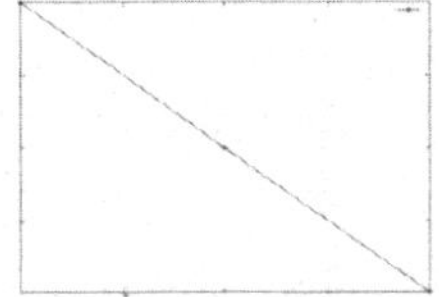

Figure 4: Our 1D DCT example input

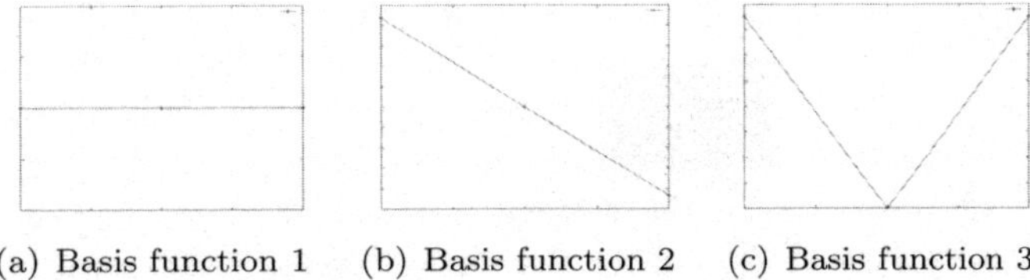

(a) Basis function 1   (b) Basis function 2   (c) Basis function 3

Figure 5: Basis Functions for a DCT of length 3

and 0.[2] From these values we can see that our input contains elements of our first and second basis function, but none of the third. This should make sense since our input numbers are a straight line, so they do not contain any data which is similar to the curve in the third basis function. If our DCT formula in this example takes in 3 digits as input and we end up with 3 digits as output, how does this help us save space? The third step, quantization, is the key to this question. Quantization is basically a way to discard DCT coefficients. In this case we would discard our third DCT coefficient because it doesn't help us describe our input. So when we get to the last step in the process which is reversing all of this in order to reconstruct our original input, we will use only 2 DCT coefficients to do this.[3] The same information now takes only two-thirds of the space!

3. 2D

To work on an image as opposed to a string of input, we need to use the 2D DCT formula (Figure 6). This is basically the same as the 1D formula, except it works on a matrix. The input we'll compress in this example is in Figure 7. So again our first step is generating the

$$F(u,v) = \sum_{x=0}^{N-1} \sum_{y=0}^{N-1} w(i,j) f[x,y] \cos\frac{(2x+1)u\pi}{2N} \cos\frac{(2y+1)u\pi}{2N}$$

if i or j $= 0$, $w = \sqrt{1/N}$, and if i or j $\neq 0$, w $= \sqrt{2/N}$

Figure 6: 2D DCT formula

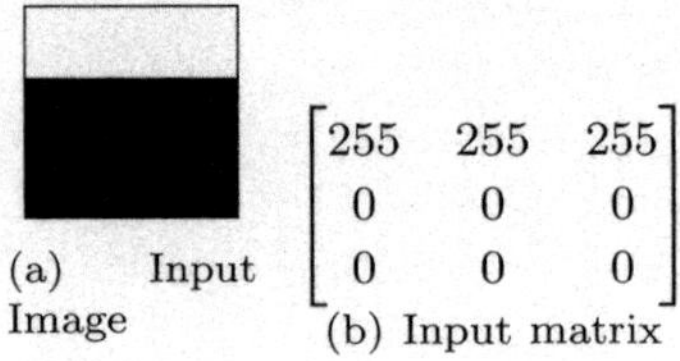

(a)   Input Image

$$\begin{bmatrix} 255 & 255 & 255 \\ 0 & 0 & 0 \\ 0 & 0 & 0 \end{bmatrix}$$

(b) Input matrix

Figure 7: Our input matrix

basis functions (Figure 8).[4] As in Figure 8, our basis functions with the lower cosine frequencies are on the top left and the basis functions with the higher cosine frequencies are on the bottom right. Next, we compare our input image to our basis functions to generate our DCT coefficients. Then, we're left with 9 DCT coefficients (Figure 9).[5] These numbers tell us our input only contains three of our nine basis functions, and one can see the graphic similarities between the basis functions on the left side of Figure 8, and our input in Figure 7. All the other basis functions do not relate. The third step is quantization. This happens by taking the DCT coefficient matrix (Figure 9) and dividing it by a quantization matrix, then rounding to the nearest integer. An example matrix is used in Figure 10. The result, when reversed (Figure 11), gets rid of one of our DCT coefficients. If we complete step four by using the quantized coefficients to reconstruct our input, we clearly have quite a big difference (Figure 12).[6] Where did that grey bar come from? EXACTLY!! We have saved a ton of space, because now we only need to transmit '250, 250, and 7 0s' to recreate our input, but our image no longer looks how it was supposed to! This is because we have discarded the high frequency basis functions, so we can no longer create sharp contrasts. But it's similar, we get the idea, and this is probably good enough.

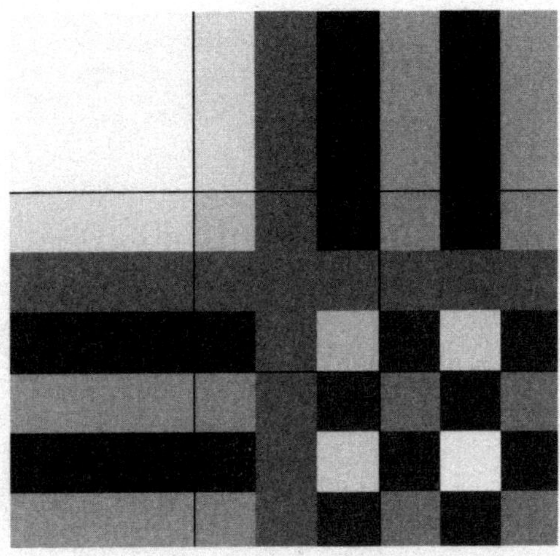

Figure 8: The 9 DCT basis functions for a 3 by 3 matrix

$$\begin{bmatrix} 255.00000 & 0 & 0 \\ 312.30994 & 0 & 0 \\ 180.31223 & 0 & 0 \end{bmatrix}$$

Figure 9: Our 9 DCT coefficients

$$\begin{bmatrix} 255.00000 & 0 & 0 \\ 312.30994 & 0 & 0 \\ 180.31223 & 0 & 0 \end{bmatrix} / \begin{bmatrix} 10 & 50 & 400 \\ 50 & 50 & 400 \\ 400 & 400 & 400 \end{bmatrix} = \begin{bmatrix} 25 & 0 & 0 \\ 6 & 0 & 0 \\ 0 & 0 & 0 \end{bmatrix}$$

Figure 10: Quantization table

$$
\begin{bmatrix} 25 & 0 & 0 \\ 6 & 0 & 0 \\ 0 & 0 & 0 \end{bmatrix} * \begin{bmatrix} 10 & 50 & 400 \\ 50 & 50 & 400 \\ 400 & 400 & 400 \end{bmatrix} = \begin{bmatrix} 250 & 0 & 0 \\ 250 & 0 & 0 \\ 0 & 0 & 0 \end{bmatrix}
$$

Figure 11: Reverse Quantization

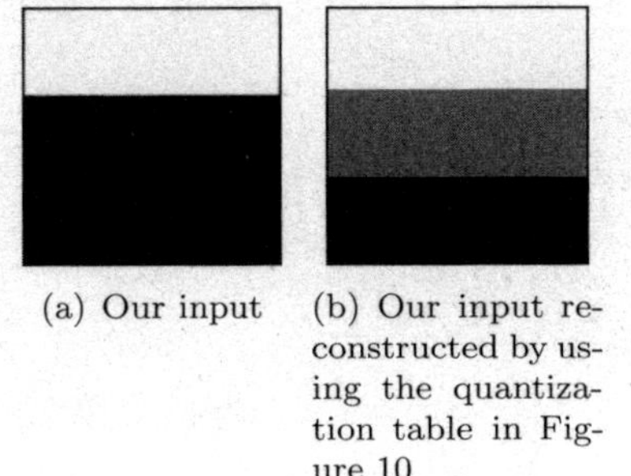

(a) Our input   (b) Our input reconstructed by using the quantization table in Figure 10

Figure 12: Reconstructing our input for our 2D 3 x 3 matrix

4. THE JOINT PHOTOGRAPHIC EXPERTS

The only difference between what we just did and a JPEG, is that a JPEG always splits the image into 8 x 8 blocks and then these 8 x 8 blocks are run through the 2D DCT. 8 x 8 blocks are used because they are small enough to have consistent spatial qualities. Even at high rates of compression, we can still make out the original image. The basis functions for a JPEG are shown in Figure 13. Also, JPEGs don't specify what quantization matrix is used. Photoshop's quantization matrix is different from Canon, etc. etc., so actually one has very little control of the discarded information. Awesome. In Figure 14 and Figure 15 we can see a sample JPEG compressed with a sample quantization matrix. Take a close look — we are recreating the image only using the top left basis function of Figure 13. Hopefully you can see now that heavily compressed JPEGs are really a bunch of 8 by 8 squares composed of only the first few low frequency basis functions of an 8 x 8 2D DCT (Figure 13). We get a 90 percent reduction in file size because we only need to send a few DCT coefficients down the line, but we get an image which is only a shadow of its former self. Welcome to the future.

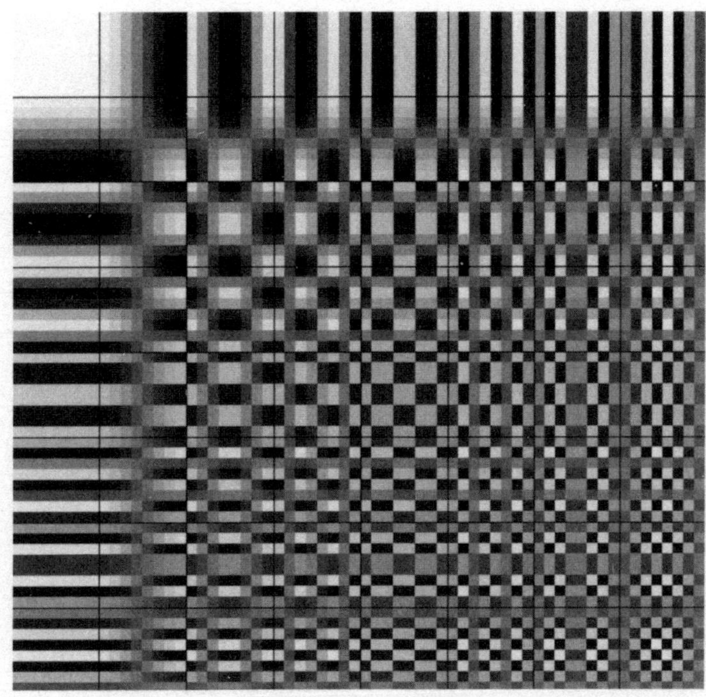

Figure 13: Our Basis functions for a JPEG

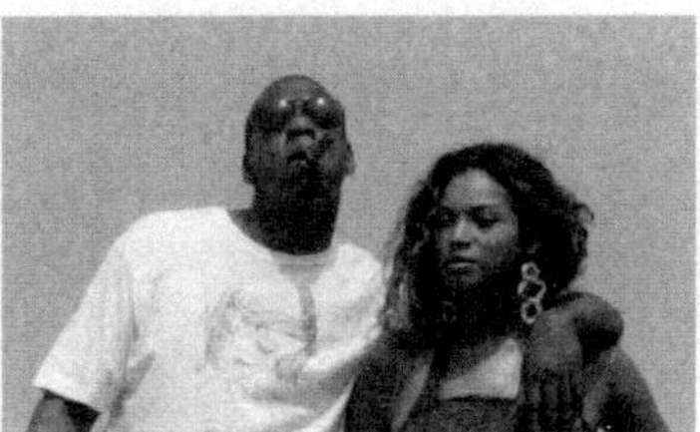

Figure 14: Our JPEG input

$$\begin{bmatrix} 51 & 101 & 151 & 201 & 251 & 301 & 351 & 401 \\ 101 & 151 & 201 & 251 & 301 & 351 & 401 & 451 \\ 151 & 201 & 251 & 301 & 351 & 401 & 451 & 501 \\ 201 & 251 & 301 & 351 & 401 & 451 & 501 & 551 \\ 251 & 301 & 351 & 401 & 451 & 501 & 551 & 601 \\ 301 & 351 & 401 & 451 & 501 & 551 & 601 & 651 \\ 351 & 401 & 451 & 501 & 551 & 601 & 651 & 701 \\ 401 & 451 & 501 & 551 & 601 & 651 & 701 & 751 \end{bmatrix}$$

Figure 15: Our JPEG quantization table

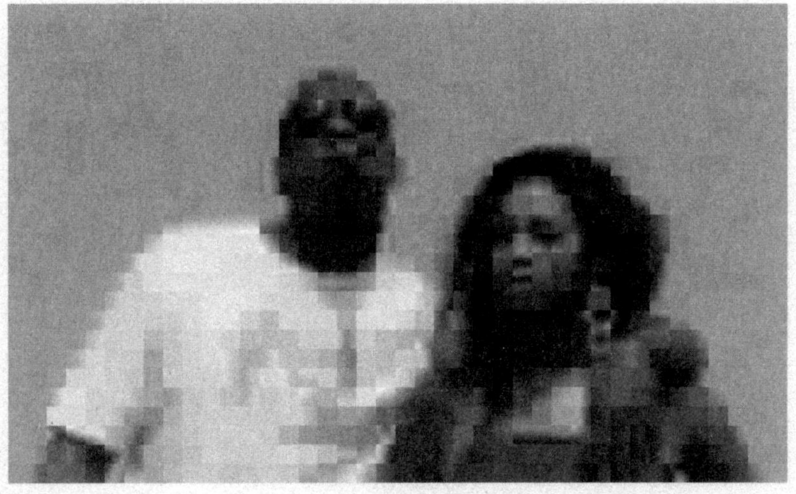

Figure 16: Our compressed JPEG using the above input and
quantization table (Figure 14 and 15)

NOTES

[1]
$$\begin{bmatrix} \cos\dfrac{(2*0+1)0\pi}{2*3} & \cos\dfrac{(2*1+1)0\pi}{2*3} & \cos\dfrac{(2*2+1)0\pi}{2*3} \end{bmatrix} = \begin{bmatrix} 1 & 1 & 1 \end{bmatrix}$$

$$\begin{bmatrix} \cos\dfrac{(2*0+1)1\pi}{2*3} & \cos\dfrac{(2*1+1)1\pi}{2*3} & \cos\dfrac{(2*2+1)1\pi}{2*3} \end{bmatrix} = \begin{bmatrix} .86603 & 6.1232e-17 & -.86603 \end{bmatrix}$$

$$\begin{bmatrix} \cos\dfrac{(2*0+1)2\pi}{2*3} & \cos\dfrac{(2*1+1)2\pi}{2*3} & \cos\dfrac{(2*2+1)2\pi}{2*3} \end{bmatrix} = \begin{bmatrix} .5 & -1 & .5 \end{bmatrix}$$

[2]
$$3.46410 = \sum_{x=0}^{2} \sqrt{1/3} * \begin{bmatrix} 3 & 2 & 1 \end{bmatrix} * \begin{bmatrix} 1 & 1 & 1 \end{bmatrix}$$

$$1.41421 = \sum_{x=0}^{2} \sqrt{2/3} * \begin{bmatrix} 3 & 2 & 1 \end{bmatrix} * \begin{bmatrix} .86603 & 6.1232e-17 & -.86603 \end{bmatrix}$$

$$0.00000 = \sum_{x=0}^{2} \sqrt{2/3} * \begin{bmatrix} 3 & 2 & 1 \end{bmatrix} * \begin{bmatrix} .5 & -1 & .5 \end{bmatrix}$$

FYI: $\;3.46410 = (\sqrt{1/3} * 3 * 1) + (\sqrt{1/3} * 2 * 1) + (\sqrt{1/3} * 1 * 1)$

[3]
$$\sqrt{1/3}*\begin{bmatrix} 1 & 1 & 1 \end{bmatrix}*3.46410+\sqrt{2/3}*\begin{bmatrix} .86603 & 6.1232e-17 & -.86603 \end{bmatrix}*1.41421 =$$
$$\begin{bmatrix} 3 & 2 & 1 \end{bmatrix}$$

[4]
$$\begin{bmatrix} \cos\frac{(2*0+1)0\pi}{2*3}*\cos\frac{(2*0+1)0\pi}{2*3} & \cos\frac{(2*0+1)0\pi}{2*3}*\cos\frac{(2*1+1)0\pi}{2*3} & \cos\frac{(2*0+1)0\pi}{2*3}*\cos\frac{(2*2+1)0\pi}{2*3} \\ \cos\frac{(2*1+1)0\pi}{2*3}*\cos\frac{(2*0+1)0\pi}{2*3} & \cos\frac{(2*1+1)0\pi}{2*3}*\cos\frac{(2*1+1)0\pi}{2*3} & \cos\frac{(2*1+1)0\pi}{2*3}*\cos\frac{(2*2+1)0\pi}{2*3} \\ \cos\frac{(2*2+1)0\pi}{2*3}*\cos\frac{(2*0+1)0\pi}{2*3} & \cos\frac{(2*2+1)0\pi}{2*3}*\cos\frac{(2*1+1)0\pi}{2*3} & \cos\frac{(2*2+1)0\pi}{2*3}*\cos\frac{(2*2+1)0\pi}{2*3} \end{bmatrix}$$

$$\begin{bmatrix} 1 & 1 & 1 \\ 1 & 1 & 1 \\ 1 & 1 & 1 \end{bmatrix}$$

$$\begin{bmatrix} \cos\frac{(2*0+1)0\pi}{2*3}*\cos\frac{(2*0+1)1\pi}{2*3} & \cos\frac{(2*0+1)0\pi}{2*3}*\cos\frac{(2*1+1)1\pi}{2*3} & \cos\frac{(2*0+1)0\pi}{2*3}*\cos\frac{(2*2+1)1\pi}{2*3} \\ \cos\frac{(2*1+1)0\pi}{2*3}*\cos\frac{(2*0+1)1\pi}{2*3} & \cos\frac{(2*1+1)0\pi}{2*3}*\cos\frac{(2*1+1)1\pi}{2*3} & \cos\frac{(2*1+1)0\pi}{2*3}*\cos\frac{(2*2+1)1\pi}{2*3} \\ \cos\frac{(2*2+1)0\pi}{2*3}*\cos\frac{(2*0+1)1\pi}{2*3} & \cos\frac{(2*2+1)0\pi}{2*3}*\cos\frac{(2*1+1)1\pi}{2*3} & \cos\frac{(2*2+1)0\pi}{2*3}*\cos\frac{(2*2+1)1\pi}{2*3} \end{bmatrix} =$$

$$\begin{bmatrix} .86603 & 6.1232e-17 & -.86603 \\ .86603 & 6.1232e-17 & -.86603 \\ .86603 & 6.1232e-17 & -.86603 \end{bmatrix}$$

$$\begin{bmatrix} \cos\frac{(2*0+1)0\pi}{2*3}*\cos\frac{(2*0+1)2\pi}{2*3} & \cos\frac{(2*0+1)0\pi}{2*3}*\cos\frac{(2*1+1)2\pi}{2*3} & \cos\frac{(2*0+1)0\pi}{2*3}*\cos\frac{(2*2+1)2\pi}{2*3} \\ \cos\frac{(2*1+1)0\pi}{2*3}*\cos\frac{(2*0+1)2\pi}{2*3} & \cos\frac{(2*1+1)0\pi}{2*3}*\cos\frac{(2*1+1)2\pi}{2*3} & \cos\frac{(2*1+1)0\pi}{2*3}*\cos\frac{(2*2+1)2\pi}{2*3} \\ \cos\frac{(2*2+1)0\pi}{2*3}*\cos\frac{(2*0+1)2\pi}{2*3} & \cos\frac{(2*2+1)0\pi}{2*3}*\cos\frac{(2*1+1)2\pi}{2*3} & \cos\frac{(2*2+1)0\pi}{2*3}*\cos\frac{(2*2+1)2\pi}{2*3} \end{bmatrix} =$$

$$\begin{bmatrix} .5 & -1 & .5 \\ .5 & -1 & .5 \\ .5 & -1 & .5 \end{bmatrix}$$

$$\begin{bmatrix} \cos\frac{(2*0+1)1\pi}{2*3}*\cos\frac{(2*0+1)0\pi}{2*3} & \cos\frac{(2*0+1)1\pi}{2*3}*\cos\frac{(2*1+1)0\pi}{2*3} & \cos\frac{(2*0+1)1\pi}{2*3}*\cos\frac{(2*2+1)0\pi}{2*3} \\ \cos\frac{(2*1+1)1\pi}{2*3}*\cos\frac{(2*0+1)0\pi}{2*3} & \cos\frac{(2*1+1)1\pi}{2*3}*\cos\frac{(2*1+1)0\pi}{2*3} & \cos\frac{(2*1+1)1\pi}{2*3}*\cos\frac{(2*2+1)0\pi}{2*3} \\ \cos\frac{(2*2+1)1\pi}{2*3}*\cos\frac{(2*0+1)0\pi}{2*3} & \cos\frac{(2*2+1)1\pi}{2*3}*\cos\frac{(2*1+1)0\pi}{2*3} & \cos\frac{(2*2+1)1\pi}{2*3}*\cos\frac{(2*2+1)0\pi}{2*3} \end{bmatrix} =$$

$$\begin{bmatrix} 8.6603e-01 & 8.6603e-01 & 8.6603e-01 \\ 6.1232e-17 & 6.1232e-17 & 6.1232e-17 \\ -8.6603e-01 & -8.6603e-01 & -8.6603e-01 \end{bmatrix}$$

$$\begin{bmatrix} \cos\frac{(2*0+1)1\pi}{2*3}*\cos\frac{(2*0+1)1\pi}{2*3} & \cos\frac{(2*0+1)1\pi}{2*3}*\cos\frac{(2*1+1)1\pi}{2*3} & \cos\frac{(2*0+1)1\pi}{2*3}*\cos\frac{(2*2+1)1\pi}{2*3} \\ \cos\frac{(2*1+1)1\pi}{2*3}*\cos\frac{(2*0+1)1\pi}{2*3} & \cos\frac{(2*1+1)1\pi}{2*3}*\cos\frac{(2*1+1)1\pi}{2*3} & \cos\frac{(2*1+1)1\pi}{2*3}*\cos\frac{(2*2+1)1\pi}{2*3} \\ \cos\frac{(2*2+1)1\pi}{2*3}*\cos\frac{(2*0+1)1\pi}{2*3} & \cos\frac{(2*2+1)1\pi}{2*3}*\cos\frac{(2*1+1)1\pi}{2*3} & \cos\frac{(2*2+1)1\pi}{2*3}*\cos\frac{(2*2+1)1\pi}{2*3} \end{bmatrix} =$$

$$\begin{bmatrix} 7.5000e-01 & 5.3029e-17 & -7.5000e-01 \\ 5.3029e-17 & 3.7494e-33 & -5.3029e-17 \\ -7.5000e-01 & -5.3029e-17 & 7.5000e-01 \end{bmatrix}$$

$$\begin{bmatrix} \cos\frac{(2*0+1)1\pi}{2*3}*\cos\frac{(2*0+1)2\pi}{2*3} & \cos\frac{(2*0+1)1\pi}{2*3}*\cos\frac{(2*1+1)2\pi}{2*3} & \cos\frac{(2*0+1)1\pi}{2*3}*\cos\frac{(2*2+1)2\pi}{2*3} \\ \cos\frac{(2*1+1)1\pi}{2*3}*\cos\frac{(2*0+1)2\pi}{2*3} & \cos\frac{(2*1+1)1\pi}{2*3}*\cos\frac{(2*1+1)2\pi}{2*3} & \cos\frac{(2*1+1)1\pi}{2*3}*\cos\frac{(2*2+1)2\pi}{2*3} \\ \cos\frac{(2*2+1)1\pi}{2*3}*\cos\frac{(2*0+1)2\pi}{2*3} & \cos\frac{(2*2+1)1\pi}{2*3}*\cos\frac{(2*1+1)2\pi}{2*3} & \cos\frac{(2*2+1)1\pi}{2*3}*\cos\frac{(2*2+1)2\pi}{2*3} \end{bmatrix} =$$

$$\begin{bmatrix} 4.3301e-01 & -8.6603e-01 & 4.3301e-01 \\ 3.0616e-17 & -6.1232e-17 & 3.0616e-17 \\ -4.3301e-01 & 8.6603e-01 & -4.3301e-01 \end{bmatrix}$$

$$\begin{bmatrix} \cos\frac{(2*0+1)2\pi}{2*3}*\cos\frac{(2*0+1)0\pi}{2*3} & \cos\frac{(2*0+1)2\pi}{2*3}*\cos\frac{(2*1+1)0\pi}{2*3} & \cos\frac{(2*0+1)2\pi}{2*3}*\cos\frac{(2*2+1)0\pi}{2*3} \\ \cos\frac{(2*1+1)2\pi}{2*3}*\cos\frac{(2*0+1)0\pi}{2*3} & \cos\frac{(2*1+1)2\pi}{2*3}*\cos\frac{(2*1+1)0\pi}{2*3} & \cos\frac{(2*1+1)2\pi}{2*3}*\cos\frac{(2*2+1)0\pi}{2*3} \\ \cos\frac{(2*2+1)2\pi}{2*3}*\cos\frac{(2*0+1)0\pi}{2*3} & \cos\frac{(2*2+1)2\pi}{2*3}*\cos\frac{(2*1+1)0\pi}{2*3} & \cos\frac{(2*2+1)2\pi}{2*3}*\cos\frac{(2*2+1)0\pi}{2*3} \end{bmatrix} =$$

$$\begin{bmatrix} .5 & .5 & .5 \\ -1 & -1 & -1 \\ .5 & .5 & .5 \end{bmatrix}$$

$$\begin{bmatrix} \cos\frac{(2*0+1)2\pi}{2*3}*\cos\frac{(2*0+1)1\pi}{2*3} & \cos\frac{(2*0+1)2\pi}{2*3}*\cos\frac{(2*1+1)1\pi}{2*3} & \cos\frac{(2*0+1)2\pi}{2*3}*\cos\frac{(2*2+1)1\pi}{2*3} \\ \cos\frac{(2*1+1)2\pi}{2*3}*\cos\frac{(2*0+1)1\pi}{2*3} & \cos\frac{(2*1+1)2\pi}{2*3}*\cos\frac{(2*1+1)1\pi}{2*3} & \cos\frac{(2*1+1)2\pi}{2*3}*\cos\frac{(2*2+1)1\pi}{2*3} \\ \cos\frac{(2*2+1)2\pi}{2*3}*\cos\frac{(2*0+1)1\pi}{2*3} & \cos\frac{(2*2+1)2\pi}{2*3}*\cos\frac{(2*1+1)1\pi}{2*3} & \cos\frac{(2*2+1)2\pi}{2*3}*\cos\frac{(2*2+1)1\pi}{2*3} \end{bmatrix} =$$

$$\begin{bmatrix} 4.3301e-01 & 3.0616e-17 & -4.3301e-01 \\ -8.6603e-01 & -6.1232e-17 & 8.6603e-01 \\ 4.3301e-01 & 3.0616e-17 & -4.3301e-01 \end{bmatrix}$$

$$\begin{bmatrix} \cos\frac{(2*0+1)2\pi}{2*3}*\cos\frac{(2*0+1)2\pi}{2*3} & \cos\frac{(2*0+1)2\pi}{2*3}*\cos\frac{(2*1+1)2\pi}{2*3} & \cos\frac{(2*0+1)2\pi}{2*3}*\cos\frac{(2*2+1)2\pi}{2*3} \\ \cos\frac{(2*1+1)2\pi}{2*3}*\cos\frac{(2*0+1)2\pi}{2*3} & \cos\frac{(2*1+1)2\pi}{2*3}*\cos\frac{(2*1+1)2\pi}{2*3} & \cos\frac{(2*1+1)2\pi}{2*3}*\cos\frac{(2*2+1)2\pi}{2*3} \\ \cos\frac{(2*2+1)2\pi}{2*3}*\cos\frac{(2*0+1)2\pi}{2*3} & \cos\frac{(2*2+1)2\pi}{2*3}*\cos\frac{(2*1+1)2\pi}{2*3} & \cos\frac{(2*2+1)2\pi}{2*3}*\cos\frac{(2*2+1)2\pi}{2*3} \end{bmatrix} =$$

$$\begin{bmatrix} 0.25000 & .5 & 0.25 \\ -.5 & 1 & -.5 \\ 0.25000 & -.5 & 0.25 \end{bmatrix}$$

$$^5\ 255.00000 = \sum_{x=0}^{2}\sum_{y=0}^{2} sqrt(1/3)*\begin{bmatrix} 1 & 1 & 1 \\ 1 & 1 & 1 \\ 1 & 1 & 1 \end{bmatrix}*sqrt(1/3)*\begin{bmatrix} 255 & 255 & 255 \\ 0 & 0 & 0 \\ 0 & 0 & 0 \end{bmatrix}$$

$$0 = \sum_{x=0}^{2}\sum_{y=0}^{2} sqrt(1/3)*\begin{bmatrix} .86603 & 6.1232e-17 & .86603 \\ .86603 & 6.1232e-17 & .86603 \\ .86603 & 6.1232e-17 & .86603 \end{bmatrix}*sqrt(2/3)*\begin{bmatrix} 255 & 255 & 255 \\ 0 & 0 & 0 \\ 0 & 0 & 0 \end{bmatrix}$$

$$0 = \sum_{x=0}^{2}\sum_{y=0}^{2} sqrt(1/3)*\begin{bmatrix} .5 & -1 & .5 \\ .5 & -1 & .5 \\ .5 & -1 & .5 \end{bmatrix}*sqrt(2/3)*\begin{bmatrix} 255 & 255 & 255 \\ 0 & 0 & 0 \\ 0 & 0 & 0 \end{bmatrix}$$

$$312.30994 = \sum_{x=0}^{2}\sum_{y=0}^{2} sqrt(2/3)*\begin{bmatrix} 8.6603e-01 & 8.6603e-01 & 8.6603e-01 \\ 6.1232e-17 & 6.1232e-17 & 6.1232e-17 \\ -8.6603e-01 & -8.6603e-01 & -8.6603e-01 \end{bmatrix}*$$

$$sqrt(1/3)*\begin{bmatrix} 255 & 255 & 255 \\ 0 & 0 & 0 \\ 0 & 0 & 0 \end{bmatrix}$$

$$0 = \sum_{x=0}^{2}\sum_{y=0}^{2} sqrt(2/3)* \begin{bmatrix} 7.5000e-01 & 5.3029e-17 & -7.5000e-01 \\ 5.3029e-17 & 3.7494e-33 & -5.3029e-17 \\ -7.5000e-01 & -5.3029e-17 & 7.5000e-01 \end{bmatrix} *sqrt(2/3)*$$

$$\begin{bmatrix} 255 & 255 & 255 \\ 0 & 0 & 0 \\ 0 & 0 & 0 \end{bmatrix}$$

$$0 = \sum_{x=0}^{2}\sum_{y=0}^{2} sqrt(2/3)* \begin{bmatrix} 4.3301e-01 & -8.6603e-01 & 4.3301e-01 \\ 3.0616e-17 & -6.1232e-17 & 3.0616e-17 \\ -4.3301e-01 & 8.6603e-01 & -4.3301e-01 \end{bmatrix} *sqrt(2/3)*$$

$$\begin{bmatrix} 255 & 255 & 255 \\ 0 & 0 & 0 \\ 0 & 0 & 0 \end{bmatrix}$$

$$180.31223 = \sum_{x=0}^{2}\sum_{y=0}^{2} sqrt(2/3)* \begin{bmatrix} .5 & .5 & .5 \\ -1 & -1 & -1 \\ .5 & .5 & .5 \end{bmatrix} *sqrt(1/3)* \begin{bmatrix} 255 & 255 & 255 \\ 0 & 0 & 0 \\ 0 & 0 & 0 \end{bmatrix}$$

$$0 = \sum_{x=0}^{2}\sum_{y=0}^{2} sqrt(2/3)* \begin{bmatrix} 4.3301e-01 & 3.0616e-17 & -4.3301e-01 \\ -8.6603e-01 & -6.1232e-17 & 8.6603e-01 \\ 4.3301e-01 & 3.0616e-17 & -4.3301e-01 \end{bmatrix} *sqrt(2/3)*$$

$$\begin{bmatrix} 255 & 255 & 255 \\ 0 & 0 & 0 \\ 0 & 0 & 0 \end{bmatrix}$$

$$0 = \sum_{x=0}^{2}\sum_{y=0}^{2} sqrt(2/3)* \begin{bmatrix} 0.25000 & .5 & 0.25000 \\ -.5 & 1 & -.5 \\ 0.25000 & -.5 & 0.25000 \end{bmatrix} *sqrt(2/3)* \begin{bmatrix} 255 & 255 & 255 \\ 0 & 0 & 0 \\ 0 & 0 & 0 \end{bmatrix}$$

$$^6\ \sqrt{1/3}*250*\sqrt{1/3}* \begin{bmatrix} 1 & 1 & 1 \\ 1 & 1 & 1 \\ 1 & 1 & 1 \end{bmatrix} + \sqrt{1/3}*0*\sqrt{2/3}* \begin{bmatrix} .86603 & 6.1232e-17 & .86603 \\ .86603 & 6.1232e-17 & .86603 \\ .86603 & 6.1232e-17 & .86603 \end{bmatrix} +$$

$$\sqrt{1/3}*0*\sqrt{2/3}* \begin{bmatrix} .5 & -1 & .5 \\ .5 & -1 & .5 \\ .5 & -1 & .5 \end{bmatrix} + \sqrt{2/3}*250*\sqrt{1/3}* \begin{bmatrix} 8.6603e-01 & 8.6603e-01 & 8.6603e\cdot \\ 6.1232e-17 & 6.1232e-17 & 6.1232e\cdot \\ -8.6603e-01 & -8.6603e-01 & -8.6603e \end{bmatrix}$$

$$\sqrt{2/3}*0*\sqrt{2/3}* \begin{bmatrix} 7.5000e-01 & 5.3029e-17 & -7.5000e-01 \\ 5.3029e-17 & 3.7494e-33 & -5.3029e-17 \\ -7.5000e-01 & -5.3029e-17 & 7.5000e-01 \end{bmatrix} + \sqrt{2/3}*0*$$

$$\sqrt{2/3}* \begin{bmatrix} 4.3301e-01 & -8.6603e-01 & 4.3301e-01 \\ 3.0616e-17 & -6.1232e-17 & 3.0616e-17 \\ -4.3301e-01 & 8.6603e-01 & -4.3301e-01 \end{bmatrix} + \sqrt{2/3}*0*\sqrt{1/3}* \begin{bmatrix} .5 & .5 & .5 \\ -1 & -1 & -1 \\ .5 & .5 & .5 \end{bmatrix} +$$

$$\sqrt{2/3}*0*\sqrt{2/3}* \begin{bmatrix} 4.3301e-01 & 3.0616e-17 & -4.3301e-01 \\ -8.6603e-01 & -6.1232e-17 & 8.6603e-01 \\ 4.3301e-01 & 3.0616e-17 & -4.3301e-01 \end{bmatrix} + \sqrt{2/3}*0*$$

$$\sqrt{2/3} \qquad\qquad * \qquad\qquad \begin{bmatrix} 0.25000 & .5 & 0.25000 \\ -.5 & 1 & -.5 \\ 0.25000 & -.5 & 0.25000 \end{bmatrix}$$

Special thanks to Danny Comer for helping with these concepts.

B — FOR BIOPOLITICS

The keywords "biopolitics" or "biopower," which have played an increasing role in debates in recent years, are used to describe the "concept of mechanisms of power," introduced in 1976 by the philosopher Michel Foucault in his book *The Will to Knowledge*.[4] He used it to describe the tendency of the modern state towards ever stricter control over the human body. (→ OUR OWN COMMUNITY) (→ NERD) This tendency, for Foucault, first appeared in the 17th century. From this moment on, the focus shifted from death to life: "One might say that the ancient right to take life or let live was replaced by a power to foster life or disallow it to the point of death."[5] Biopolitics, Foucault writes, is distinguished from the power of sovereignty by its non-repressive relation to life. It is a technique that operates on life to increase production in order to engender ever more of it—like neo-liberalism it is subject to an imperative of optimization. (→ XMAS BUY, BUY, BUY) According to the linguist Michael Hardt and the political scientist Antonio Negri, who have elaborated this concept in their studies, biopolitics also marks a new relationship between nature and culture and a blurring of the boundaries between them. Biopolitics seizes human nature and refers to a horizon of hybrid subjectivities; the boundaries between man and machine, and between man and animal become ever more diffuse.[6] (→ IDENTITY MARKETING) (→ YOUTUBE)

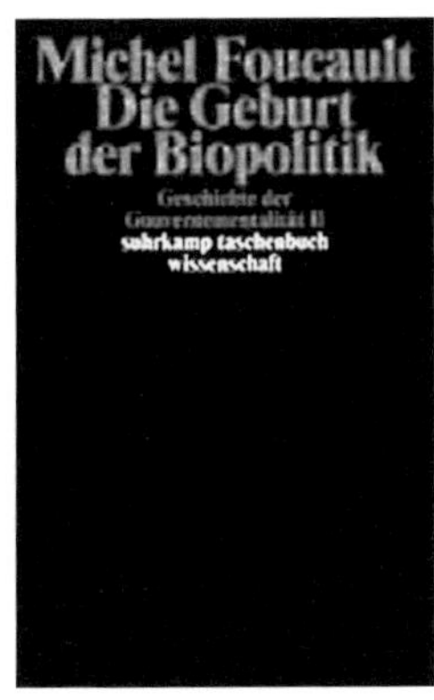

Unter den Stichworten «Biopolitik» oder «Biomacht», welche seit einigen Jahren immer stärker diskutiert werden, versteht man das «Konzept von Machtmechanismen», welches der Philosoph Michel Foucault im Jahr 1976 in seinem Buch *Der Wille zum Wissen* einführte.[7] Damit bezeichnet er eine Tendenz des modernen Staats, den menschlichen Körper immer stärker zu kontrollieren.

(→ OUR OWN COMMUNITY) (→ NERD) Gemäss Foucault zeigt sich diese Tendenz ab dem 17. Jahrhundert. Ab diesem Zeitpunkt verschiebt sich der Fokus vom Tod zum Leben: «Man könnte sagen, das alte Recht, sterben zu machen oder leben zu lassen, wurde abgelöst von einer Macht, leben zu machen oder in den Tod zu stossen.»[8] Foucault bezeichnete mit «Biopolitik» die Tendenz des modernen (Sozial-)Staates, den menschlichen Körper immer stärker zu kontrollieren. Die Biopolitik ist eine anhand Leben produktionssteigernde Technik, um noch mehr davon zu fördern – die Biopolitik ist wie der Neoliberalismus auch einem Optimierungsimperativ unterworfen. (→ XMAS BUY, BUY, BUY) Für den Sprachtheoretiker Michael Hardt und den Politikwissenschaftler Antonio Negri, die mit den Begriff weiter in ihren Studien ausgeführt haben, markiert Biopolitik auch eine neue Relation von Natur und Kultur und die Implosion der Grenzen dazwischen. Biopolitik macht nicht Halt vor der menschlichen Natur und verweist auf einen Horizont hybrider Subjektivitäten, wobei die Grenzen sowohl zwischen Mensch und Maschine als auch zwischen Mensch und Tier immer mehr verschwinden.[9] (→ IDENTITY MARKETING) (→ YOUTUBE)

C — FOR CARNIVALESQUE

In his seminal study *Rabelais and His World*, the literary theorist Mikhail Bakhtin (1895–1975) examined the phenomenon of popular culture as a form of counterculture, as suggested by the subtitle of his book.[10] His findings led Bakhtin to develop the concept of carnivalization, which continues to operate in contemporary debates. The annual carnival season is regarded as a vent that permits a society to temporarily undermine rigid political and hierarchical structures using humor and laughter, and to imagine a new organization of the world. (→ HAHAHA OR HYPERREALITY MEETS HYPERMENTAL) This blurring of boundaries and departure from the norm, enabled by the breaking of taboos, thus also allows a short-lived undermining of the boundaries between high and popular cultures. (→ WAR OF FORMS) This in turn suggests that the carnivalesque is accompanied by an impulse toward equality. Whether the carnivalesque functions to stabilize the system or, in its aesthetic and performative strategies of inversion, disfiguration and undermining, harbors a genuine subversive potential, is a question that remains controversial to this day.[11] In an age of globalization, in particular, its opponents have sought to reactivate the carnivalesque, as is evident, for example, in the "Reclaim the Street" movement.[12] Today, the carnivalesque is also considered in the context of a "performative act," in discussions that often revolve around the body in its grotesque and transgressive form.[13] (→ SHANA MOULTON) (→ RYAN TRECARTIN & LIZZIE FITCH)

In seinem grundlegenden Werk *Rabelais und seine Welt* untersuchte der Literaturtheoretiker Michail Bachtin (1895–1975) das Phänomen der Volkskultur als Form von Gegenkultur – so auch der Untertitel der Studie.[14] Davon ausgehend, definierte Bachtin das bis heute verwendete Stichwort der

---

4—Neither Foucault nor Hardt/Negri offer a clear distinction between the terms "biopower" and "biopolitics." See Jacques Rancière's discussion of this problem: "Biopolitique ou politique?," *Multitude* no. 1, Paris 2000, 88–93. The concepts of "biopower" and "biopolitics" are first introduced in Michel Foucault, *The History of Sexuality*, vol. 1: *The Will to Knowledge*, London 1976 (French original: Michel Foucault, *La volonté de savoir*, Paris 1976). In recent years, Giorgio Agamben, Michael Hardt/Antonio Negri, and others have elaborated these concepts and revived the debate: Giorgio Agamben, *Homo Sacer. Sovereign Power and Bare Life*, Stanford 1998 (Italian original: Giorgio Agamben, *Homo sacer. Il potere sovrano e la nuda vita*, Turin 1995); Michael Hardt, Antonio Negri, *Empire*, Cambridge, Mass. 2000.
5—Foucault, *The Will to Knowledge*, 138.
6—Cf. Michael Hardt, Antonio Negri, *Labour of Dionysos: A Critique of the State-Form*, Minnesota 1994, 29.
7—Zwischen den Begriffen «Biomacht» und «Biopolitik» unterscheiden weder Foucault noch Hardt/Negri klar. Zu dieser Problematik veröffentlichte Jacques Rancière einen Aufsatz, vgl. ders., «Biopolitique ou politique?», in: *Multitude*, Nr. 1, S. 88–93, Paris 2000.
Die Begriffe «Biomacht»/«Biopolitik» werden eingeführt in: Michel Foucault, *Der Wille zum Wissen. Sexualität und Wahrheit*, Frankfurt 1977 (Erstveröffentlichung in Französisch: Michel Foucault, *La volonté de savoir*, Paris 1976).
Durch u.a. Giorgio Agamben, Michael Hardt und Antonio Negri wurde der Begriff in den letzten Jahren weiter ausgearbeitet und erneut diskutiert: Giorgio Agamben, *Homo sacer. Die Souveränität der Macht und das nackte Leben*, Frankfurt 2002 (Erstveröffentlichung in Italienisch: Giorgio Agamben, *Homo sacer. Il potere sovrano e la nuda vita*, Torino 1995).
Michael Hardt, Antonio Negri, *Empire – Die neue Weltordnung*, Frankfurt 2002 (Erstveröffentlichung in Englisch: Michael Hardt, Antonio Negri, *Empire*, Cambridge 2000).

8—Foucault 1976 (wie Anm. 4), S. 165.
9—Vgl. Michael Hardt, Antonio Negri, *Die Arbeit des Dionysos. Materialistische Staatskritik in der Postmoderne*, Berlin 1997, S. 19 (Erstveröffentlichung in Englisch: Michael Hardt, Antonio Negri, *Labour of Dionysos: A Critique of the State-Form*, Minnesota 1994).
10—The study was written as a dissertation in 1940, but for political reasons could not be published until 1965. See Mikhail Bakhtin, *Rabelais and His World*, Helene Iswolsky (trans.), Cambridge, Mass. 1968 (Russian original: Mikhail Bakhtin, *Tvorchestvo Fransua Rable i narodnaia kultura srednevekovia i Renessansa*, Moscow 1965).
11—Cf. Sönke Gau, Katharina Schlieben (eds.), *Spektakel, Lustprinzip oder das Karnevaleske?* Berlin 2008.
12—Naomi Klein's book *No Logo. Taking Aim at the Brand Bullies*, New York 2000, describes the re-conquest of the street.
13—See also Erika Fischer-Lichte, *Die Ästhetik des Performativen*, Frankfurt 2004.
14—Die Arbeit ist 1940 als Dissertation entstanden; sie konnte jedoch aus politischen Gründen erst 1965 publiziert werden.
Vgl. Michail Bachtin, *Rabelais und seine Welt*, Frankfurt 1995 (Erstveröffentlichung in Russisch: 1965).

Karnevalisierung. Die alljährliche Karnevalszeit gilt dabei als Ventil einer Gesellschaft, in welcher durch Humor und Lachen starre politische und hierarchische Strukturen temporär untergraben und ästhetische Überschreitungen gewagt werden sowie eine Weltorganisation neu gedacht wird. (→ HAHAHA OR HYPERREALITY MEETS HYPERMENTAL) Dieses Moment der Entgrenzung und des Aufbruchs durch den Tabubruch ermöglichte somit auch eine kurzfristige Untergrabung der Grenzen zwischen Hoch- und Populärkultur. (→ WAR OF FORMS) Dies wiederum zeigt, dass dem Karnevalesken ein utopisches Moment der Gleichwertigkeit verschiedener Kulturen innewohnt. Die Beurteilung der Funktion des Karnevalesken, ob es nun lediglich eine Stabilisierung des Systems oder doch ein subversives Potenzial in sich trägt – in seinen ästhetischen und performativen Strategien der Umdrehung, Entstellung und Unterwanderung –, wird bis heute kontrovers diskutiert.[15] Gerade im Zuge der Globalisierung haben deren Gegner versucht, das Karnevaleske zu reaktivieren, wie am Beispiel der «Reclaim the Street»-Bewegung zu sehen ist.[16] Im Zusammenhang mit dem Karnevalesken wird heute auch von einem «performative turn» gesprochen, wobei der Körper häufig in seiner grotesken, transgressiven Form als Dreh- und Angelpunkt diskutiert wird.[17] (→ SHANA MOULTON) (→ RYAN TRECARTIN & LIZZIE FITCH)

D — FOR D(O)I(T)Y(OURSELF) AND BRICOLAGE

In the middle of the first decade of the 21st century, as contemporary art experienced a veritable boom, we observed how economic circumstances shaped the way artists produced, and more and more works reached a market whose production had already consumed gigantic sums of money. (→ XMAS AND BUY, BUY, BUY) A number of artists, however, consciously resisted such a mode of production, opting instead for one derived from the idea of bricolage, as framed by the ethnologist Claude Lévi-Strauss. We can trace this concept through the 20th century as it reappears time and again in various artistic movements, such as the Situationists or Punk, which introduced the idea of DIY ("Do It Yourself").[18] (→ CORY ARCANGEL) (→ PAPER RAD) (→ SHANA MOULTON) (→ RYAN TRECARTIN & LIZZIE FITCH) This use of bricolage and DIY is shaped by self-organization, individual initiative, distrust of established authorities, and a "critical pleasure." (→ OUR OWN COMMUNITY) (→ CARNIVALESQUE) The concept of "DIY" must clearly be understood as opposing the (professional) specialist, and it resists passive consumerism—yet it does so not with a simple gesture of refusal but with one of (counter) production. (→ LOW TECH) (→ JUNK-STORE AESTHETICS) Still, this form of action cannot be described using the concept of the "amateur," for the latter has no political dimension.[19] "DIY" frequently engenders new collective artistic practices and the possibility of opening up and employing a new repertoire of communicative means outside the established circulation systems of production and distribution. (→ YOUTUBE)

Mitten in der ersten Dekade des 21. Jahrhunderts, während die zeitgenössische Kunst einen regelrechten Boom erlebte, konnte beobachtet werden, wie ökonomische Verhältnisse sich auf den

Produktionsmodus von Künstlern auswirkten und immer mehr Werke den Markt erreichten, die bereits Riesensummen für ihre Produktion verschlungen hatten. (→ XMAS AND BUY, BUY, BUY) Jedoch widersetzte sich eine ganze Reihe von Kunstschaffenden bewusst einem solchen Produktionsmodus und entschied sich vielmehr für einen, der von der Idee der Bricolage des Ethnologen Claude Lévi-Strauss ausging. Dieses Konzept lässt sich durch das 20. Jahrhundert hindurch immer wieder bei verschiedenen Kunstbewegungen orten – so bei den Situationisten oder der Punk-Bewegung, wo der Begriff des «DIY» («Do It Yourself») eingeführt wurde.[20] (→ CORY ARCANGEL) (→ PAPER RAD) (→ SHANA MOULTON) (→ RYAN TRECARTIN & LIZZIE FITCH) Dieser Einsatz von Bricolage und DIY ist geprägt von Selbstorganisation, Eigeninitiative, Misstrauen gegenüber etablierten Autoritäten und einer «kritischen Lust». (→ OUR OWN COMMUNITY) (→ CARNIVALESQUE) Der Begriff «DIY» ist klar als Gegensatz zum (professionellen) Spezialistentum zu verstehen und widersetzt sich dem passiven Konsumverhalten – jedoch nicht mit einer simplen Geste der Verweigerung, sondern mit einer der (Gegen-)Produktion. (→ LOW TECH) (→ JUNK-STORE AESTHETICS) Wobei diese Form des Handelns nicht mit dem Begriff des «Amateurs» beschrieben werden kann, da diesem jegliche politische Dimension fehlt.[21] Oftmals kommt es dabei zu neuen kollektiv-künstlerischen Praxen und der Möglichkeit, ein neues kommunikatives Repertoire ausserhalb der etablierten Produktions- und Distributionskreisläufe zu öffnen und zu benutzen. (→ YOUTUBE)

E — FOR EXPERIMENTAL FILM / VIDEO

The interrelations between pop music, film and the visual arts have intensified over the past few decades. (→ RHIZOME) (→ HAHAHA OR HYPERREALITY MEETS HYPERMENTAL) As well as collaborations between individual genres and artistic styles, we can also see increasing amalgamations of these domains. (→ CORY ARCANGEL) (→ PAPER RAD) Such blurring of boundaries and even fusions be-

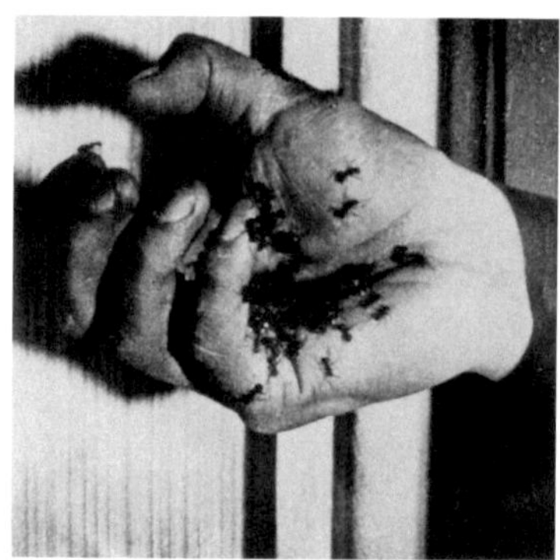

Still from *Un chien andalou*, directed by Salvador Dalí, Luis Buñuel, 1929

tween art and music could be observed already in the early 20th century in the visual arts, in groups such as the Dadaists, the Bauhaus, or De Stijl, but also, for example, in groups associated with Absolute Film.[22] We can read this phenomenon as one of the many lines that make up the heterogeneous history of experimental film. With the triumphant rise of MTV in the 1980s at the latest, the medium of video was not only taken up by the music industry as a means of distribution, but also re-

---

15—Vgl. Sönke Gau, Katharina Schlieben (Hrsg.), *Spektakel, Lustprinzip oder das Karnevaleske?*, Berlin 2008.

16—Im Buch *No Logo* von Naomi Klein wird die Rückeroberung der Strasse von einer jungen Generation Globalisierungsgegner beschrieben. Vgl. dies., *No Logo – Der Kampf der Global Player um Marktmacht*, München 2002.

17—Vgl. auch Erika Fischer-Lichte, *Die Ästhetik des Performativen*, Frankfurt 2004.

18—The concept of "bricolage" is here understood not in its traditional artistic sense but, like Lévi-Strauss's *La pensée sauvage*, as a process in which an object with defined socio-cultural connotations is translated, and contributes to a new cultural identity. The concept also implies that there is no ready set of formal instruments that the artist draws on; an explicit and joyful experimentation is crucial—just as "wild thinking" is a psychic function that has combinatorial but not (yet) rational-analytical capabilities. Cf. Claude Lévi-Strauss, *The Savage Mind*, Chicago 1966 (French original: Claude Lévi-Strauss, *La pensée sauvage*, Paris 1962) and Craig O'Hara, *The Philosophy of Punk*, London 1992.

19—In this context, we might also mention Andrew Keen's controversial *The Cult of the Amateur—How Blogs, MySpace, YouTube, and the Rest of Today's User-Generated Media Are Destroying Our Economy, Our Culture, and Our Values*, New York 2007.

20—Der Begriff der «Bricolage» wird dabei nicht in seiner traditionell künstlerischen Funktion verstanden, sondern wie in Lévi-Strauss' Abhandlung *La pensée sauvage* als Prozess, bei dem ein Objekt mit einer bestimmten soziokulturellen Konnotation übersetzt wird und zu einer neuen kulturellen Identität beiträgt. Der Begriff impliziert auch, dass nicht ein bereits vorgefertigtes formales Instrumentarium zur Verfügung steht, sondern eine explizite Experimentierfreudigkeit voransteht – so ist das «wilde Denken» eine psychische Funktion, die (noch) nicht über rational-analytische, wohl aber über kombinatorische Fähigkeiten verfügt. Vgl. Claude Lévi-Strauss, *La pensée sauvage*, Paris 1962, sowie Craig O'Hara, *The Philosophy of Punk*, London 1992.

21—In diesem Zusammenhang liesse sich etwa die umstrittene Publikation von Andrew Keen, *The Cult of the Amateur – How Blogs, MySpace, YouTube, and the Rest of Today's User-Generated Media Are Destroying Our Economy, Our Culture, and Our Values*, New York 2007, anfügen.

22—Cf. Ulrike Gross, Markus Müller, *Make it Funky. Crossover zwischen Musik, Pop, Avantgarde und Kunst*, Cologne 2003, 9–20.

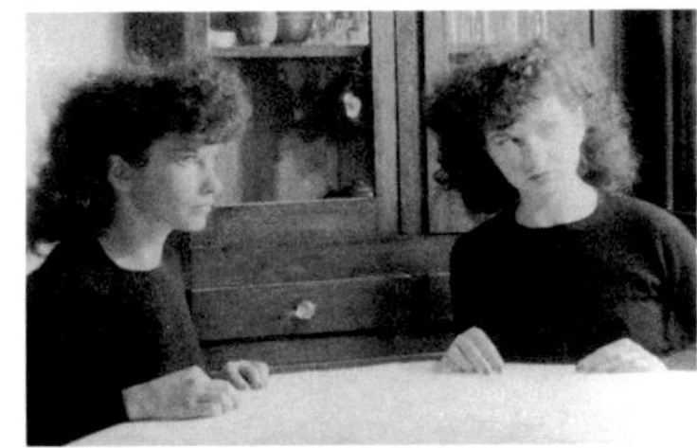

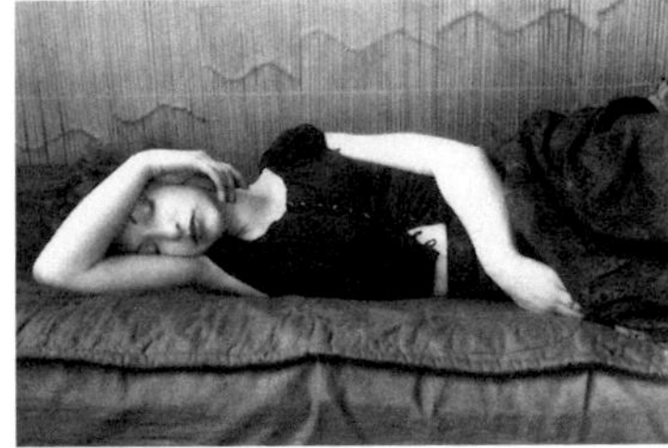

Stills from *Meshes of the Afternoon*, directed by Maya Deren , Alexander Hammid, 1943

flected on and exploited by visual artists. From a distance, we can recognize that the era of the lavishly produced music video is already mostly over, thanks to the radical transformation of the music market over the past ten years. Yet the post-Surrealist and highly significative filmicvisual language of directors such as Michel Gondry, Chris Cunningham, or Spike Jonze, whose work marks the heyday of this movement, has left traces in the art of a younger generation of visual artists. In particular, the forms in which time is shaped, in its abstractness and irrationality, has always been a central aspect of experimental film. (→ FICTION AND NARRATIVE METHODS) As well as this general set of problems, a similarly excessive density of signs can be noted in the films of Matthew Barney or what is the opposite pole in terms of formal aesthetic, the videos of Pipilotti Rist, who rose to prominence at the same time (→ SPECTACULAR, SPECTACULAR EXCESS)—two positions that can also be read as dialectically opposed to commercial TV culture. According to the literary theorist Fredric Jameson, the medium of video has always stood in such dialectical interrelation. It is interesting that this reciprocity and mutual quotation between the media have become normal over the past few decades. (→ QUOTES) Influences in artistic work come not only from music videos, but also from advertising spots, the serial structure of soap operas, or the casting format. (→ RYAN TRECARTIN & LIZZIE FITCH) (→ SHANA MOULTON) Whereas experimental film used to live in the shadows, not least because far fewer distribution options were available for films of this genre, its status has now changed for the better thanks to the innumerable online video streaming platforms. (→ YOUTUBE)

In den letzten Jahrzehnten haben sich die Beziehungen zwischen Pop-Musik, Film und bildender Kunst immer mehr intensiviert. (→ RHIZOME) (→ HAHAHA OR HYPERREALITY MEETS HYPERMENTAL) Nebst Kollaborationen zwischen den einzelnen Gattungen und Kunstrichtungen lässt sich auch eine zunehmende Amalgamierung dieser Bereiche feststellen. (→ CORY ARCANGEL) (→ PAPER RAD) Diese Entgrenzungen und Verschmelzungen von Kunst und Musik lassen sich bereits seit Beginn des 20. Jahrhunderts von Seiten der bildenden Kunst bei Gruppierungen wie den Dadaisten, dem Bauhaus oder De Stijl beobachten, aber auch bei solchen, die beispielsweise beim Absoluten Film angesiedelt sind.[23] Dies kann als eine der vielen Linien der heterogenen Geschichte des Experimentalfilms gelesen werden. Spätestens mit dem Siegeszug von MTV in den 1980er Jahren wurde das Medium Video nicht einzig von der Musikindustrie als Distributionsmittel aufgegriffen, sondern ebenfalls von bildenden Künstlern reflektiert und verwertet. Aus der heutigen zeitlichen Distanz lässt sich die Hauptära von kostspielig produzierten Musikvideos aufgrund des radikalen

Wandels des Musikmarkts in den letzten zehn Jahren als bereits wieder abgeschlossen betrachten. Die postsurrealistische, zeichengeladene Filmbildsprache der Regisseure Michel Gondry, Chris Cunningham oder Spike Jonze, welche die Blütezeit dieser Bewegung markieren, hat jedoch bei einer jüngeren Generation bildender Künstler ihre Spuren hinterlassen: Gerade die Gestaltungsform von Zeit, in ihrer Abstraktion und Irrationalität, bildet im Experimentalfilm immer wieder ein zentrales Moment. (→ FICTION AND NARRATIVE METHODS) Nicht nur diese Problematik, sondern auch eine ähnlich exzessive Zeichendichte lässt sich bei den Filmen von Matthew Barney oder, in ihrer formalästhetischen Gegenposition, den Videos von Pipilotti Rist finden, die im selben Zeitraum bekannt wurde. (→ SPECTACULAR, SPECTACULAR EXCESS) Zwei Positionen, die auch in einer Dialektik mit der kommerziellen Fernsehkultur gelesen werden können. Nach Literaturtheoretiker Frederic Jameson stand das Medium Video schon immer in einer solch dialektischen Beziehung. Es erscheint interessant, dass sich in den letzten Jahrzehnten diese Wechselwirkung und das gegenseitige Zitieren zu einer Normalität entwickelt haben. (→ QUOTES) So fliessen nicht nur das Musikvideo, sondern auch Werbespots, das Serielle einer Soap Opera oder das Casting-Format in künstlerische Arbeiten ein. (→ RYAN TRECARTIN & LIZZIE FITCH) (→ SHANA MOULTON) Während das Schattendasein des Experimentalfilms auch darin begründet lag, dass es für Filme dieses Genres sehr viel weniger Distributionsmöglichkeiten gab, hat sich sein Status heute dank den unzähligen Videoplattformen auf dem Internet positiv verändert. (→ YOUTUBE)

F — FOR FICTION AND NARRATIVE METHODS

The term "fiction" can designate a cultural technique that practices the creation of a world(view) or of a representation of a world by means of literature, film, painting, or other artistic forms.[24] Experimentation with narrative methods and the fragmentation of linear textuality are things that both high culture and pop culture have explored again and again, be it in Virginia Woolf's "stream of consciousness" or in Steve Jackson's and Ian Livingstone's interactive fantasy novels.[25] With the invention of the Internet or of hypertext, the most extravagant expectations regarding an experimental alternative model of narrative seemed to come true. (→ RHIZOME) The description of hypertext as a perfect rhizomatic medium fails

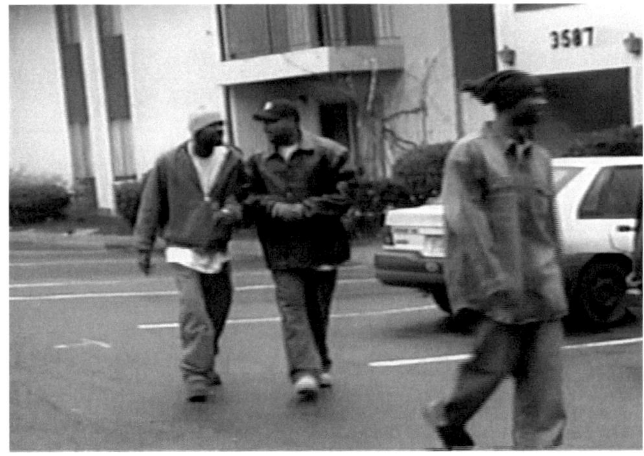

Paper Rad
P-Unit Mixtape 2005
2005

23—Vgl. Ulrike Gross, Markus Mülle, *Make it Funky – Crossover zwischen Musik, Pop, Avantgarde und Kunst*, Köln 2003, S. 9–20.

24—Vgl. Gérard Genette, *Fiction and Diction*, trans. Catherine Porter, Ithaca 1993 (French original: Gérard Genette, *Fiction et diction*, Paris 1991).
25—In these so-called interactive novels, the reader exercised immediate influence over the plot. Conceptually, the book is divided into ca. 300 to 400 numbered sections—the reader begins with section 1, at the end of which he is given a choice of sections with which to continue. This process continues until the reader reaches the end of the book—usually also the last numbered section—or reaches a textual dead-end, i.e. dies, on his way there. These books were especially popular in the 1980s. Among the protagonists of this movement are the fantasy authors Ian Livingstone and Steve Jackson with their *Fighting Fantasy* series; cf. Ian Livingstone, Steve Jackson, *The Warlock of Firetop Mountain*, London 1982. For more information see http://www.fightingfantasygamebooks.com.

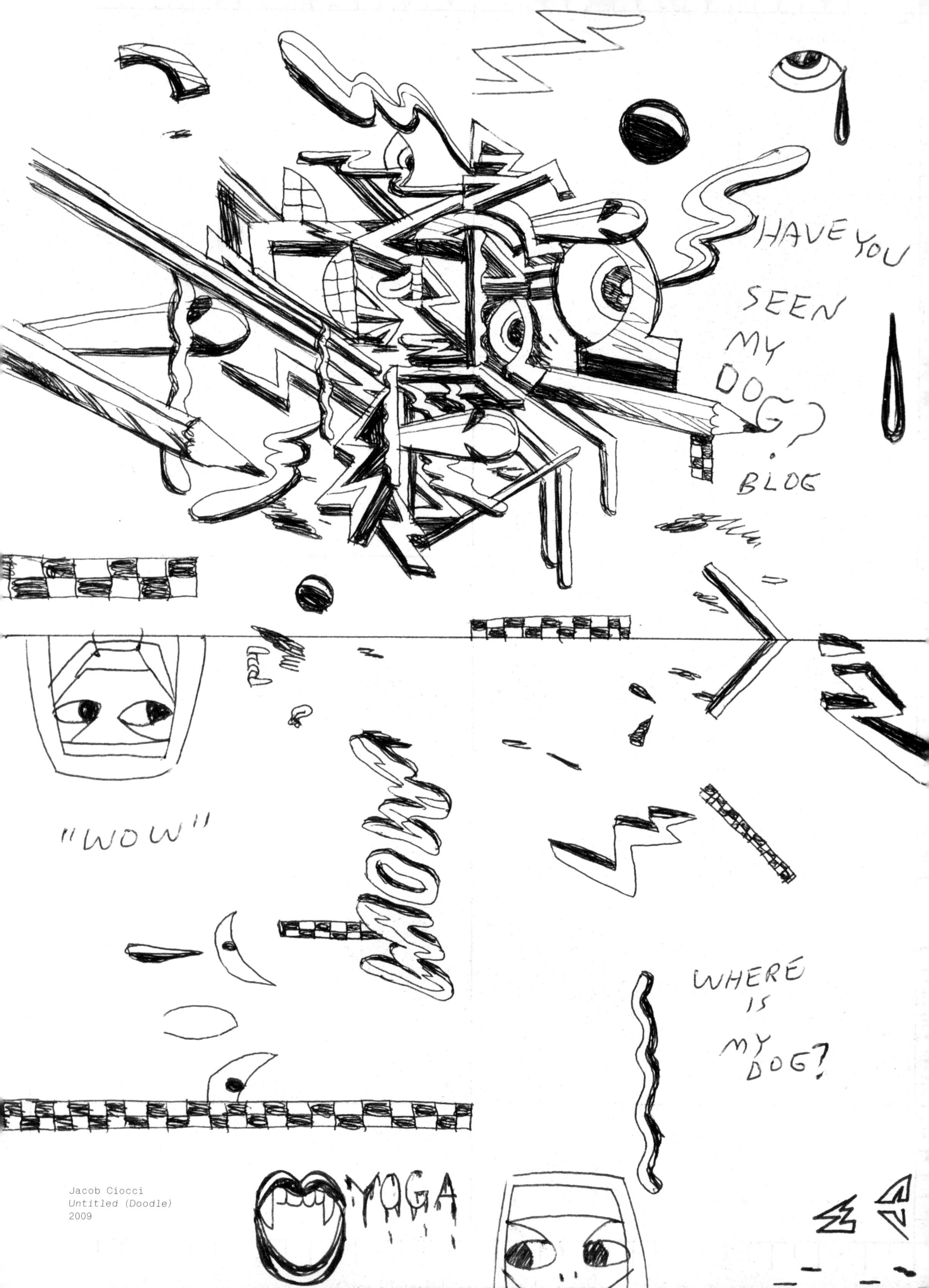
HAVE YOU
SEEN
MY
DOG?
BLOG
"WOW"
WOW
WHERE
IS
MY
DOG?
YOGA

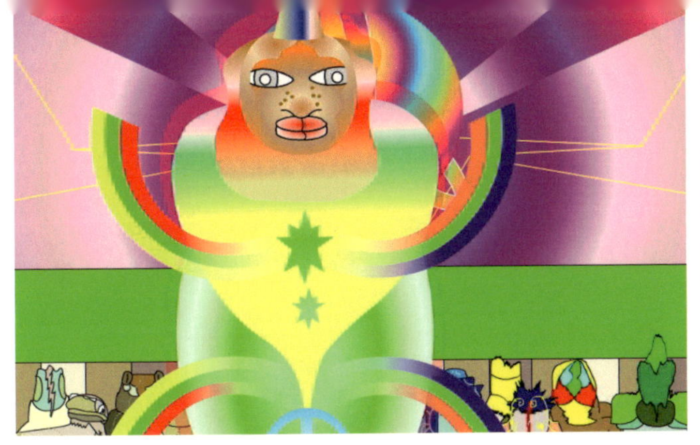
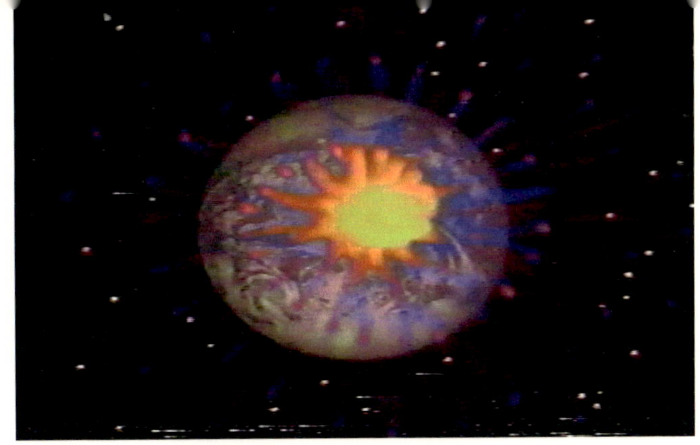
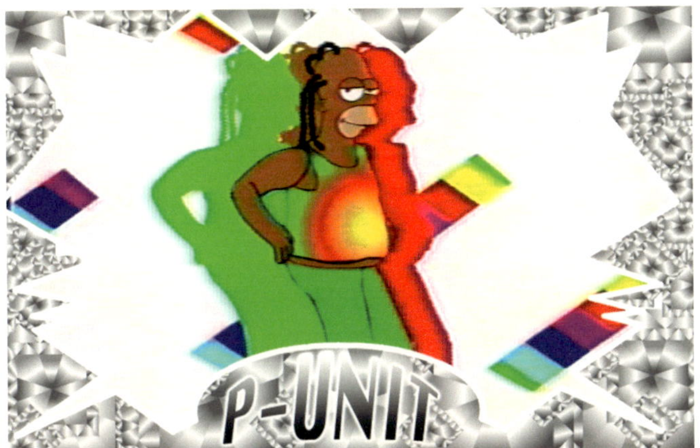
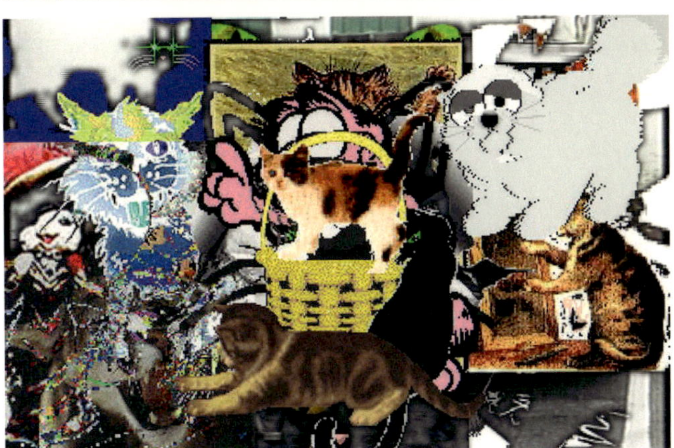
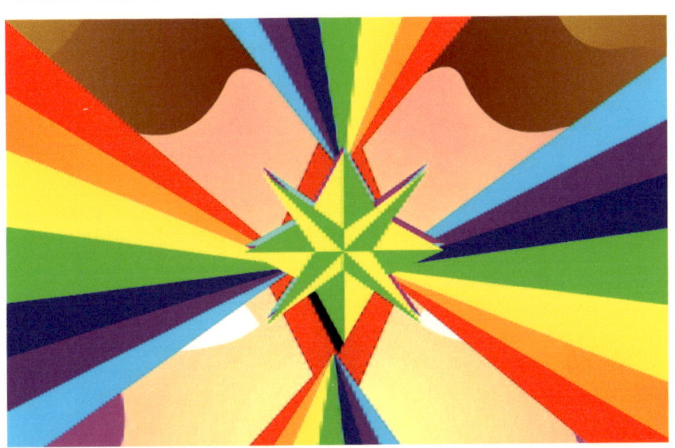
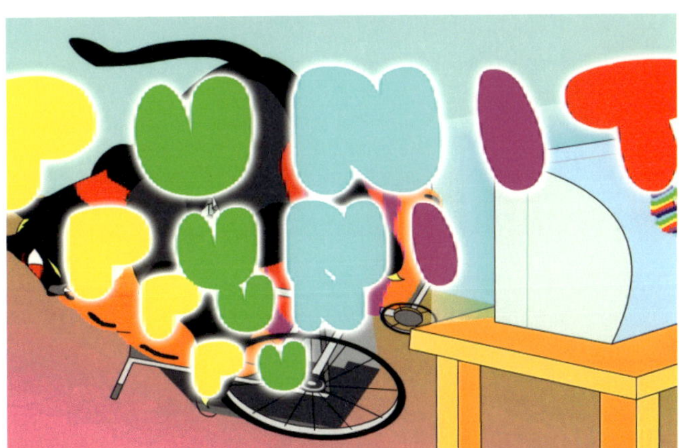
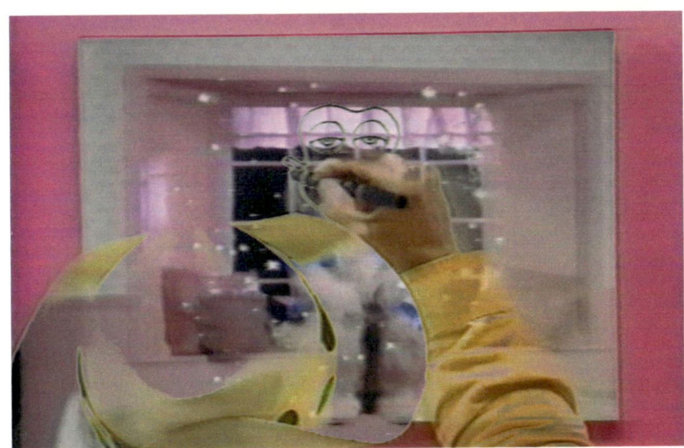
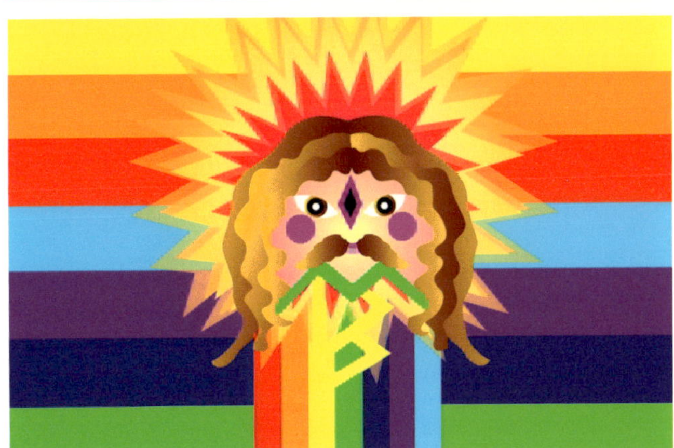
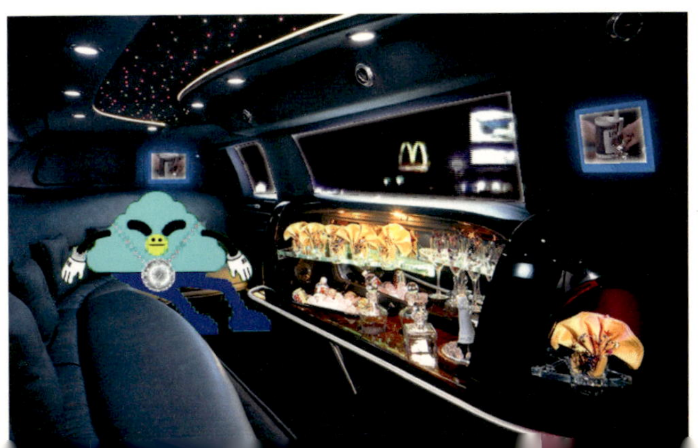

Paper Rad
P-Unit Mixtape 2005
2005

to acknowledge that however deeply nested, it remains a linear text to the extent that it originates in an author and is often not susceptible to manipulation of its form by the reader. Similar forms of narrative, which would perhaps best be described as circular in form, can be found in computer games. (→ ZAK MCKRACKEN AND THE ALIEN MINDBENDERS) But the television culture of 24/7 zapping likewise evinces an alternative form of reading formats that lend themselves to temporally linear consumption. (→ WAR OF FORMS) It mixes the most diverse formats, from soap opera to TV advertising, from the reality casting show to animated cartoons, to create a single gigantic storm of imagery. (→ PAPER RAD) (→ SHANA MOULTON) (→ SPECTACULAR, SPECTACULAR EXCESS) More generally, filmic narration can always be described as a shaping of time that can be viewed through a variety of technologies. In accelerated representation ("fast motion"), for instance, a motion picture is recorded with a smaller number of frames per second than will be shown in the subsequent projection. A parallel phenomenon is the inverse technique: deceleration (or "slow motion"). Time-lapse, or the elision of images, and the expansion of time, in which the filmic time of narration becomes longer than the time narrated by the film, and flashbacks and flash-forwards, as ways of showing past or future events, are other possibilities. Such turning to the past or the future represents knowledge that can only be communicated by an off-screen narrator or a character. Parallel montage, in which shots from two narrative strands are cut in alternation, creates the impression that actions take place simultaneously. These are only a few of the many ways of allocating time in a filmic space. (→ RYAN TRECARTIN & LIZZIE FITCH)

Unter dem Begriff der «Fiktion» kann eine Kulturtechnik verstanden werden, die eine Schaffung einer eigenen Welt(ansicht) oder -darstellung durch Literatur, Film, Malerei oder andere Kunstformen praktiziert.[26] Das Experimentieren mit Erzählmethoden und das Durchbrechen eines linearen Textes wurden sowohl in der Hochkultur als auch in der Pop-Kultur immer wieder aufs Neue getestet, sei es anhand des «stream of consciousness» von Virginia Woolf oder der interaktiven Fantasy-Romane von Steve Jackson und Ian Livingstone.[27] Mit der Erfindung des Internets oder dem Hypertext schien die kühnste Hoffnung auf ein experimentelles, alternatives Erzählmodell in Erfüllung gegangen zu sein. (→ RHIZOME) Den Hypertext als vollkommen rhizomatisches Medium zu bezeichnen, unterschlägt, dass ein Hypertext – wie verschachtelt auch immer – insofern weiterhin ein linearer Text bleibt, als er von einem Autor ausgeht und in seiner Form vom Leser oftmals nicht mehr verändert werden kann. Ähnliche Formen der Narration, die sich vielleicht am besten als zirkuläre Formen beschreiben liessen, findet man in Computerspielen. (→ ZAK MCKRACKEN AND THE ALIEN MINDBENDERS) Aber auch in der Fernsehkultur des «24/7 Zapping» lässt sich eine alternative Leseform von zeitlich linear konsumierbaren Formaten beobachten. (→ WAR OF FORMS) So vermischen sich die verschiedensten Formate – von der Soap Opera zur Fernsehwerbung, der Reality-Casting-Show zum Animationsfilm zu einem gigantischen Bildersturm. (→ PAPER RAD) (→ SHANA MOULTON) (→ SPECTACULAR, SPECTACULAR EXCESS) Generell kann man filmisches Erzählen auch immer als Gestaltung von Zeit, die mit unterschiedlichen Techniken geschehen kann, beschreiben. Bei der Beschleunigung («fast motion») werden beispielsweise die Bewegungsaufnahmen mit einer geringeren Bildzahl pro Sekunde gedreht, als in der anschliessenden Projektion zu sehen sind. Parallel dazu existiert auch deren technische Umkehrung: die Verlangsamung («slow

motion»). Die Zeitraffung durch Auslassung oder Zeitdehnung, wenn die Erzählzeit des Films länger als die Realzeit des Films wird, der Rückblende (Flashback) oder dem Vorgreifen (Flashforward), dem Zeigen von Vergangenem bzw. Zukünftigem, sind weitere Möglichkeiten. Unter der Zuwendung zu Vergangenheit bzw. Zukunft versteht man das Wissen, das nur durch einen Off-Erzähler oder eine Figur transportiert wird. Die Parallelmontage, in welcher Einstellungen aus zwei Handlungssträngen nacheinander im Wechsel montiert werden, erzeugt den Eindruck der Gleichzeitigkeit von Handlungen. Dies sind nur einige wenige der vielen Möglichkeiten, die Zeit in einem filmischen Raum anzuordnen. (→ RYAN TRECARTIN & LIZZIE FITCH)

G — FOR GARFIELD AND GUMBY

Gumby is a green humanoid clay figure from the 1950s; Garfield is a comic strip character, a fat cat with a coat of orange fur from the late 1970s: both are icons in the world of comic strips and animation, and familiar to audiences far beyond the community of comic experts.[28] Both characters appear as references to pop culture in contemporary art. (→ PAPER RAD)

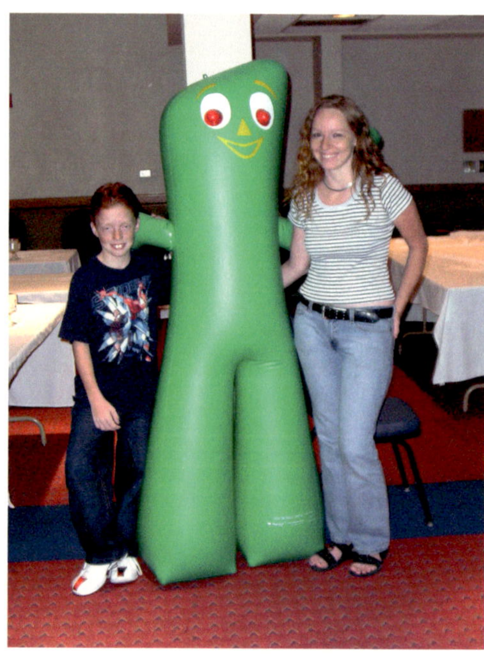

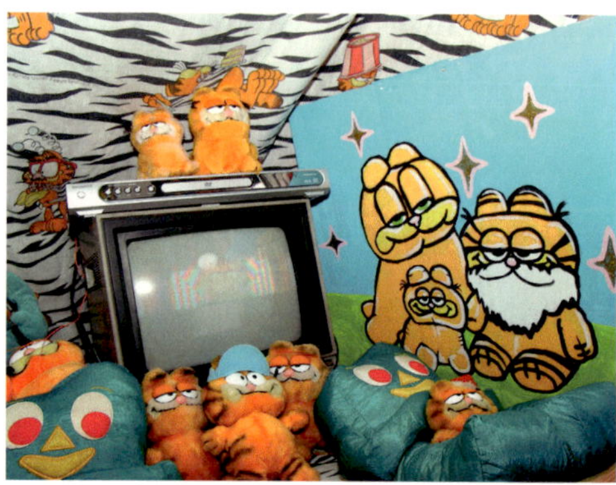

Gumby ist eine grüne, menschenähnliche Lehmfigur aus den 1950er Jahren – Garfield eine gezeichnete, orangefarbene dicke Katze aus den späten 1970er Jahren: Beide sind Ikonen in der Welt des Comics und Zeichentrickfilms und alles andere als nur Comic-Experten bekannt.[29] Beide Figuren tauchen als Referenzen der Pop-Kultur in der Gegenwartskunst auf. (→ PAPER RAD)

26—Vgl. Gérard Genette, *Fiction et diction*, Paris 1991.
27—In diesen als interaktiv bezeichneten Romanen konnte der Leser direkt Einfluss auf die Handlung nehmen. Konzeptuell ist das Buch in circa 300 bis 400 nummerierte Abschnitte unterteilt – der Leser beginnt bei Abschnitt 1 und kann am Ende des Abschnitts die Entscheidung treffen, bei welchem Abschnitt er weiterlesen möchte. Dies setzt sich so lange fort, bis man entweder das Ende des Buchs erreicht – meist auch den letzten nummerierten Abschnitt – oder man auf dem Weg dorthin in einer textuellen Sackgasse landet bzw. stirbt. Die Bücher waren vor allem in den 1980er Jahren sehr populär. Die Fantasy-Autoren Ian Livingstone und Steve Jackson können als Protagonisten einer solchen Bewegung mit ihrer *Fighting Fantasy*-Serie angeführt werden, vgl. Ian Livingstone, Steve Jackson, *The Warlock of Firetop Mountain*, London 1982. Mehr Informationen: http://www.fightingfantasygamebooks.com.

28—See: http://www.gumby.com; http://www.garfield.com.
29—Siehe: http://www.gumby.com; http://www.garfield.com.

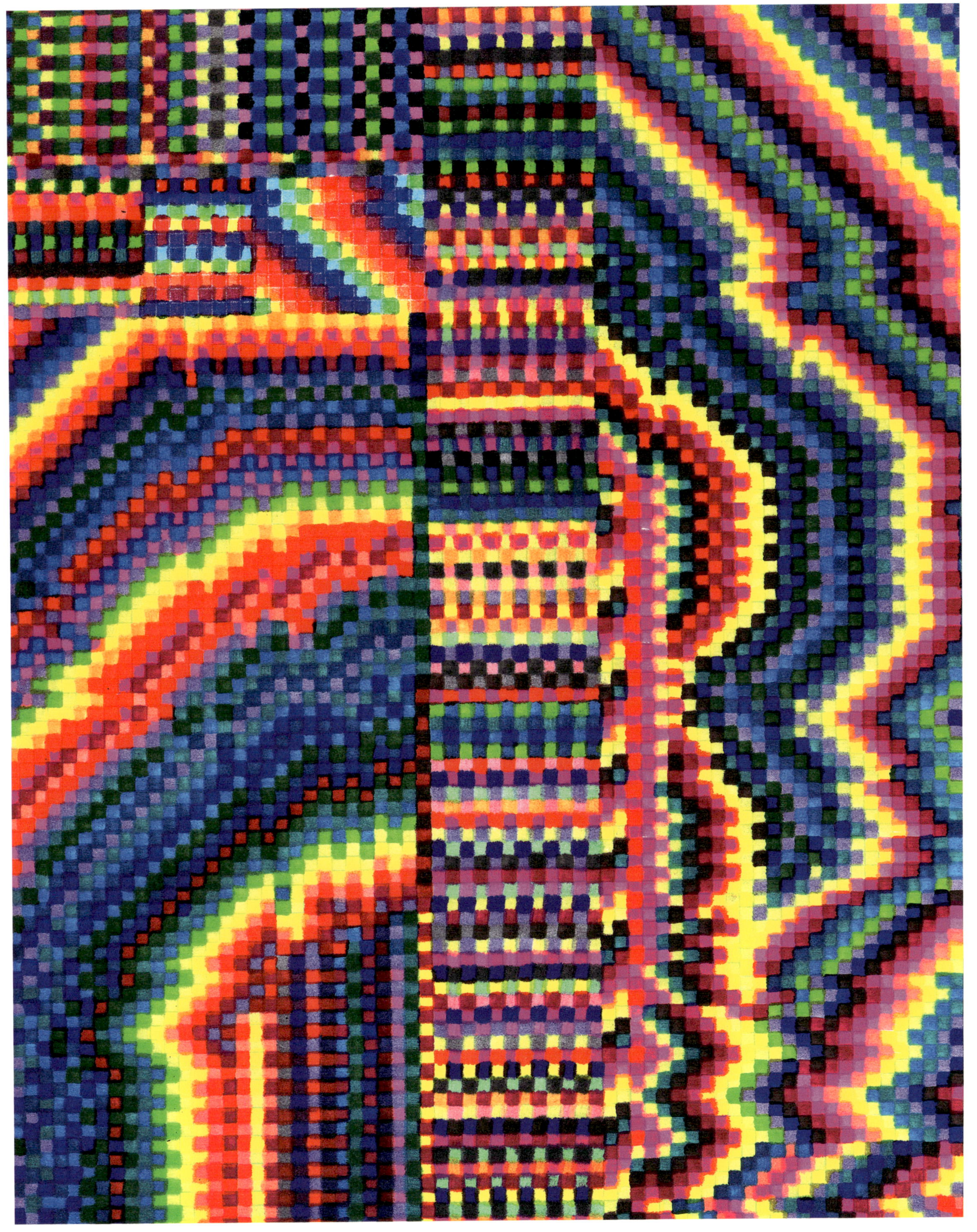

Jessica Ciocci
Untitled (Grid Drawings)
2009

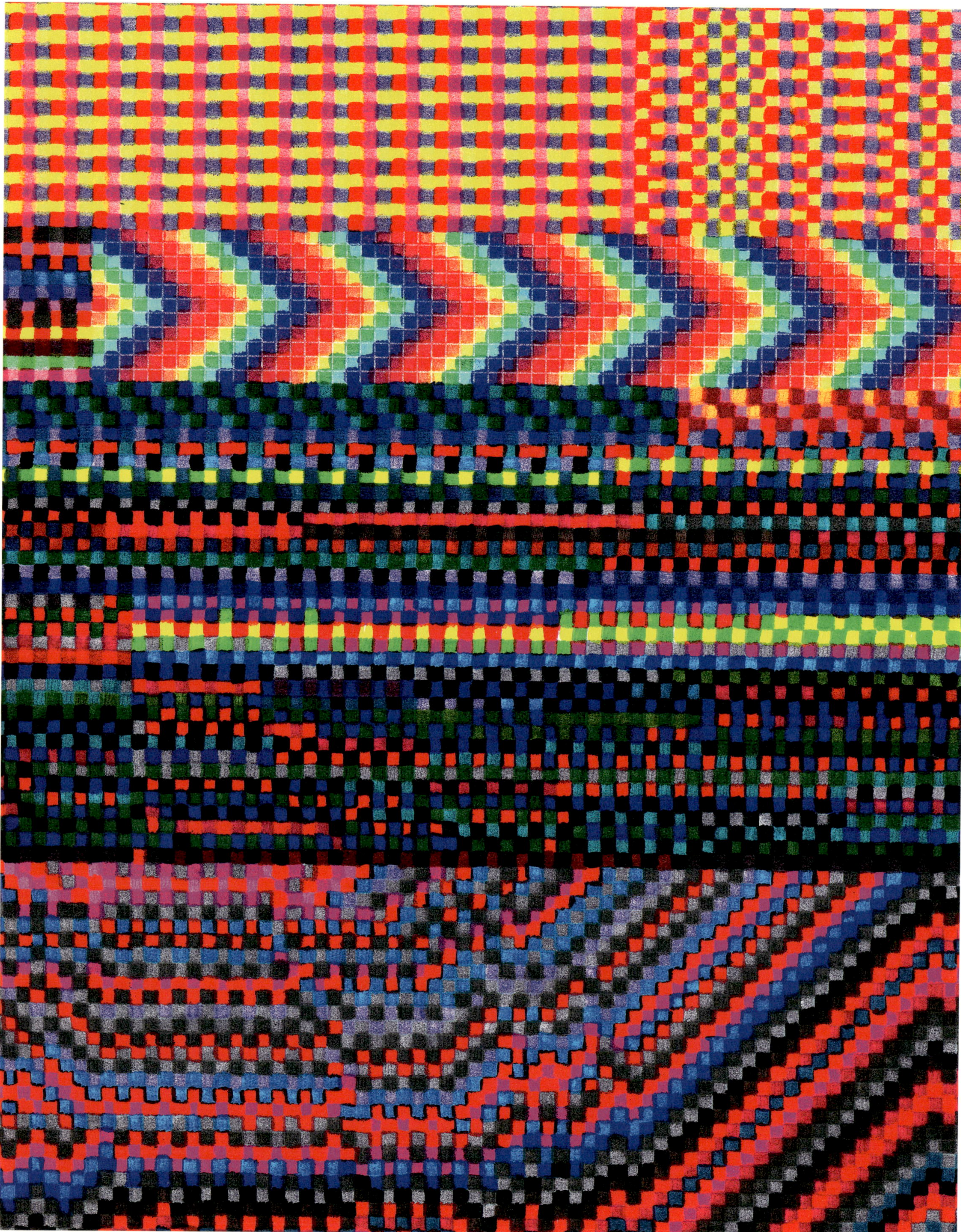

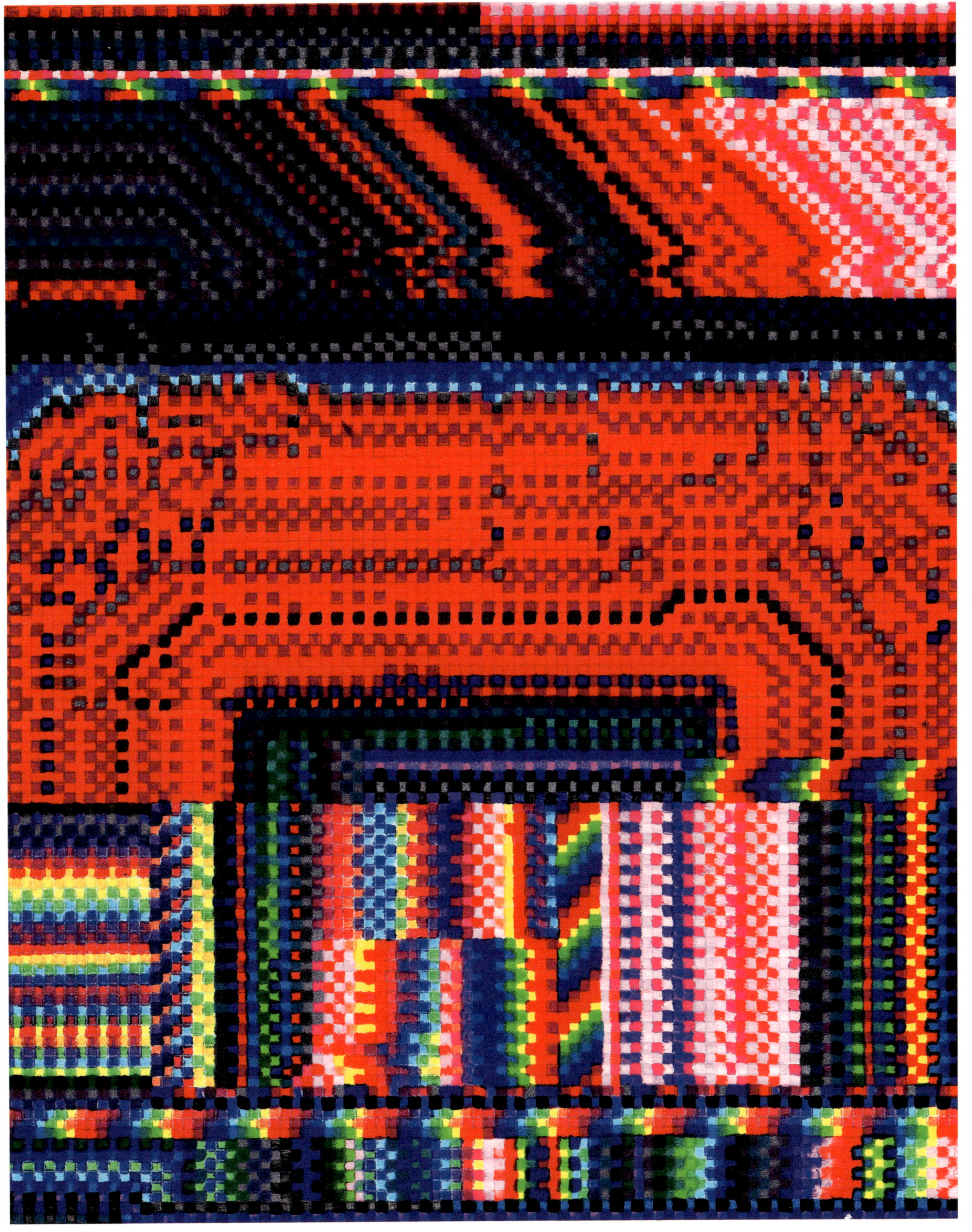

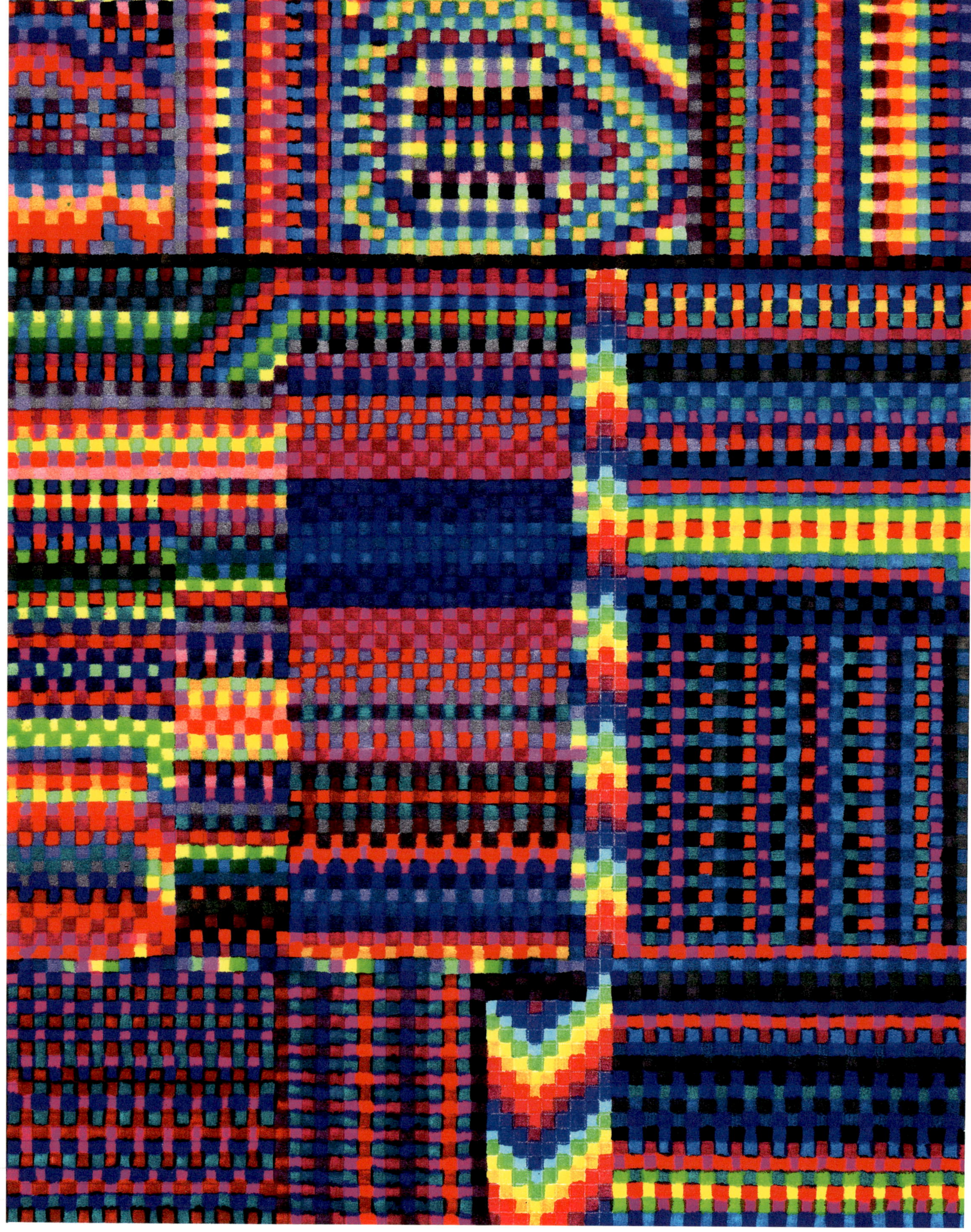

H—FOR HAHAHA OR HYPERREALITY MEETS HYPERMENTAL

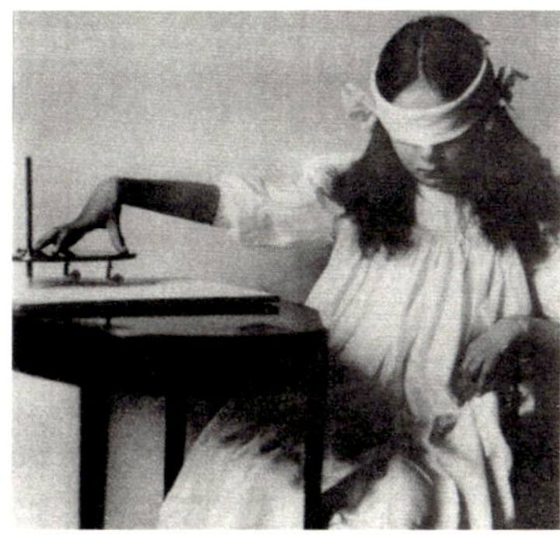

In an exhibition entitled "Hypermental," this keyword served to situate "post-Surrealist" tendencies and aspects that were manifest in works of art in a great variety of genres and styles during the second half of the 20th century, including the most recent art.[30] Surrealism was here conceived not so much as an autonomous system whose history came to a conclusion after its heyday in the first half of the 20th century, but instead as a philosophical and conceptual order that continues to influence the artistic praxis of younger artists to this day. (→ SHANA MOULTON) The original definition offered by André Breton has lost its revolutionary spirit. The methods he proposed, such as 'écriture automatique,' which was meant to help uncover the subconscious, did not prevail.[31] Yet the idea remains current that the surreal can come to the fore in a dialogue with the other, which can appear in the form of a dream, the miraculous, or the uncanny. Surrealist thinking, then, evinces a heightened interest in the issues of sexuality, drives, obsessions and wishes. (→ IDENTITY MARKETING) Probably the most

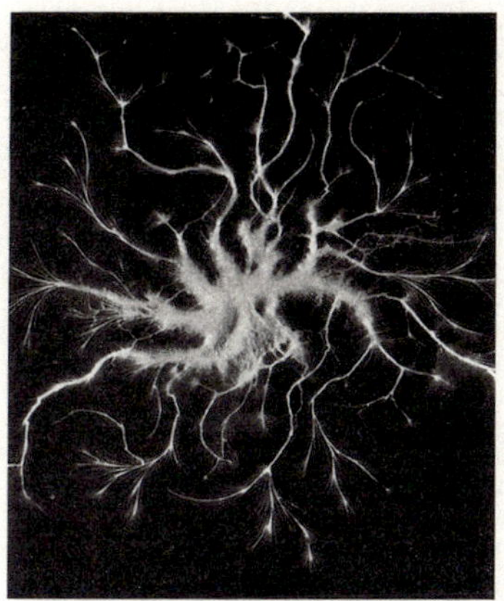

Abb. 1 »L'image, telle qu'elle se produit dans l'écriture automatique« (Abbildung zu André Breton, »La beauté sera convulsive«, in: *Minotaure*, Nr. 5, 1934)

important Surrealist filmmaker was Luis Buñuel (1900–1983), in whose films subversion, provocation, insurrection against the church and the bourgeoisie, compulsions, obsessions, and the "battle of the sexes" were thematic constants.[32] (→ CARNIVALESQUE) Among the filmic means Buñuel used were not only the so-called 'shock images' ('image choc'), but also an aesthetic that interwove filmic reality with dream sequences; he also used stylistic means from the tradition of grotesque comedy.[33] (→ SPECTACULAR, SPECTACULAR EXCESS) In the filmic production of visual artists in particular, Surrealist film has (once again) found a firm place in the canon. (→ EXPERIMENTAL FILM / VIDEO)

Unter dem Schlagwort «Hypermental» wurden in der gleichnamigen Ausstellung «postsurrealistische» Tendenzen und Aspekte verortet, die sich in der zweiten Hälfte des 20. Jahrhunderts in den Werken verschiedenster Kunstrichtungen – teilweise bis in die Gegenwart – manifestieren.[34] Der Surrealismus wird hier weniger als eigenständiges, historisch abgeschlossenes System begriffen, welches in der ersten Hälfte des 20. Jahrhunderts seine Blütezeit erlebte, als vielmehr als philosophisch-gedankliche Ordnung, die bis heute in die künstlerische Praxis jüngerer Künstler einfliesst. (→ SHANA MOULTON) Dabei hat die ursprüngliche Definition von André Breton ihren revolutionären Geist eingebüsst. Die von ihm vorgeschlagenen Methoden wie die «écriture automatique», die dazu dienen sollte, das Unterbewusstsein freizulegen, hat sich nicht durchgesetzt.[35] Die Idee jedoch, dass das Surreale im Dialog mit dem Anderen, welches in Form des Traums, des Wunderbaren oder des Unheimlichen auftreten kann, ist immer noch akzeptiert. So bringt das surrealistische Denken dem Thema der Sexualität, der Triebe, der Obsessionen und Wünsche ein verstärktes Interesse entgegen. (→ IDENTITY MARKETING) Als wohl wichtigster surrealistischer Filmemacher kann Luis Buñuel (1900–1983) bezeichnet werden, der in seinen Filmen Subversion, Provokation, die Auflehnung gegen die Kirche und das Bürgertum, Triebe und Obsessionen sowie den «Kampf der Geschlechter» zu seinen thematischen Konstanten gemacht hat.[36] (→ CARNIVALESQUE) Als filmische Mittel verwendete Buñuel dabei nebst den sogenannten Schockbildern («image choque») auch eine Ästhetik, welche die filmische Realität mit Traumsequenzen durchsetzte, und er verwendete Stilmittel, die in der Tradition der grotesken Komik standen.[37] (→ SPECTACULAR, SPECTACULAR EXCESS) Gerade im filmischen Schaffen bildender Künstler hat der surrealistische Film heute (erneut) seinen Platz gefunden. (→ EXPERIMENTAL FILM / VIDEO)

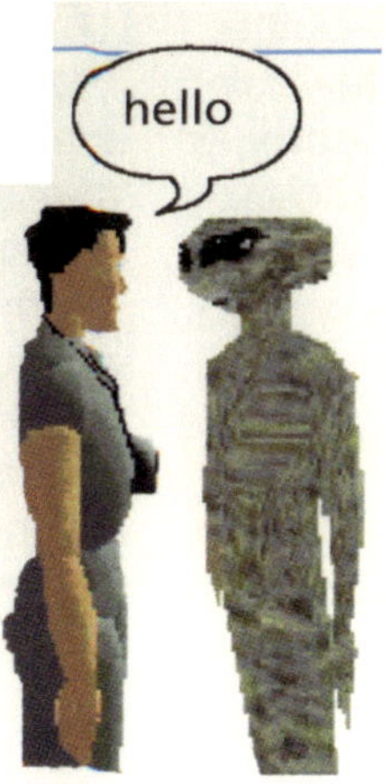

Avatars talking in Active Worlds

30—*Hypermental – Wahnhafte Wirklichkeit 1950–2000 von Salvador Dalí bis Jeff Koons*, curated by Bice Curiger, at the Kunsthaus Zürich (2000). See the exh. cat. of the same title, Bice Curiger (ed.), Ostfildern-Ruit 2000.
31—He defines Surrealism as a "psychic automatism in its pure state, by which one proposes to express—verbally, by means of the written word or any other manner—the actual functioning of thought, in the absence of any control exercised by reason, exempt from any aesthetic or moral concern." Cf. André Breton, "Le Manifeste du Surréalisme," in: *Œuvres complètes*, Marguerite Bonnet (ed.), Paris 1952.
32—Cf. Bruce Babington, Peter William, "The Life of the Interior: Dreams in the Films of Luis Buñuel," *Critical Quarterly* 27, Pittsburgh 1986, 5–20.

33—Cf. Uwe M. Schneede, "Surrealistische Filme — Das Prinzip der Schockmontage," in *Surrealismus*, Peter Bürger (ed.), Darmstadt 1973, 313–321.
34—Im Jahr 2000 kuratierte Bice Curiger für das Kunsthaus Zürich die Ausstellung *Hypermental – Wahnhafte Wirklichkeit 1950–2000 von Salvador Dalí bis Jeff Koons* (gleichnamiger Ausstellungskatalog, hrsg. von Bice Curiger, Ostfildern-Ruit 2000).
35—Seine Definition für den Surrealismus lautet: «Der Surrealismus ist ein reiner psychischer Automatismus, durch welchen man, sei es mündlich, sei es schriftlich, sei es auf jede andere Weise, den wirklichen Ablauf des Denkens auszudrücken sucht.» Vgl. André Breton, «Le Manifeste du Surréalisme», in: *Œuvres complètes*, hrsg. von Marguerite Bonnet, Paris 1952.
36—Vgl. Bruce Babington, Peter William, «The Life of the Interior: Dreams in the Films of Luis Buñuel», in: *Critical Quarterly*, Vol. 27, Pittsburgh 1986, S. 5–20.
37—Vgl. Uwe M. Schneede, «Surrealistische Filme – Das Prinzip der Schockmontage», in: *Surrealismus*, hrsg. von Peter Bürger, Darmstadt 1973, S. 313–321.

One thing the writer Naomi Klein addresses in detail in her much-debated bestseller *No Logo*, which has been read widely, especially among a younger generation of anti-globalization activists, is the situation in which marketing found itself in the late 1980s and early 1990s. Klein connects this situation to academic debates over racial, gender, and social politics with a view to issues of representation.[38] She describes the socio-political demand her generation had expressed: that brand imperia such as MTV, CNN, and Calvin Klein do a better job of representing previously marginalized groups. The idea was that a society whose variety is better reflected in its representations would become more tolerant and inclusive as well—according to a model that bears resemblance to stimulus-response theory. Marketing experts soon analyzed such "quantitative" demands. After "Marlboro Friday," in August 1992, marketing entered a profound crisis of faith, which led to a fundamental revision of policies aimed at generating new audiences. (→ XMAS AND BUY, BUY, BUY) The set of possible identities accepted by society at large was expanded by the addition of types such as the "happy gay," "lesbian chic," "black pride," or the "sassy confident girlie." These new proto-consumers were introduced across the entire pop-cultural spectrum—from soap operas to lifestyle magazines. (→ FICTION AND NARRATIVE METHODS) That these identities, in the concrete shape they took, were no less determined and just as commodified, was not what the followers of Judith Butler, who had taken the stage with her critique of the concepts of identity and subjectivity, of normative heterosexuality and a materialization of gender, had intended.[39] Butler's model hypothesis of gender as a performative construct remains, it is fair to say, one of her most important contributions to this day; it offers ways in which to conceive masculinity and femininity as reflections of social actions and not as biologically determined materializations—in Queer Studies, in particular, her model has become canonical. On the Internet more than anywhere else, the idea of such a liquid gender and of identity as subject to individual shaping seems to have prevailed. Virtual online role-playing games allow users to anonymously (or so it would seem) explore the most varied identities and sexualities. (→ ZAK MCKRACKEN AND THE ALIEN MINDBENDERS) In this sense, cyberspace at least seems to confirm Butler's hypotheses. (→ SHANA MOULTON) (→ RYAN TRECARTIN & LIZZIE FITCH)

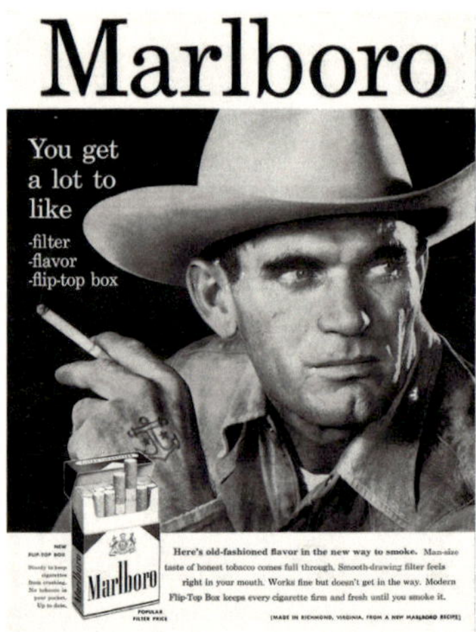

In ihrem viel diskutierten Bestseller *No Logo*, der insbesondere von einer jüngeren Generation von Globalisierungsgegnern rezipiert wurde, thematisiert die Autorin Naomi Klein unter anderem ausführlich die Marketingsituation in den späten 1980er und frühen 1990er Jahren und bringt diese unter dem Stichwort

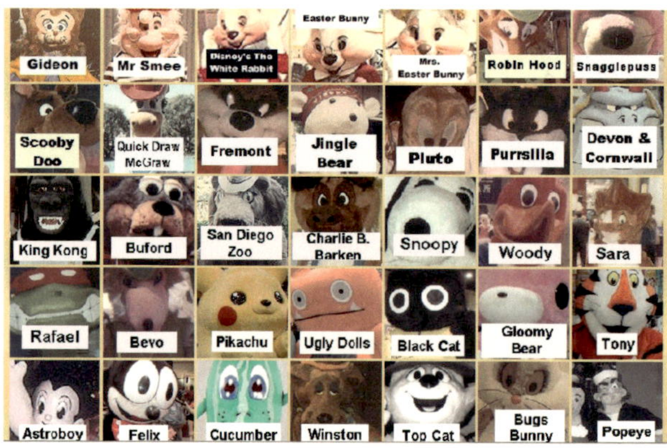

JEC

der Repräsentanz in einen Zusammenhang mit universitären Diskussionen um Rassen-, Geschlechter- und Sozialpolitik.[40] Sie beschreibt die gesellschaftspolitische Forderung ihrer Generation, Markenimperien wie MTV, CNN und Calvin Klein aufzurufen, bis anhin marginalisierte Gruppen besser zu repräsentieren. Mit dem Ziel, dass – wenn die Gesellschaft in ihrer Vielfältigkeit besser widergespiegelt wird – diese toleranter und vielfältiger werde – wie von der Stimulus-Response-Theorie dargelegt. Solche «quantitativen» Forderungen wurden schon bald von den Marketingexperten analysiert und im Zuge des «Marlboro Friday» im August 1992, als das Markenmarketing (u. a. Marlboro) in eine Glaubenskrise trat, um anschliessend eine Kehrtwende im werbestrategischen Vorgehen einzuleiten mit dem Ziel, neue Käuferschichten zu generieren. (→ XMAS AND BUY, BUY, BUY) Der Kreis möglicher, in einer breiteren Gesellschaft akzeptierten Identitäten wurde erweitert mit «Verkörperungen» wie dem «happy gay», dem «lesbian chic», dem «proud to be black» oder den «frech-selbstbewussten Girlies». Die neuen Proto-Konsumenten wurden auf der gesamten popkulturellen Bandbreite eingeführt – sei es in der Soap Opera oder im Lifestyle-Magazin. (→ FICTION AND NARRATIVE METHODS) Dass diese Identitäten auch in ihrer Ausgestaltung gleich determiniert und zur Warenförmigkeit verkamen, war nicht im Sinne der Anhänger Judith Butlers, die mit ihrer Kritik am Identitäts- und Subjektbegriff, an der normativen Heterosexualität und einer Materialisierung des Geschlechts bekannt wurden.[41] Das Thesenmodell eines performativen Geschlechts kann heute als einer von Butlers wichtigsten Beiträge angesehen werden: Sie definierte darin Kategorien wie männlich und weiblich als Reflexion sozialer Handlungen und nicht als biologisch determinierte Materialisierungen – wobei gerade in den Queer Studies ihr Modell kanonisch eingebettet ist. Nicht zuletzt im Internet scheint sich heute die Idee eines solch veränderlichen Geschlechts und einer individuell formbaren Identität durchgesetzt zu haben. Im virtuellen Online-Rollenspiel können die verschiedensten Identitäten und Sexualitäten (scheinbar) anonym ausgetestet werden. (→ ZAK MCKRACKEN AND THE ALIEN MINDBENDERS) So scheint sich wenigstens im Internetraum die These Butlers zu bestätigen. (→ SHANA MOULTON) (→ RYAN TRECARTIN & LIZZIE FITCH)

The following pages contain visual source material from:

Cory Arcangel / CA
Jessica Ciocci / JEC
Jacob Ciocci / JAC
Shana Moulton / SM

38—Naomi Klein, *No Logo. Taking Aim at the Brand Bullies*, New York 2000, 107–128.
39—Judith Butler, *Gender Trouble: Feminism and the Subversion of Identity*, New York 1990.

40—Naomi Klein, *No Logo – Der Kampf der Global Player um Marktmacht*, München 2002, S. 123 ff.
41—Judith Butler, *Gender Trouble: Feminism and the Subversion of Identity*, New York 1990.

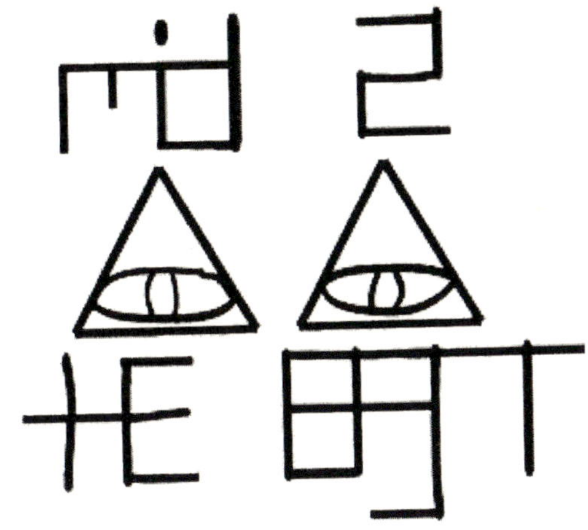

JAC

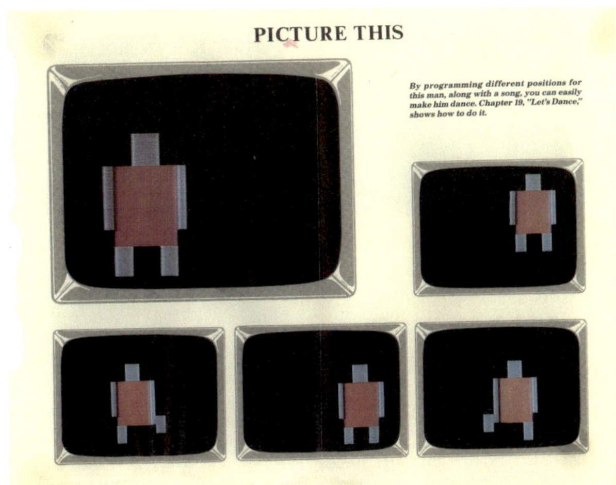

JAC

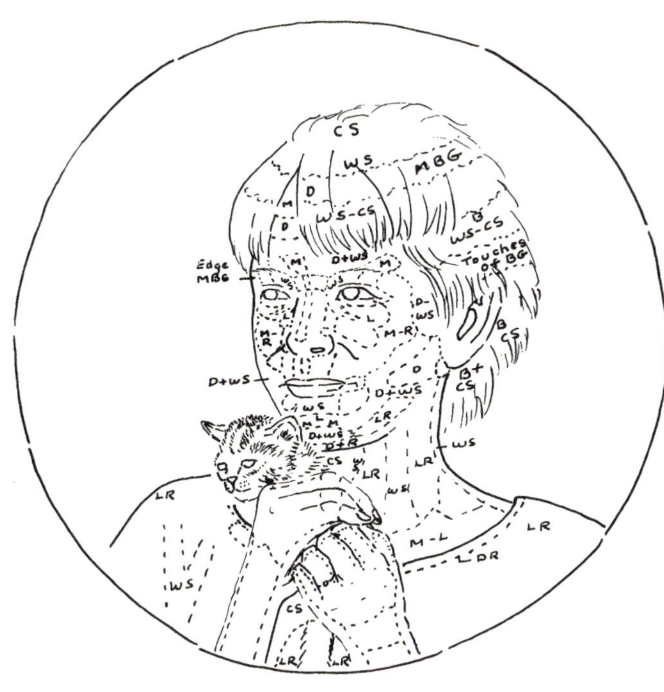

JAC

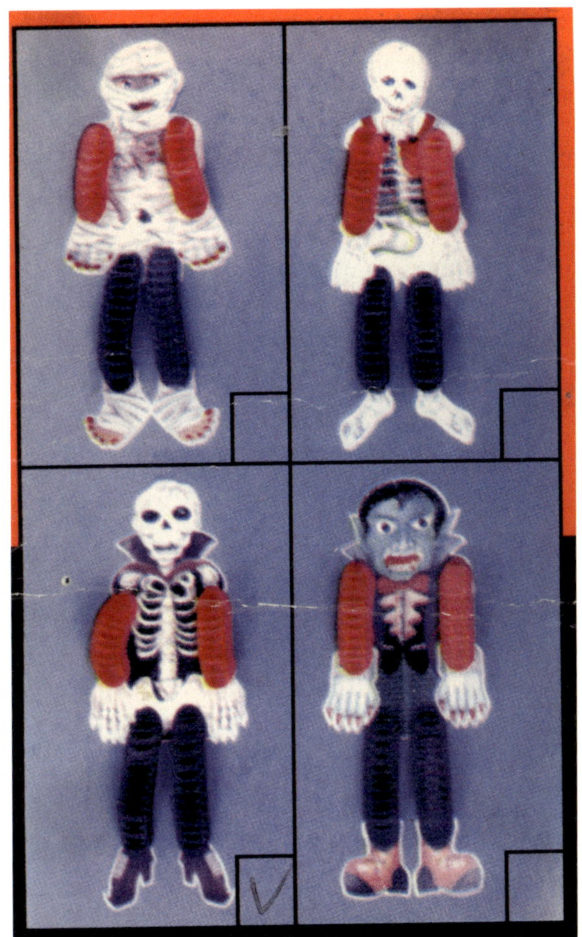

JAC

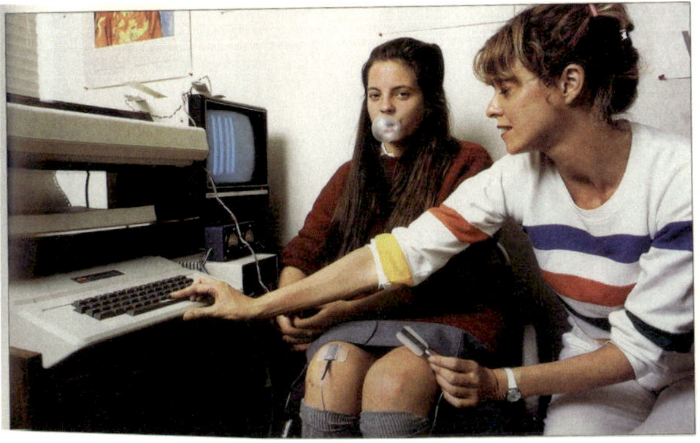

JAC

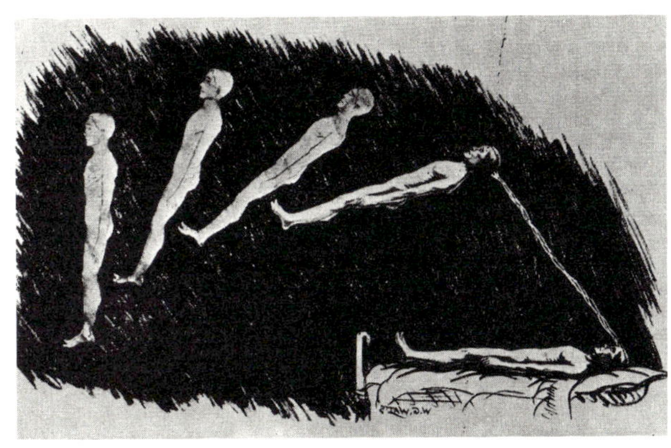

SM

FEAR OF:
DOGS
BLOGS
SPIDERS
WEB
2.0

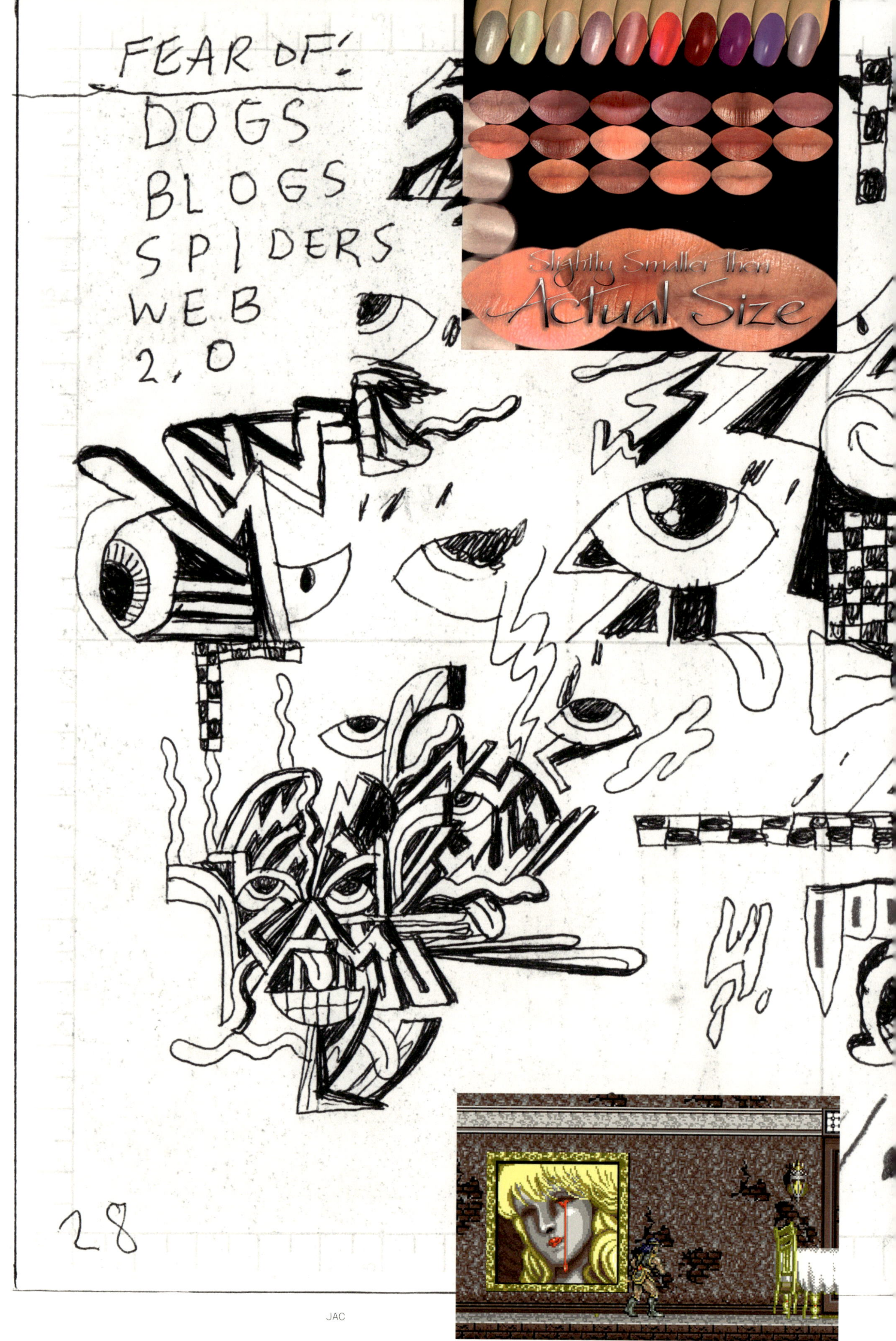

28

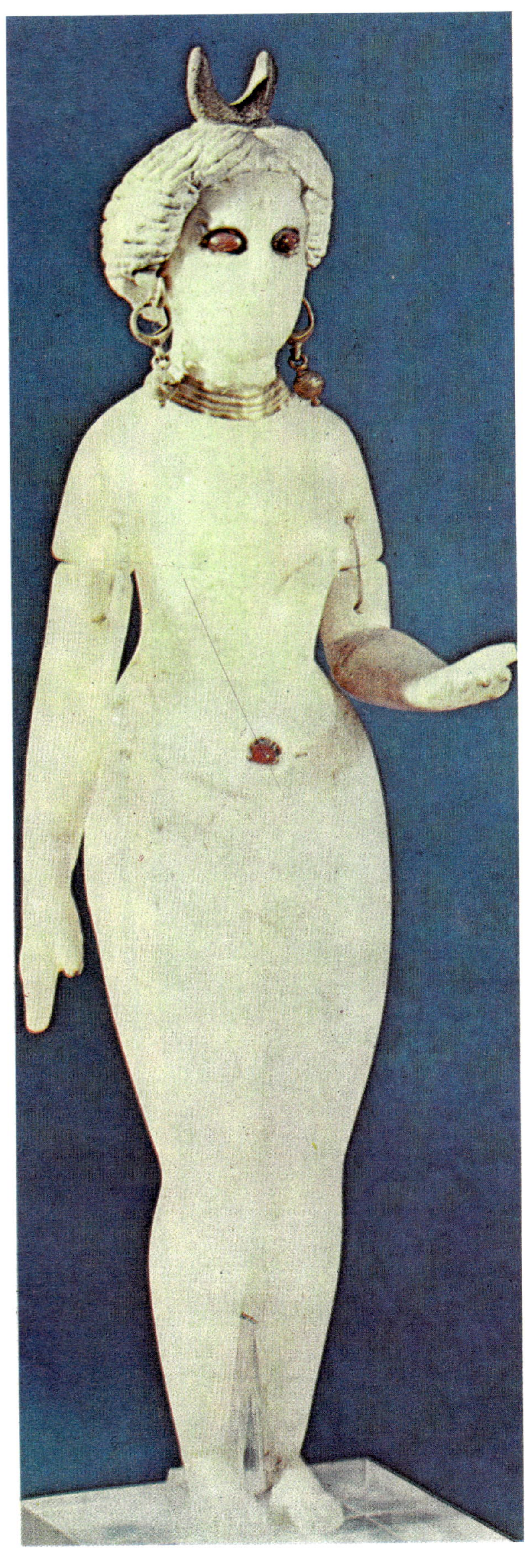

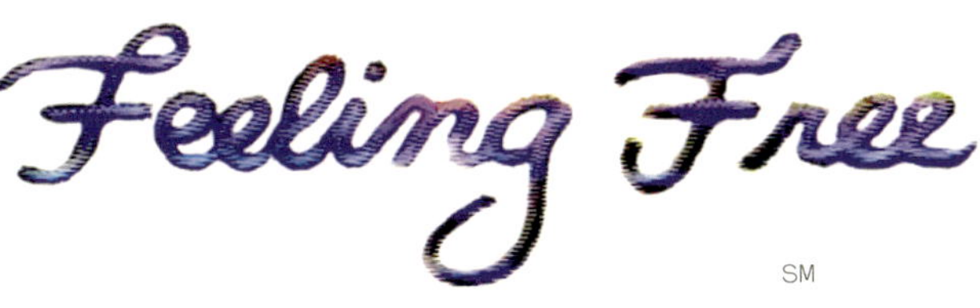

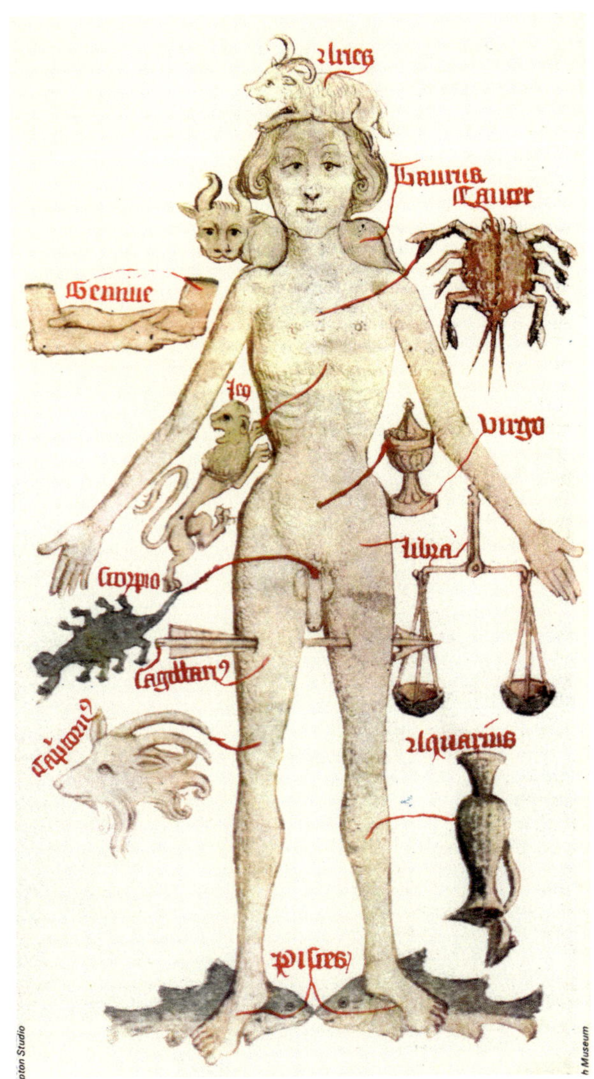

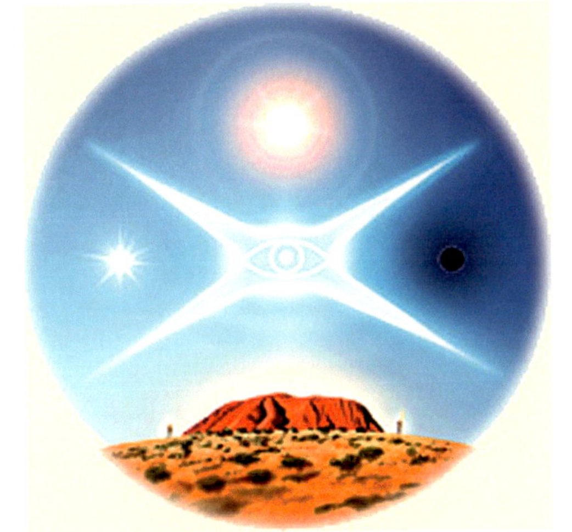

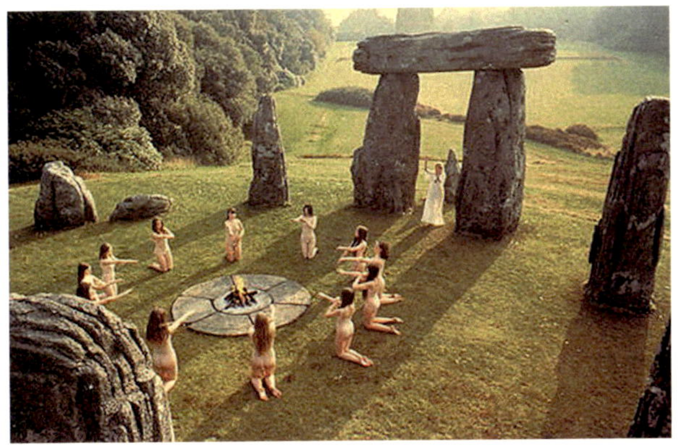

SM

DETERIORATION, THEY SAID

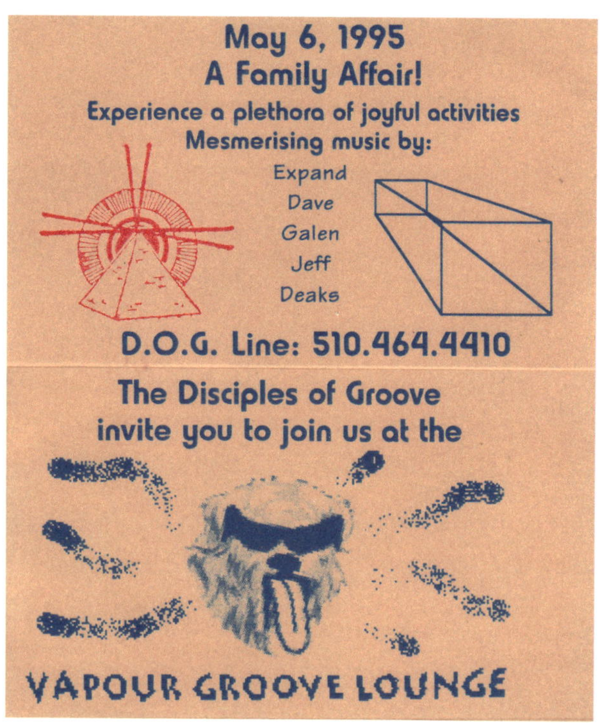

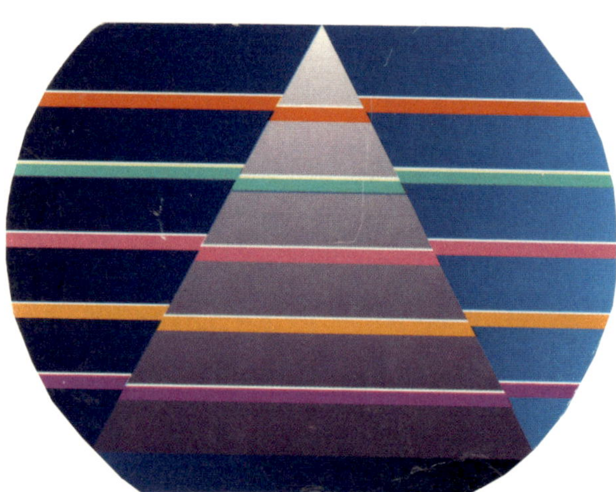

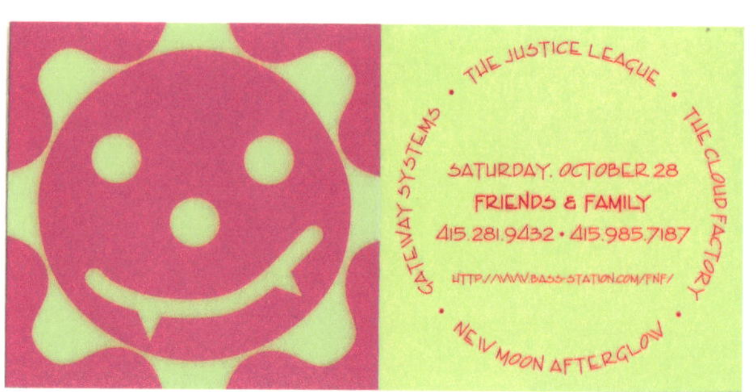

SM

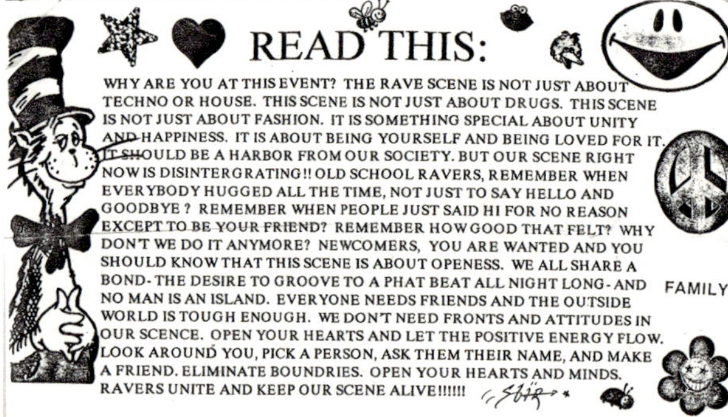

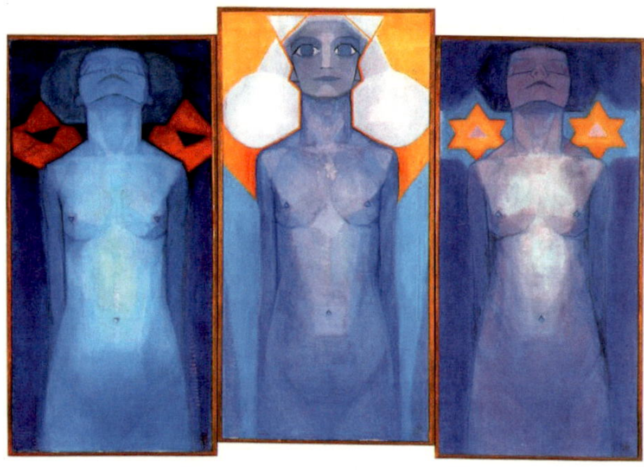

Piet Mondrian, *Evolution,* 1911
© 2009 Mondrian/Holtzman Trust c/o HCR International.

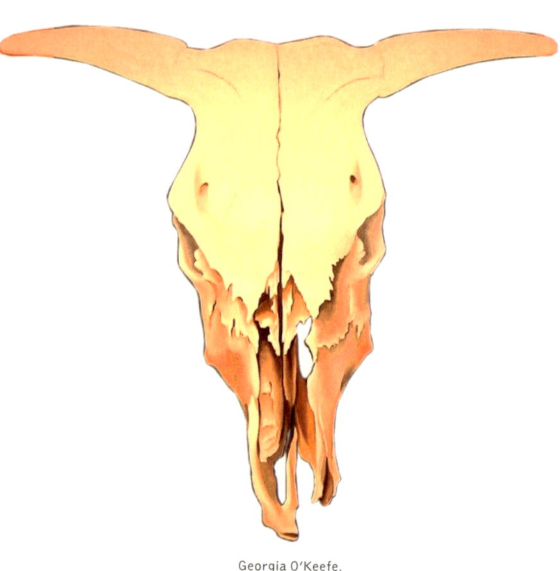

Georgia O'Keefe,
Cow's Skull: Red White and Blue, 1931

01/24/2008

Et

!Solid

CA

RAY
BOURQUE
DEFENSE
BRUINS
Dominik Hasek
Goaltender
BLACKHAWKS

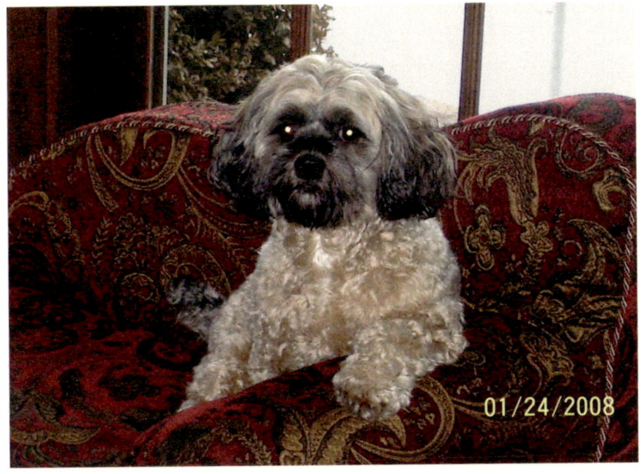

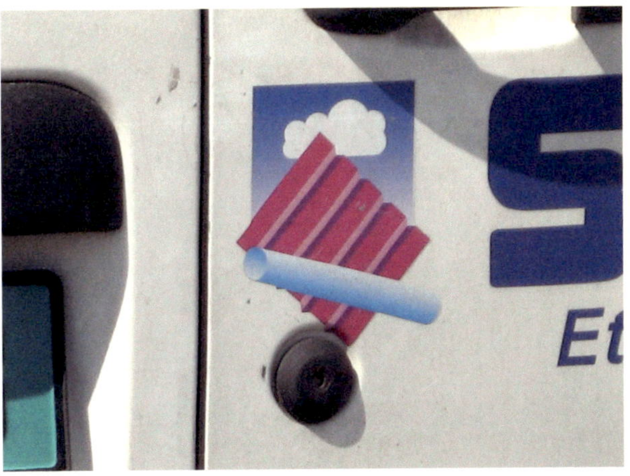

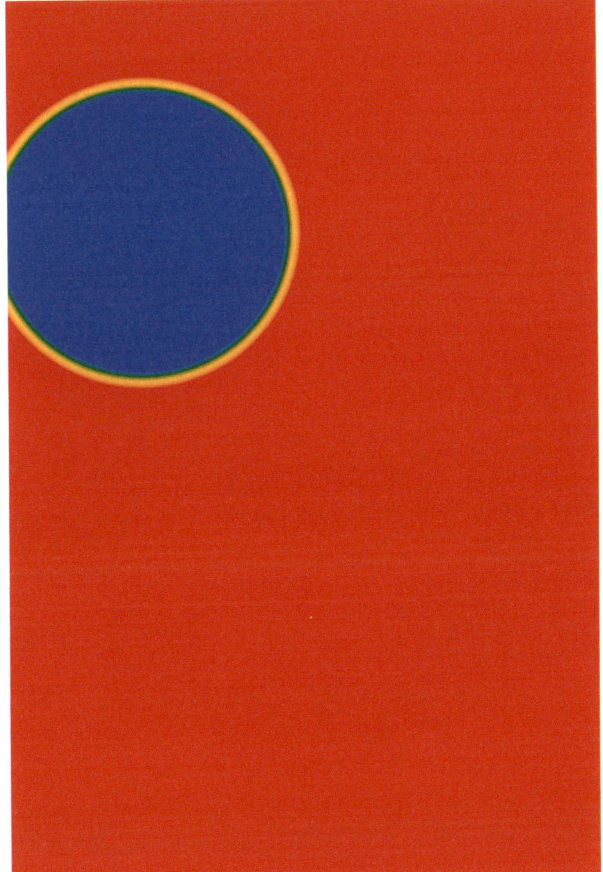

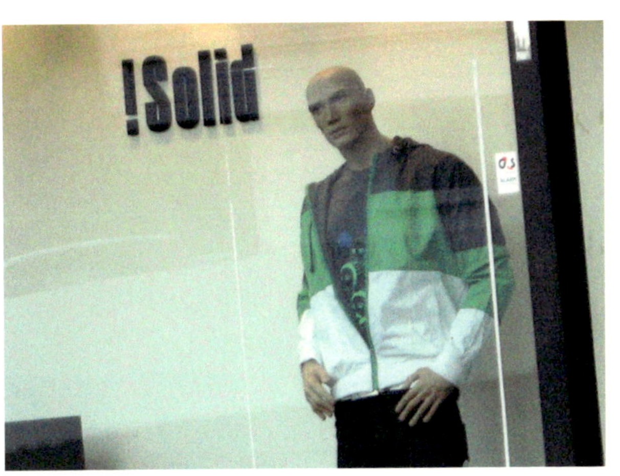

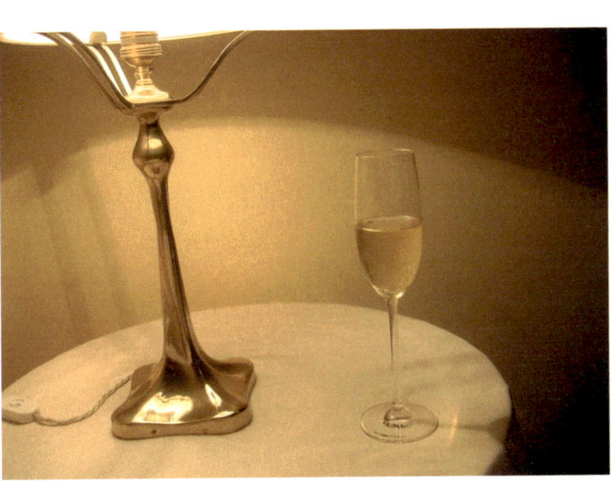

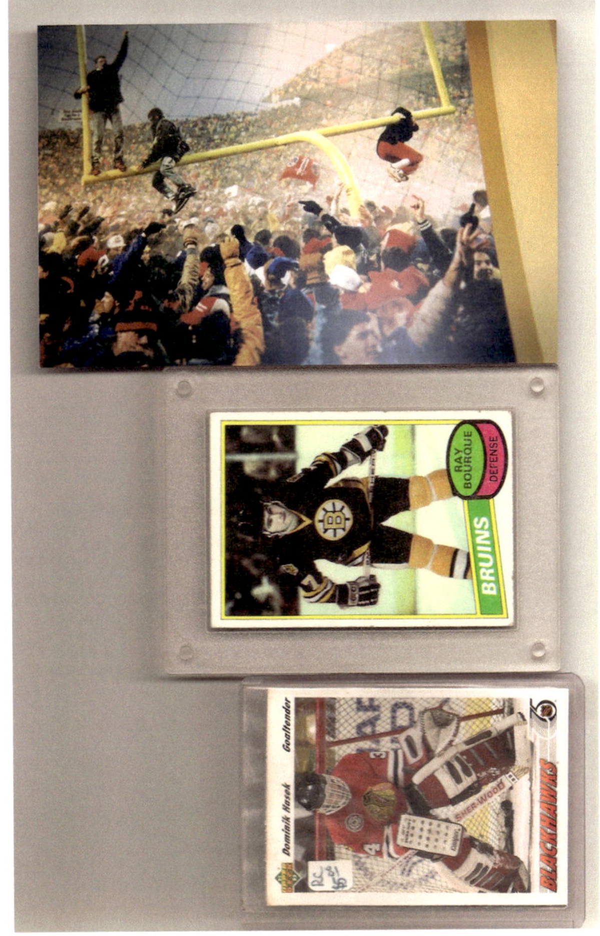

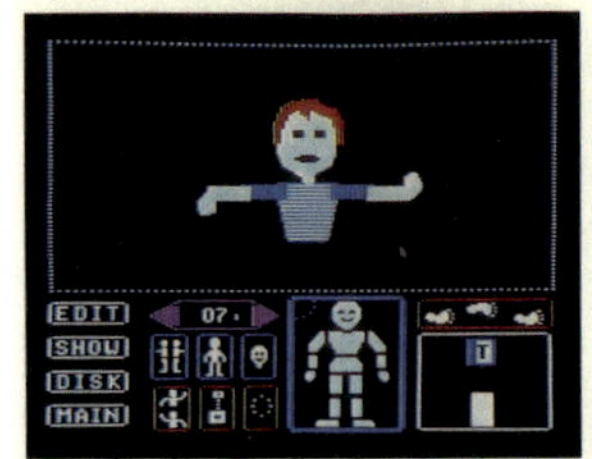
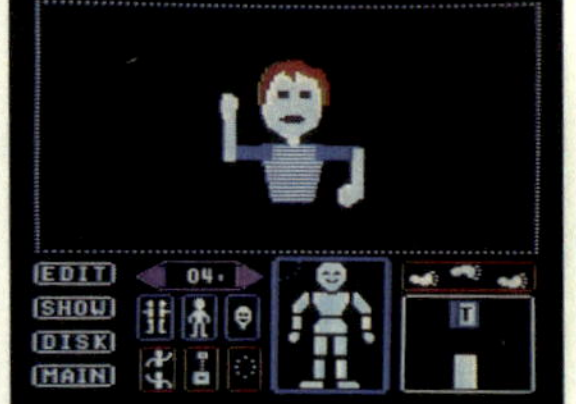
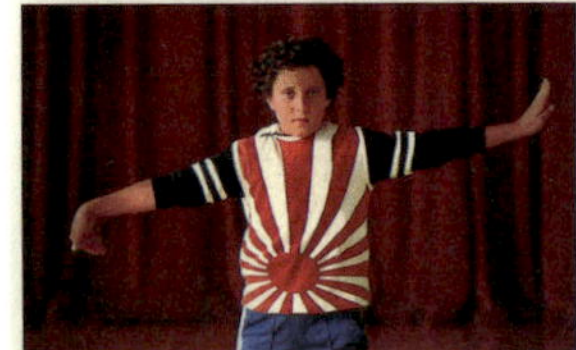
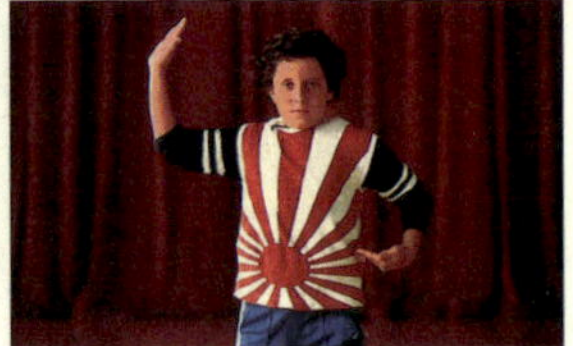

JAC

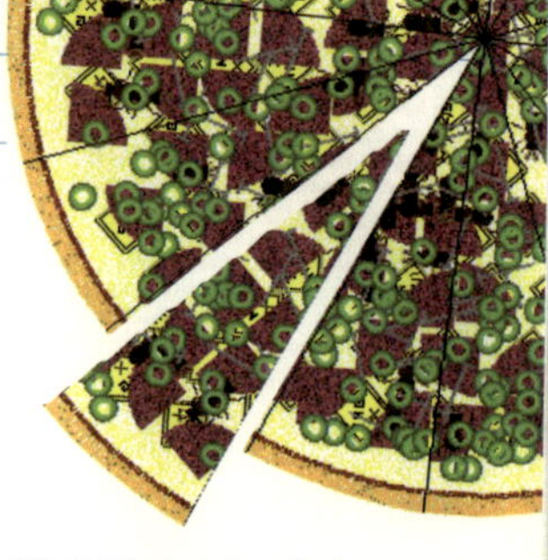

59 CREATE A VIRTUAL PIZZA

Imagine a pizza with sinks, footballs, and smiling faces as toppings. It may not sound very appetizing, but there is a Web site where you can create a virtual pizza with all kinds of strange ingredients. The Internet Pizza Server is at **http://www.ecst.csuchico.edu/~pizza/**.

To design a pizza, scroll down the home page, and click on the link to *Order and view a pizza over the Web*. You will see an online form that lists a variety of ingredients. To select a topping, place a mark in the box next to it. You could be conventional and choose olives, ground beef and green peppers. Alternatively, you could choose more unusual ingredients, such as beetles, road signs and kittens. You can create a truly bizarre combination on your virtual pizza.

When you've finished, click on *order pizza* to download your pizza. A page containing a picture of the pizza will appear on your screen.

This virtual pizza has beetles, nails, olives, salami and road signs on top.

61 PUT YOUR RECIPE ON THE WEB

JAC

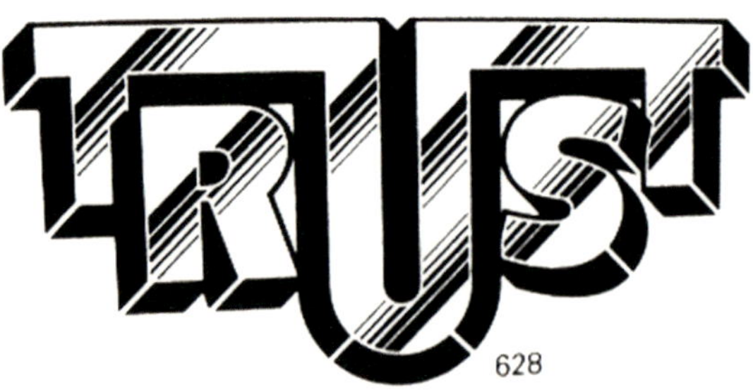

JAC

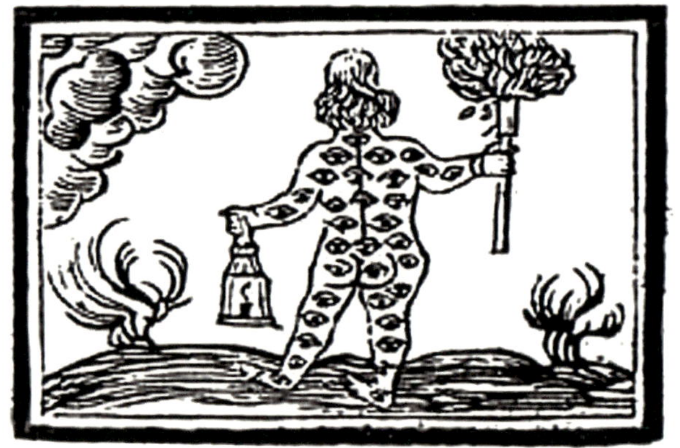

SM

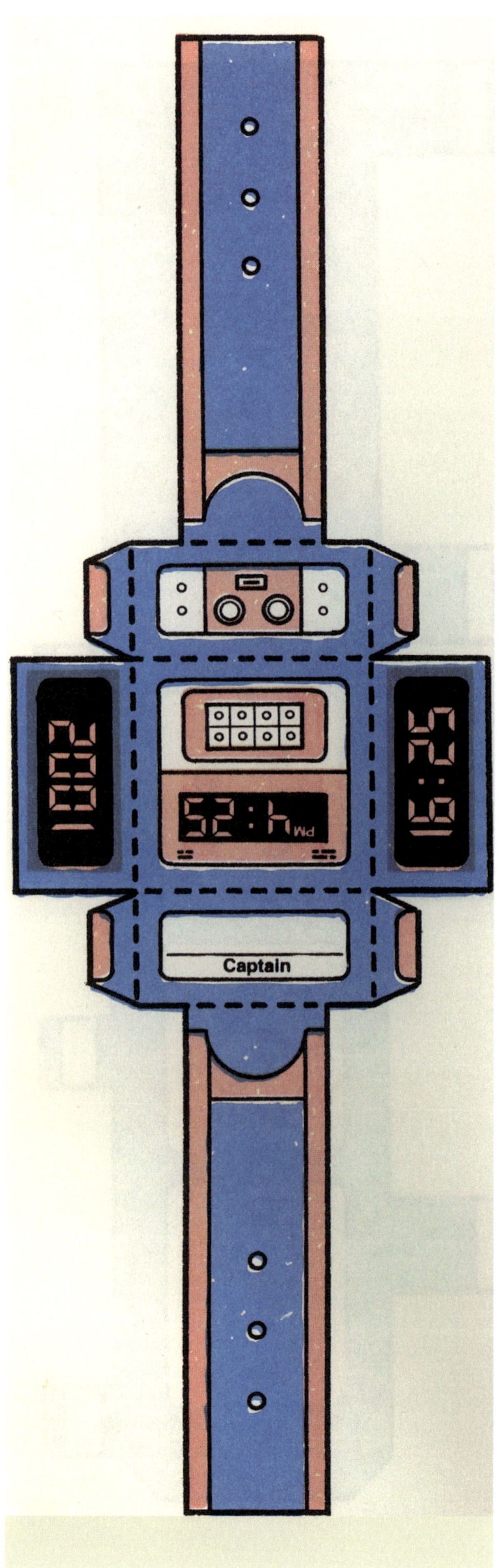

JAC

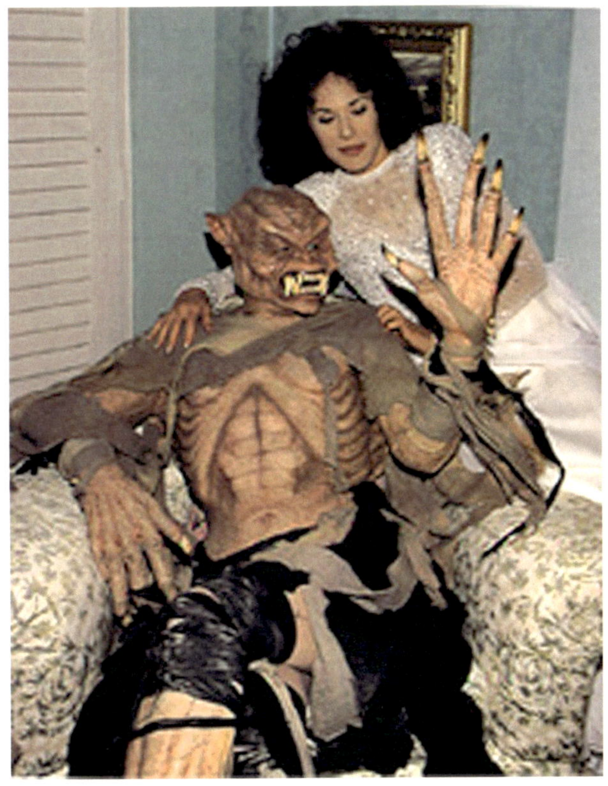

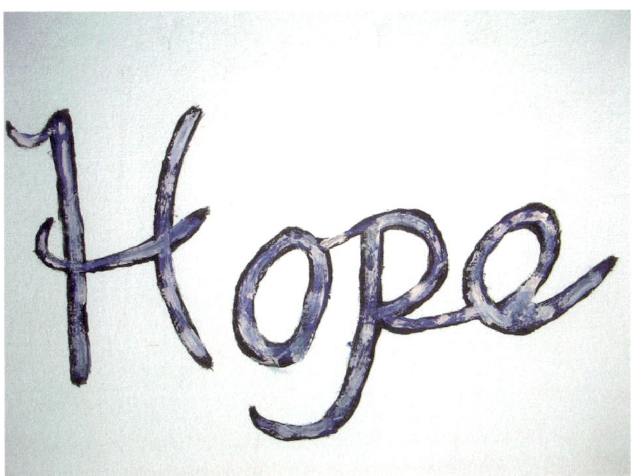

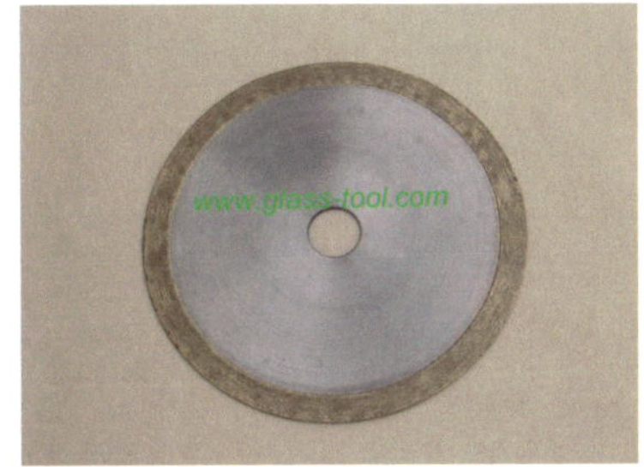

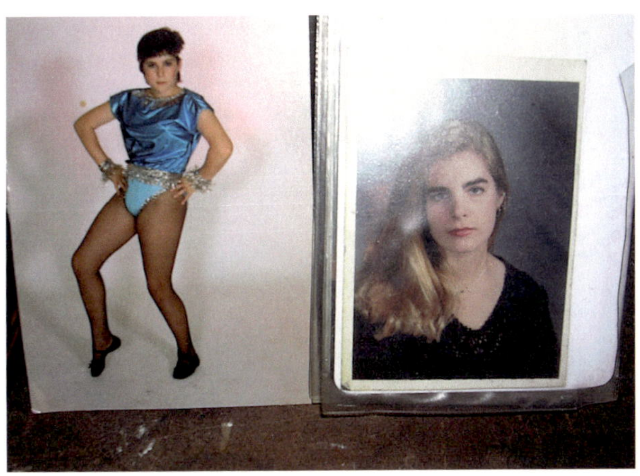

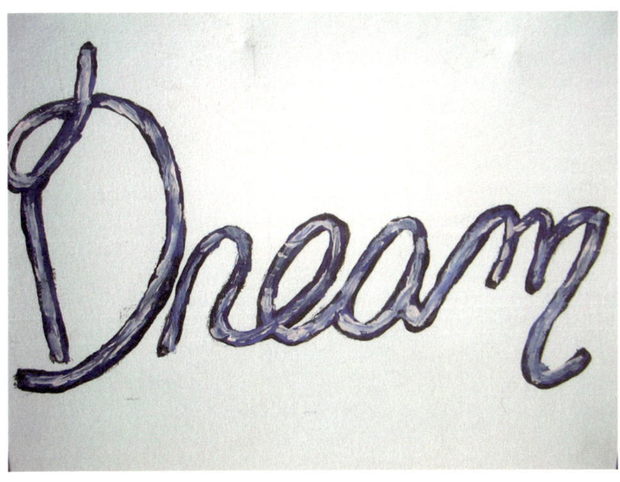

J—FOR JUNK-STORE AESTHETICS

Many of today's contemporary artists work with the debris of popular culture, complementing it with hand-made objects and forms to create inter-media sculptures and installations. (→ CORY ARCANGEL) (→ SHANA MOULTON) (→ PAPER RAD) (→ RYAN TRECARTIN & LIZZIE FITCH) Everyday objects are intertwined with the colorful and seemingly dysfunctional objects and the junk-store knickknacks of an over-saturated consumerist society. (→ XMAS AND BUY, BUY, BUY) This strong involvement of objects and characters with roots in popular culture serves as a highly humorous commentary on the usually arbitrary lines dividing high from pop culture. (→ D(O)I(T)Y(OURSELF) AND BRICOLAGE)

Viele zeitgenössische Künstler arbeiten heute mit populärkulturellem «Schutt», ergänzen diesen mit handgemachten Objekten und Formen und schaffen so intermediale Skulpturen und Installationen. (→ CORY ARCANGEL) (→ SHANA MOULTON) (→ PAPER RAD) (→ RYAN TRECARTIN & LIZZIE FITCH) Alltagsgegenstände werden mit bunten, auf den ersten Blick funktionslosen Gegenständen und Ramschladen-Schnickschnack einer übersättigten Konsumgesellschaft ineinander verflochten. (→ XMAS AND BUY, BUY, BUY) Der starke Einbezug von Objekten und Figuren, die in der populären Kultur verwurzelt sind, unterläuft mit viel Humor die meist arbiträren Grenzlinien zwischen Hochkultur und Pop-Kultur. (→ D(O)I(T)Y(OURSELF) AND BRICOLAGE)

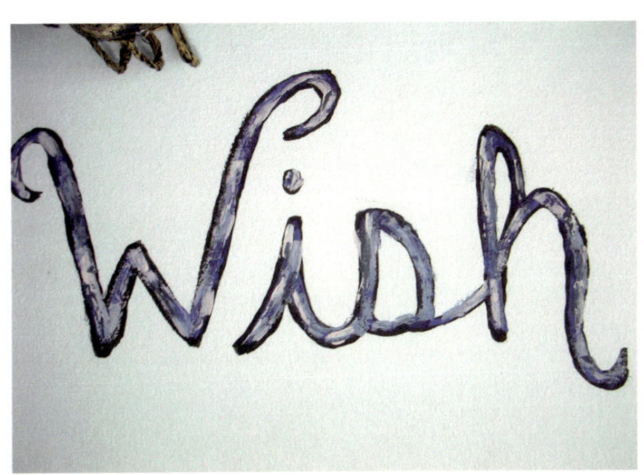

JEC

K—FOR KARMA AND OTHER NEW AGE STUFF

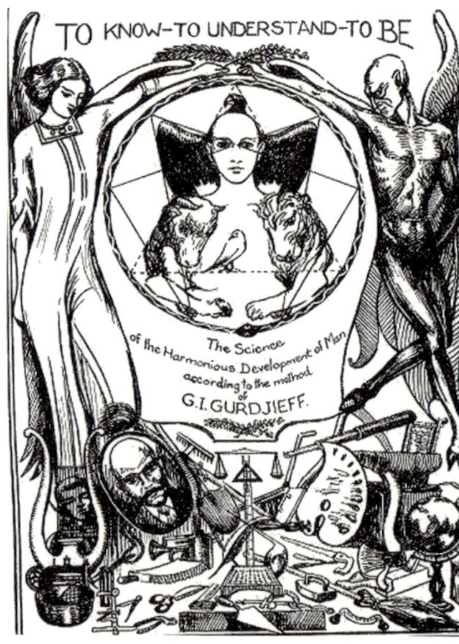

The New Age trend is not a homogeneous and closed movement that took place exclusively in California during the last third of the 20th century—even if that is where these ideas had the most visible effects on broader culture. We should instead describe New Age with a view to the 1960s as an open, alternative-leftist, pan-sophist protest movement paralleling Hippie culture, a movement that was swept up in a wave of commercialization 20 years later, which lent the term the negative connotations it now has. (→XMAS AND BUY, BUY, BUY) This sort of "exploitation" of an alternative culture seems to be of special artistic interest today. (→SHANA MOULTON) New Age-related ideas first appeared in the arts in the early 20th century, often in the context of occultism and spiritualism. Protagonists include the Russians Vladimir Sergeyevitch Solovyov (1853–1900)—a philosopher of religion who, at the age of 21, wrote the provocative book *The Crisis of Western Philosophy*—and G.I. Gurdjieff (1866–1949), the founder of the controversial doctrine of the "Fourth Way," an esoteric movement that aims at a "holistic development" of man. There is no denying the strong influence of spiritualism on Piet Mondrian, Wassily Kandinsky, or Kazimir Malevich, yet for a long time this aspect of Modernism was taboo; "modern art" was to seem as secularized and autonomous as possible.[42] (→WAR OF FORMS) Yet later artistic styles, such as Land art, which can be found in the vast expanses of California and New Mexico to this day, are likewise closely related to esoteric ideas.

Die New-Age-Bewegung bildet keine homogene, geschlossene Bewegung, die ausschliesslich im Kalifornien im letzten Drittel des 20. Jahrhunderts stattfand – auch wenn gerade dort dieses Gedankengut stark prägend wirkte. Vielmehr lässt sich New Age mit Blick auf die 1960er Jahre als offene, alternativ-linke, pansophistische Protestbewegung parallel zur Hippie-Bewegung beschreiben, die 20 Jahre später von einer Kommerzialisierungswelle erfasst und zu einem negativ konnotierten Begriff wurde. (→XMAS AND BUY, BUY, BUY) Gerade diese Form der «Ausbeutung» einer Alternativkultur erscheint heute von künstlerischem Interesse. (→SHANA MOULTON) Das Gedankengut von New Age manifestierte sich zu Beginn des 20. Jahrhunderts im kunstnahen Umfeld erstmals, vielfach in Zusammenhang mit Okkultismus und Spiritualismus. Als Protagonisten können etwa die Russen Wladimir Sergejewitsch Solowjew (1853–1900) – ein Religionsphilosoph, der im Alter von 21 Jahren das provozierende Buch *Kritik der westlichen Philosophie* schrieb – oder Georg Gurdjieff

(1866–1949), der Begründer der umstrittenen Lehre des «vierten Wegs», einer esoterischen Bewegung, die sich der «ganzheitlichen Entwicklung» des Menschen annimmt. So ist nicht von der Hand zu weisen, dass beispielsweise die Arbeiten von Piet Mondrian, Wassily Kandinsky oder Kasimir Malewitsch vom Spirituellen stark beeinflusst sind. Lange Zeit wurde jedoch dieser Aspekt der Moderne tabuisiert, damit die «moderne Kunst» möglichst säkularisiert und autonom erschiene.[43] (→WAR OF FORMS) Jedoch auch spätere Kunstrichtungen wie Land Art, die in den Weiten Kaliforniens und New Mexicos bis heute zu finden ist, hat einen engen Bezug zum esoterischen Gedankengut.

L—FOR LOW TECH

The term "low tech" marks the opposite of "high tech." The definition of "low tech" used here is a matter not so much of technological intelligence or the level of technological development—which is often quite complex even in low tech—but of its position in relation to the technology used in industry and the economy at large to increase production and, most importantly, overall economic output. In this sense, we can also speak of a social component of this technology. (→CORY ARCANGEL) Of course, low tech also includes technologies that are colloquially considered obsolete, such as video. (→SHANA MOULTON) (→PAPER RAD) (→RYAN TRECARTIN) The concept of "low tech" is moreover closely related to a mindset that seeks to use technology only to the extent that the user fully understands its operation, or to use it critically. (→D(O)I(T)Y(OURSELF) AND BRICOLAGE)

Der Begriff «Low Tech» bildet den Gegensatz zu «High Tech». Die hier verwendete Definition von «Low Tech» hat weniger mit der technologischen Intelligenz oder Entwicklungsstufe zu tun – die auch bei Low Tech vielfach höchst komplex ist –, sondern vor allem in ihrer konträren Position zu einer Technologie, die in Industrie und Wirtschaft zur Produktionssteigerung und vor allem für ein Wachstum der Wirtschaft eingesetzt wird. So kann dieser Technologie auch eine soziale Komponente zugeschrieben werden. (→CORY ARCANGEL) Natürlich zählen auch im umgangssprachlichen Sinn überholte Technologien zu Low Tech wie unter anderem das Medium Video. (→SHANA MOULTON) (→PAPER RAD) (→RYAN TRECARTIN) Der Begriff «Low Tech» steht ebenfalls in engem Zusammenhang mit der Mentalität, Technologie so weit zu nutzen, wie man sie selber noch begreifen kann bzw. diese kritisch zu benutzen. (→D(O)I(T)Y(OURSELF) AND BRICOLAGE)

M—FOR MOULTON, SHANA

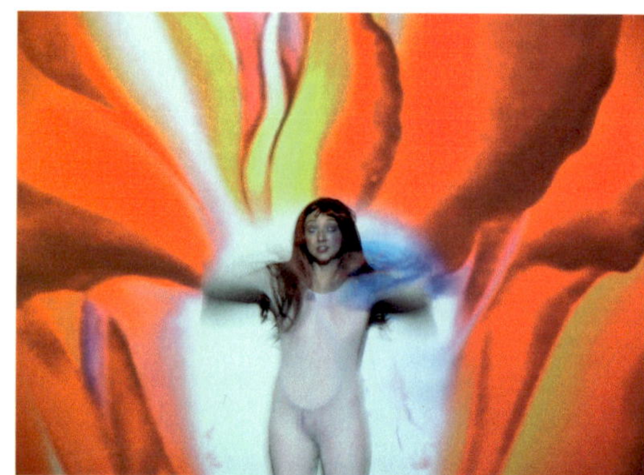

Shana Moulton's works of video and performance art are humorous examinations of the interplay between consumerism, commercialized New Age philosophies, and reminiscences of other artistic styles and individual artists, such as Mondrian (who was influenced by theosophy), the later work of Georgia O'Keeffe, or Land art. (→KARMA AND OTHER NEW AGE STUFF) (→XMAS AND BUY, BUY, BUY) Her narrative videos, into which she cuts psychedelic sequences, and which call to mind the

---

42—Cf. Noemi Smolik, "Mit Okkultem zur Subversion," in: *Psychonauten – Kunst in Ekstase*, Veit Loers (ed.), Cologne 2008.

43—Vgl. Noemi Smolik, «Mit Okkultem zur Subversion», in: *Psychonauten – Kunst in Ekstase*, hrsg. von Veit Loers, Köln 2008.

video aesthetics of the late 1970s and 1980s, were conceived
as a series entitled *Whispering Pines* (2002–). The title "quotes"
the name of the resort town in the San Joaquin valley in
Central California, an unspoiled and idyllic place. (→ QUOTES)
The project, grandly conceived, has now grown to more than
ten episodes, in which the fictional character Cynthia—who
is also an alter ego of the artist—plays a bored, hypochondriac
housewife who, as an antithesis to the fun-loving and raven-
ously adventurous female character of the sort staged by
Pipilotti Rist, is on an ongoing quest for "redemption." With
the central character in her domestic setting, but also with
her choice of format, Moulton draws on narrative concepts
developed in soap operas, thus transferring the popular genre
into the context of art.[44] (→ FICTION AND NARRATIVE METHODS) But

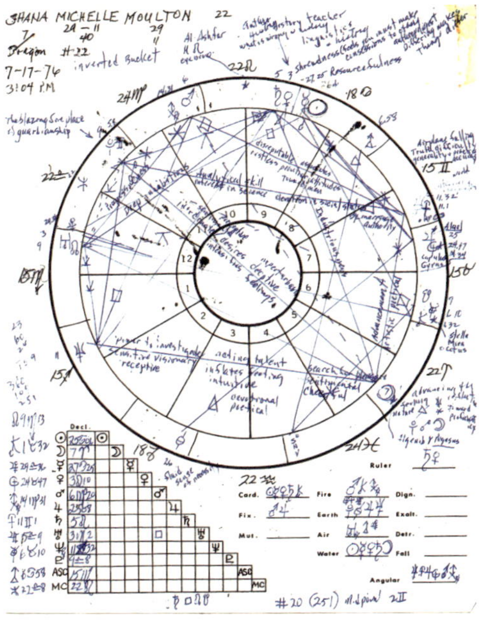

Moulton also continues a tradition of experimental film defined by protagonists such as Maya Deren, who established
her reputation with circular narrative methods in *Meshes of
the Afternoon* (1943). (→ EXPERIMENTAL FILM / VIDEO) (→ FICTION AND
NARRATIVE METHODS) The moments that illustrate the world of
Cynthia's imagination—which frequently slides into the psychedelic register—are often also marked by a "migration
of form(s)"—forms, characters and motifs drawn from the
"heights" of an already recognized history of art begin to
alternate with the "low," with "trash." (→ WAR OF FORMS) For instance, in *Whispering Pines 7* (2006), Cynthia, cleaning the
skin of her nose using a pore strip and facing a Surrealist
distorting mirror, encounters a modern Picasso-style Sphinx
sculpture, as the song *Now That I'm a Woman* from the animated movie *The Last Unicorn* (1982) can be heard playing in
the background.[45] (→ UNICORN) On a visual level, Cynthia's
face—as suggested by the song's lyrics—blends into the frag-
mented-cubist Sphinx sculpture. Moulton produces these
effects with simple masking and green-box technology. (→ LOW
TECH)

Feeling Free

44—Cf. Charlotte Brundsdon, *The Feminist, the Housewife, and the Soap Opera*, Oxford 2000.
45—The original song was recorded by the band America, who wrote the
film's soundtrack. The complete lyrics are: "Once, I can't remember/I was,
long ago, someone strange/I was innocent and wise/And full of pain/Now
that I'm a woman/Everything is strange/Once, when I was searching/Some-
where out of reach/Far away/In a place I could not find/Or heart obey/Now
that I'm a woman/Everything is changed/Everything is changed/Everything
has changed."

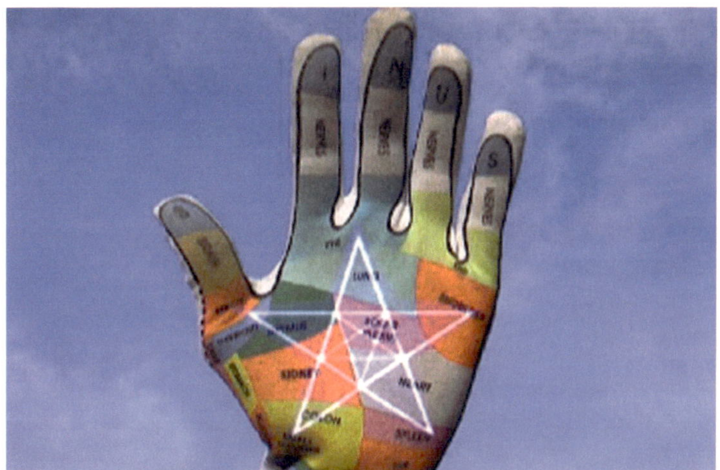

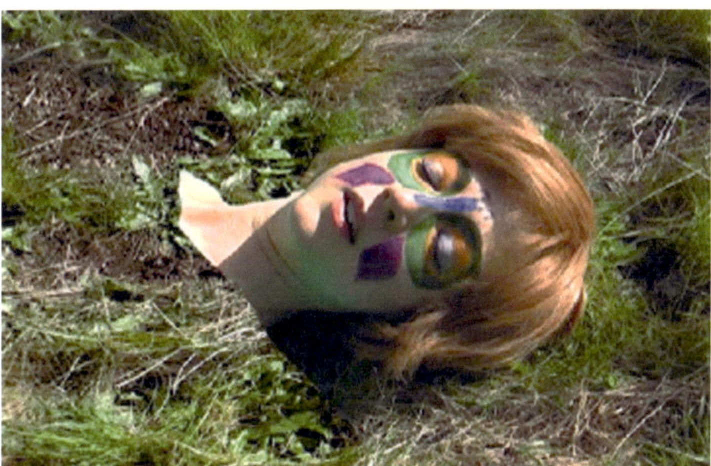

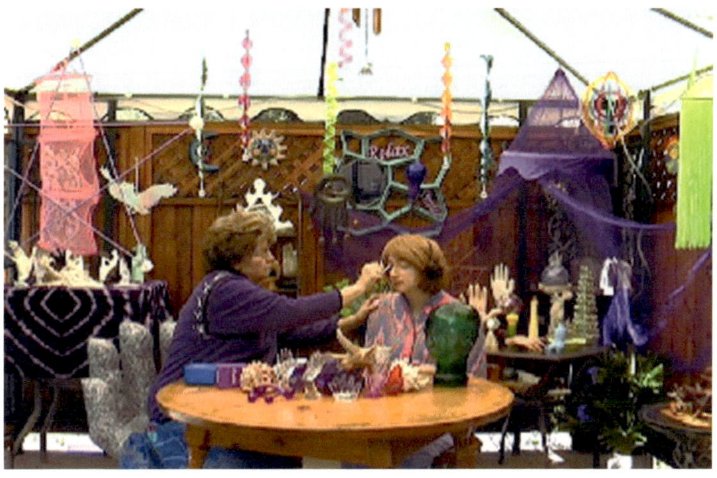

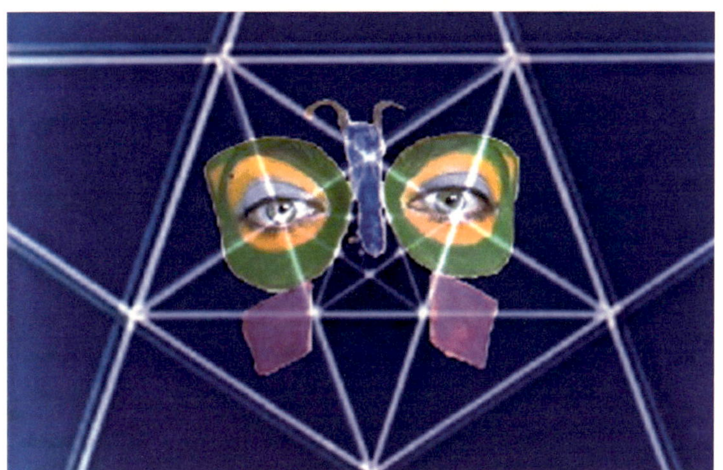

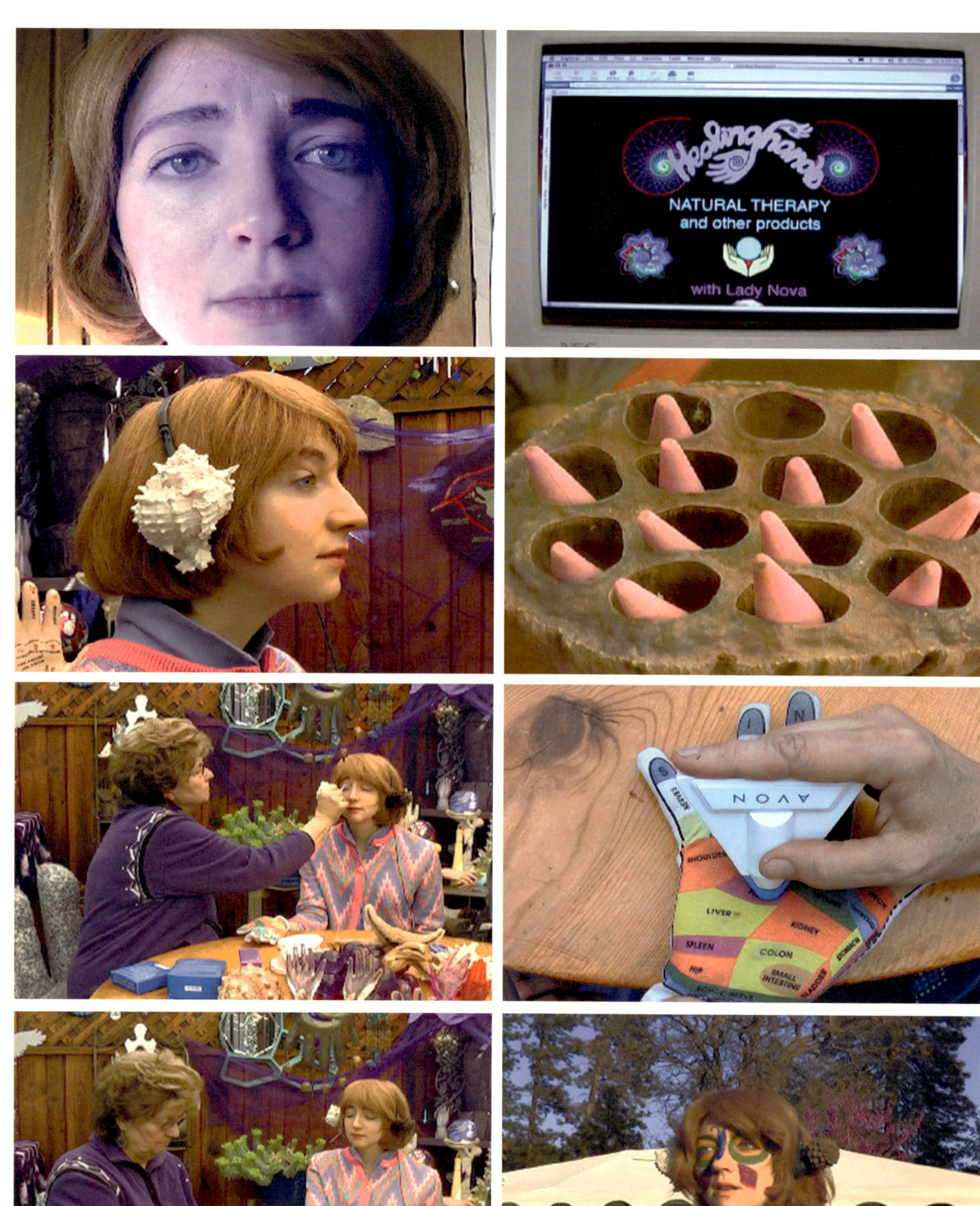

Shana Moulton
Whispering Pines 4
2007

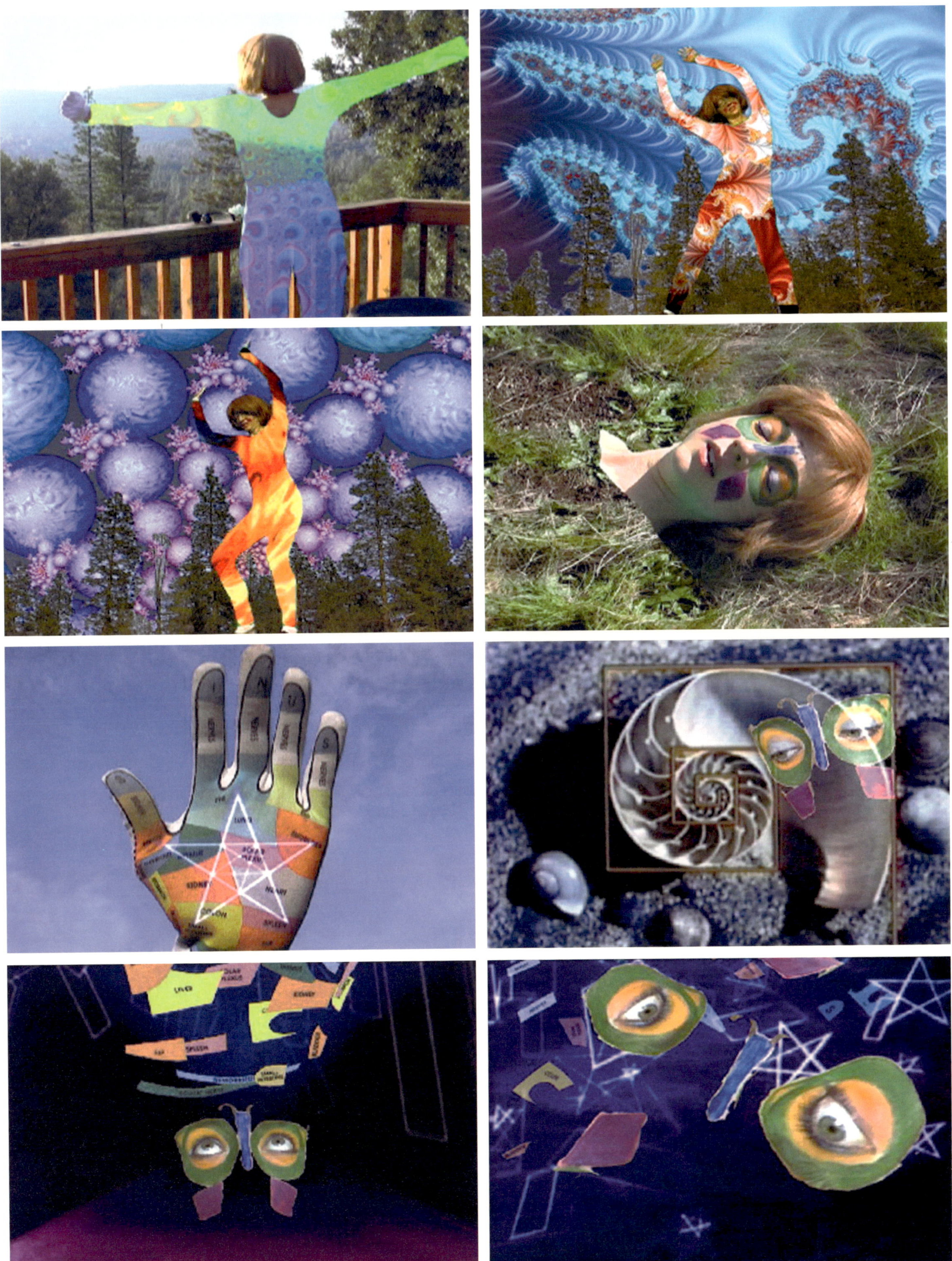

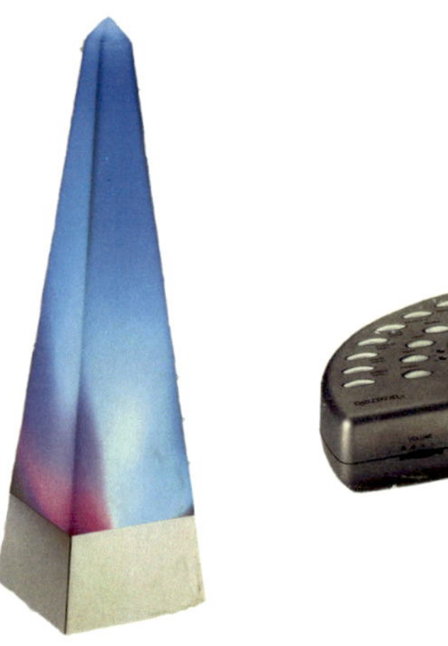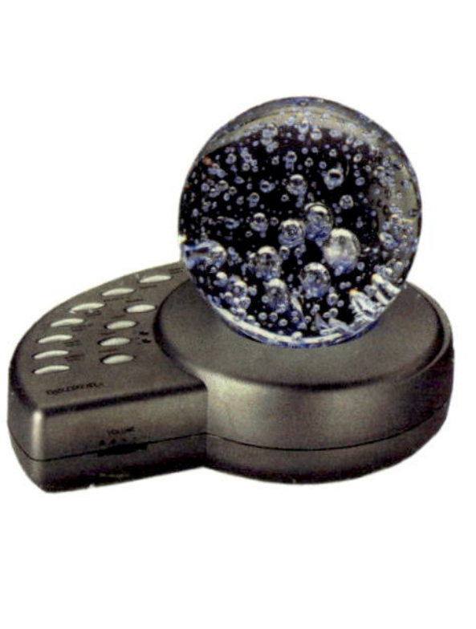

Mit Humor untersucht die Künstlerin Shana Moulton in ihren Videos und Performances die Wechselwirkung von Konsumismus, kommerzialisierten New-Age-Philosophien und Reminiszenzen anderer Kunstbewegungen und Künstlern wie beispielsweise der von der Theosophie beeinflusste Mondrian, den späteren Arbeiten Georgia O'Keeffes oder Land Art. (→ KARMA AND OTHER NEW AGE STUFF) (→ XMAS AND BUY, BUY, BUY) Die narrativen, mit psychedelischen Sequenzen versetzten Videos, die an die Videoästhetik der späten 1970er/1980er Jahre erinnern, wurden als Serie unter dem Titel *Whispering Pines* (2002 bis heute) konzipiert. Der Titel «zitiert» dabei den gleichnamigen Ferienort im San Joaquin Valley in Zentralkalifornien, einer naturverbundenen, idyllischen Ortschaft. (→ QUOTES) Mittlerweile umfasst das gross angelegte Projekt über zehn Episoden, in welchen die Kunstfigur Cynthia – die gleichzeitig als Alter Ego der Künstlerin anzusehen ist – eine hypochondrische und gelangweilte Hausfrau mimt, die gewissermassen als Antithese zu einer lebenslustigen aufbruchswütigen Frauenfigur à la Pipilotti Rist stets von neuem ihre «Erlösung» sucht. Nicht nur mittels der Hauptfigur in ihrem häuslichen Setting, sondern auch durch das gewählte Format lehnt sich Moulton an narrative Konzepte von Soap Operas an und überführt dieses populäre Genre damit in den Kunstkontext.46 (→ FICTION AND NARRATIVE METHODS) Gleichzeitig steht Moulton auch in der Tradition des Experimentalfilms und dessen Protagonistinnen wie etwa Maya Deren, die mit ihren zirkulären Erzählmethoden u. a. in *Meshes of the Afternoon* (1943) bekannt wurde. (→ EXPERIMENTAL FILM / VIDEO) (→ FICTION AND NARRATIVE METHODS) In den Momenten, die Cynthias Vorstellungswelt – die immer wieder stark ins Psychedelische kippt – illustrieren, findet oftmals auch eine «Migration der Form(en)» statt – Formen, Figuren und Motive sowohl aus dem «high» einer bereits anerkannten Kunstgeschichte, beginnen mit dem «low», dem «Abfall», zu alternieren. (→ WAR OF FORMS) So trifft Cynthia in *Whispering Pines 7* (2006) beim Porenreinigen mit einem Nasenstrip vor einem surrealistisch-verzerrten Spiegel auf eine moderne Sphinx-Skulptur à la Picasso, während im Hintergrund der Song *Now that I'm a Woman* aus dem Animationsfilm *The Last Unicorn* aus dem Jahr 1982 erklingt.47 (→ UNICORN) Auf der visuellen Ebene verschmelzen das Gesicht Cynthias – im Sinne des Songtexts – mit der fragmentiert-kubistischen Sphynx-Skulptur anhand eines einfachen Greenbox-Effekts. (→ LOW TECH)

Feeling Free

46—Vgl. Charlotte Brundsdon, *The Feminist, the Housewife, and the Soap Opera*, Oxford 2000.

47—Der Song stammt ursprünglich von der Band America, die den Soundtrack zum Film schrieb. Der komplette Text lautet: «Once, I can't remember/I was, long ago, someone strange/I was innocent and wise and full of pain/Now that I'm a woman/Everything is strange/Once, when I was searching/Somewhere out of reach/Far away/In a place I could not find/Or heart obey/Now that I'm a woman/Everything is changed/Everything is changed/Everything has changed.

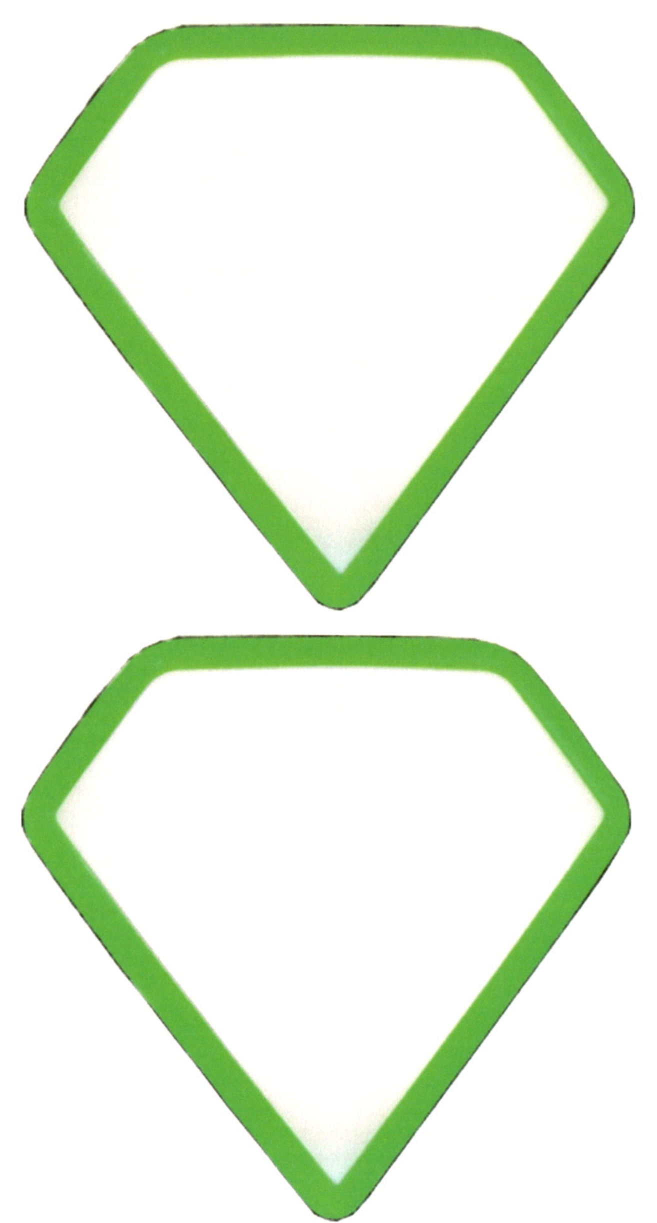

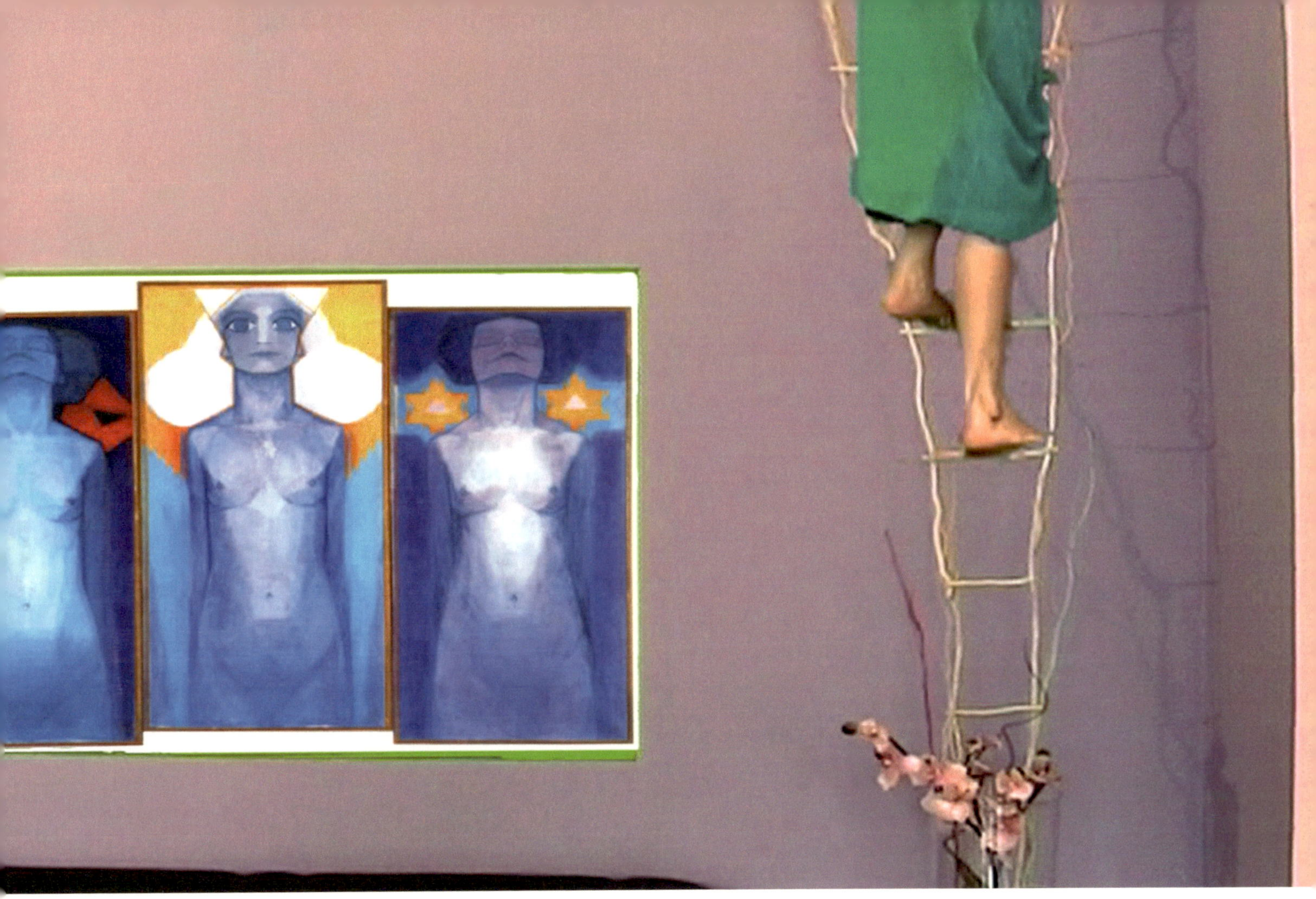

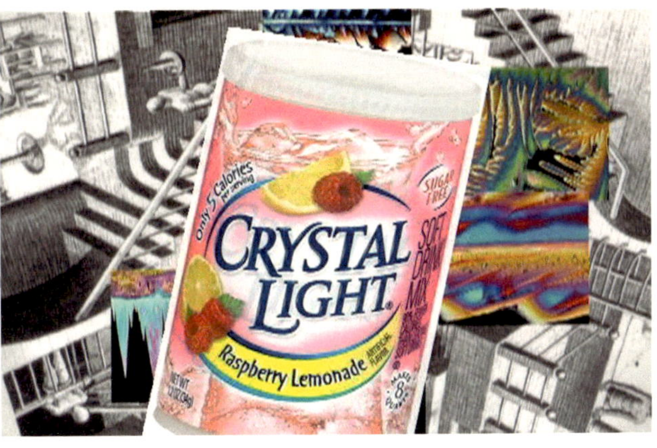

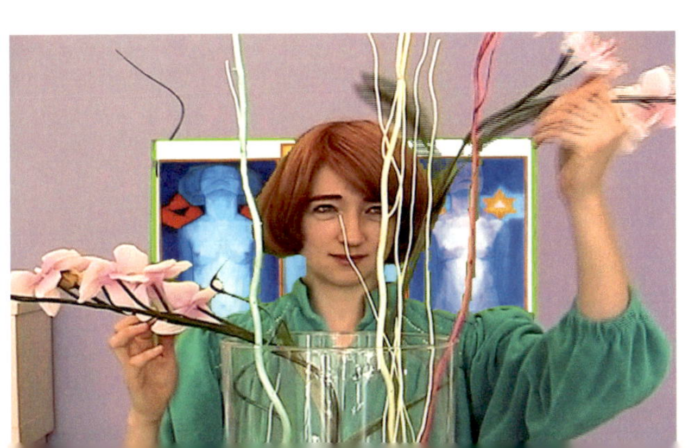

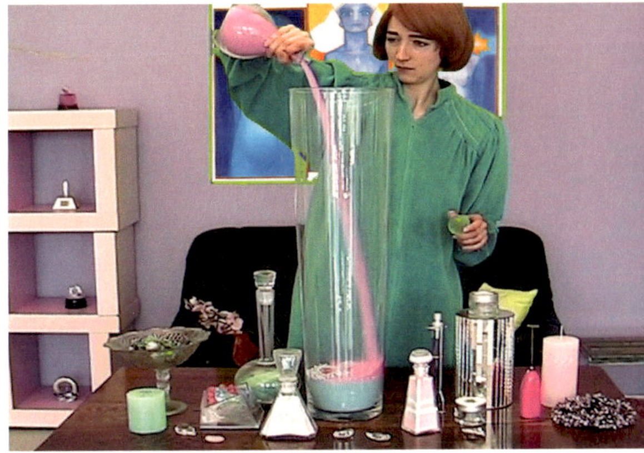

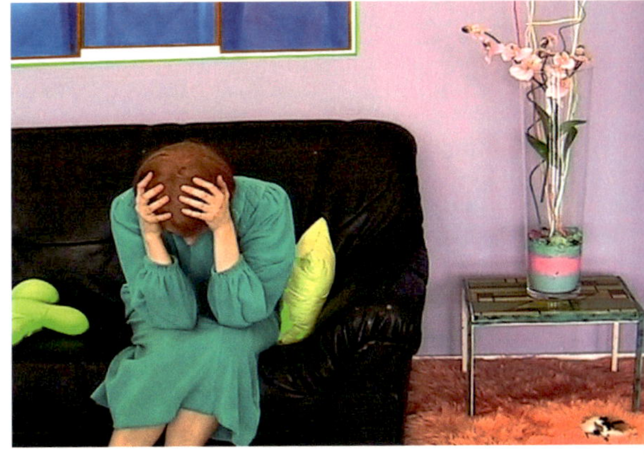

Shana Moulton
Whispering Pines 8
2006

46/47

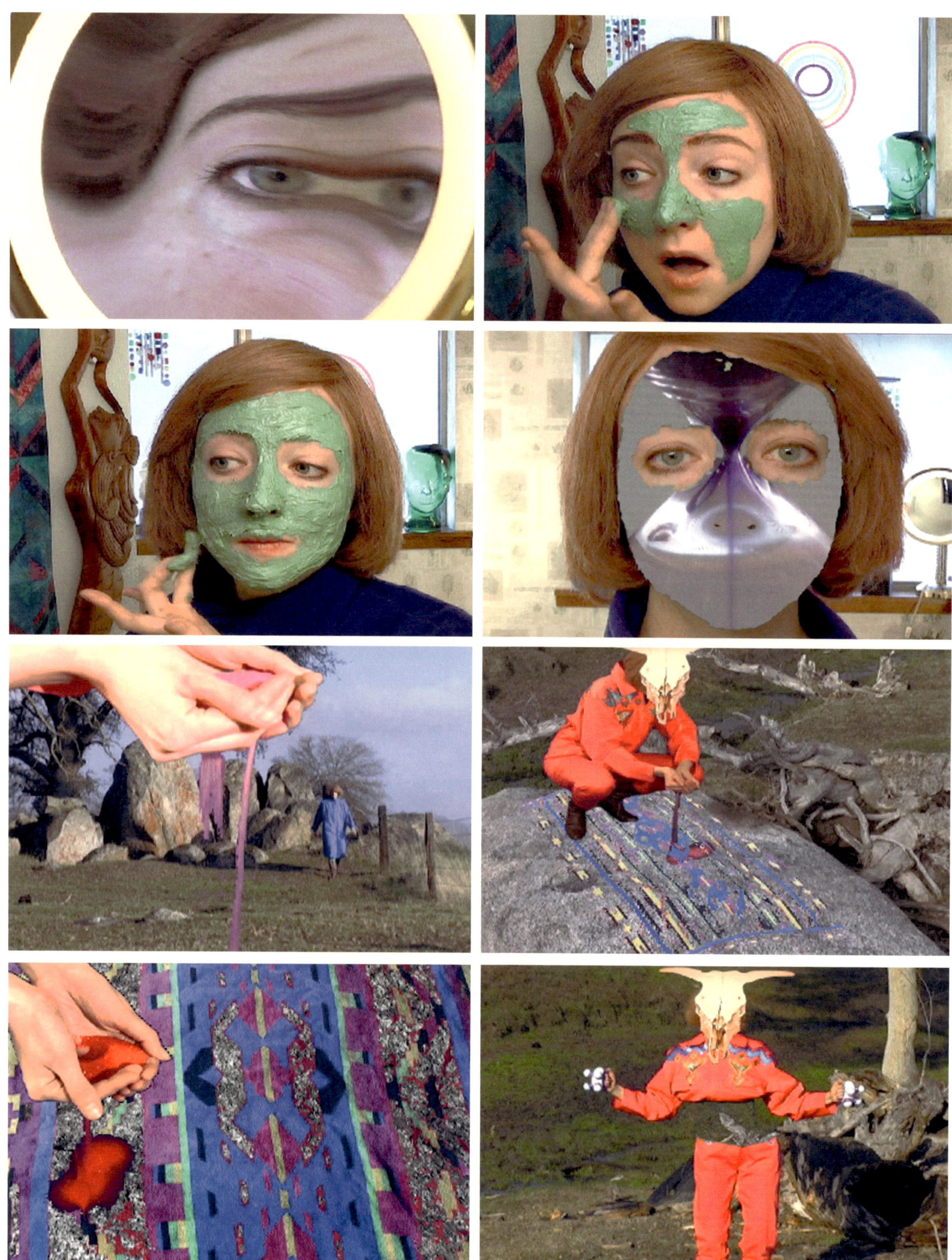

Shana Moulton
Sand Saga
2008

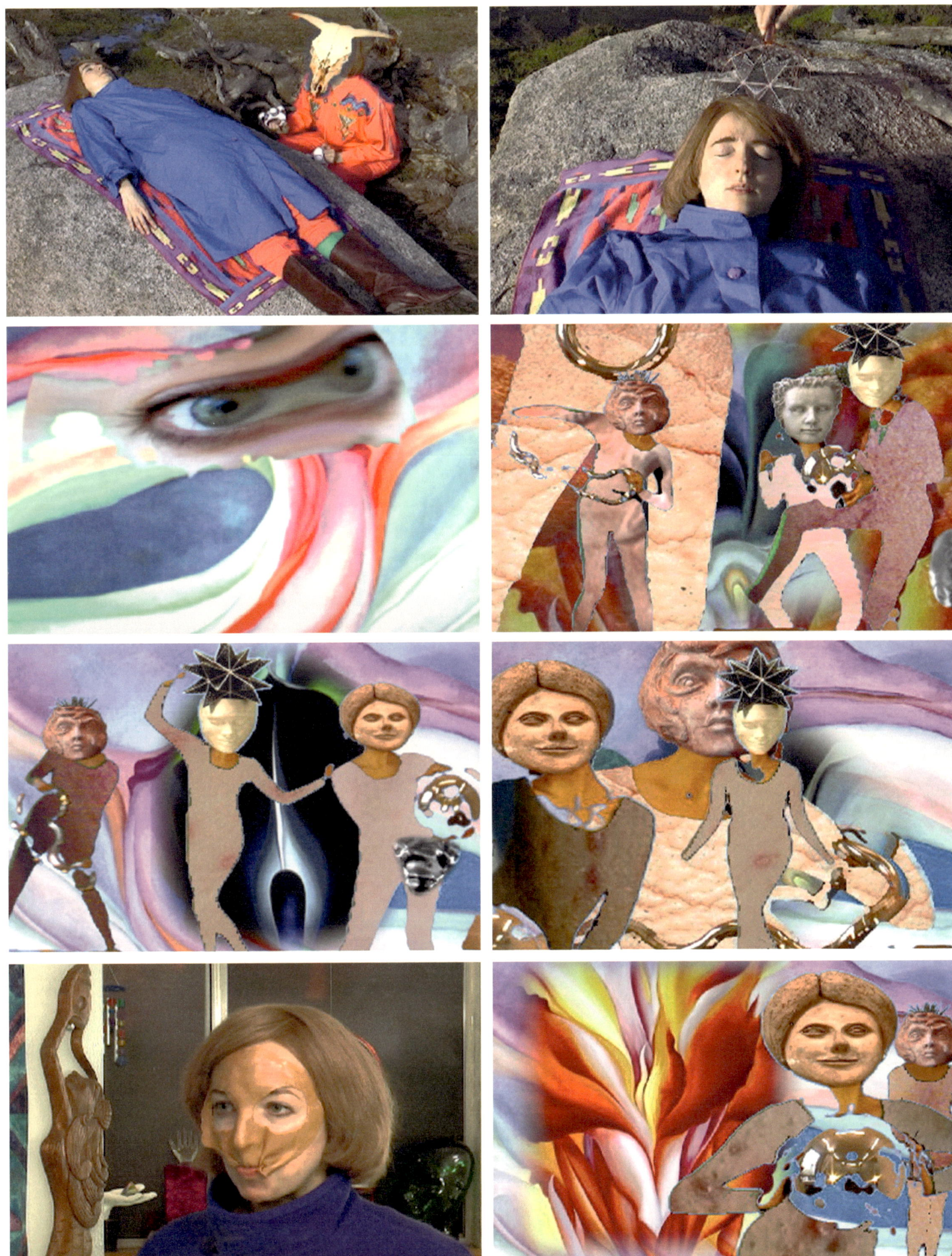

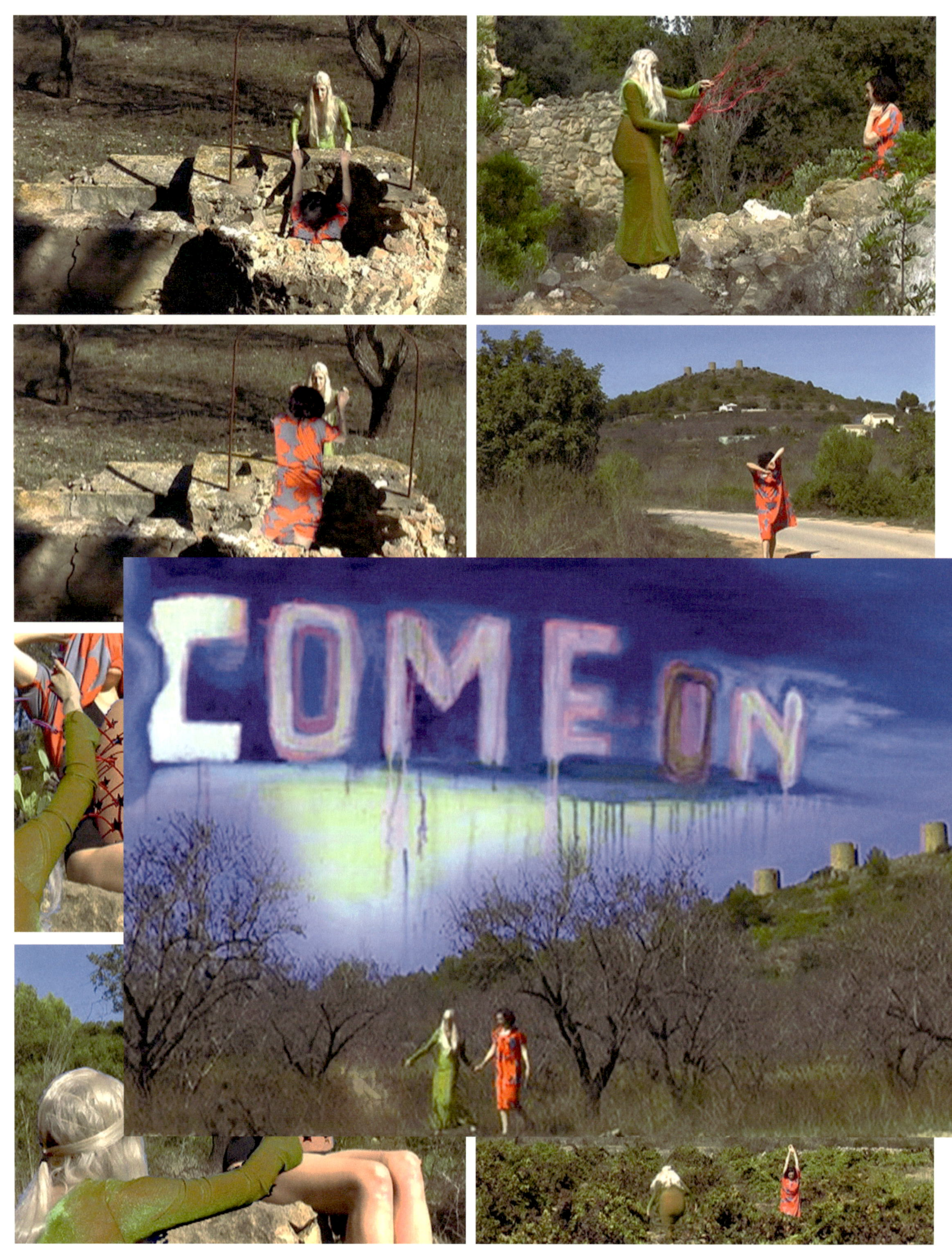

Shana Moulton
(in collaboration with Lucy Stein)
Exstasi Exstano
2008

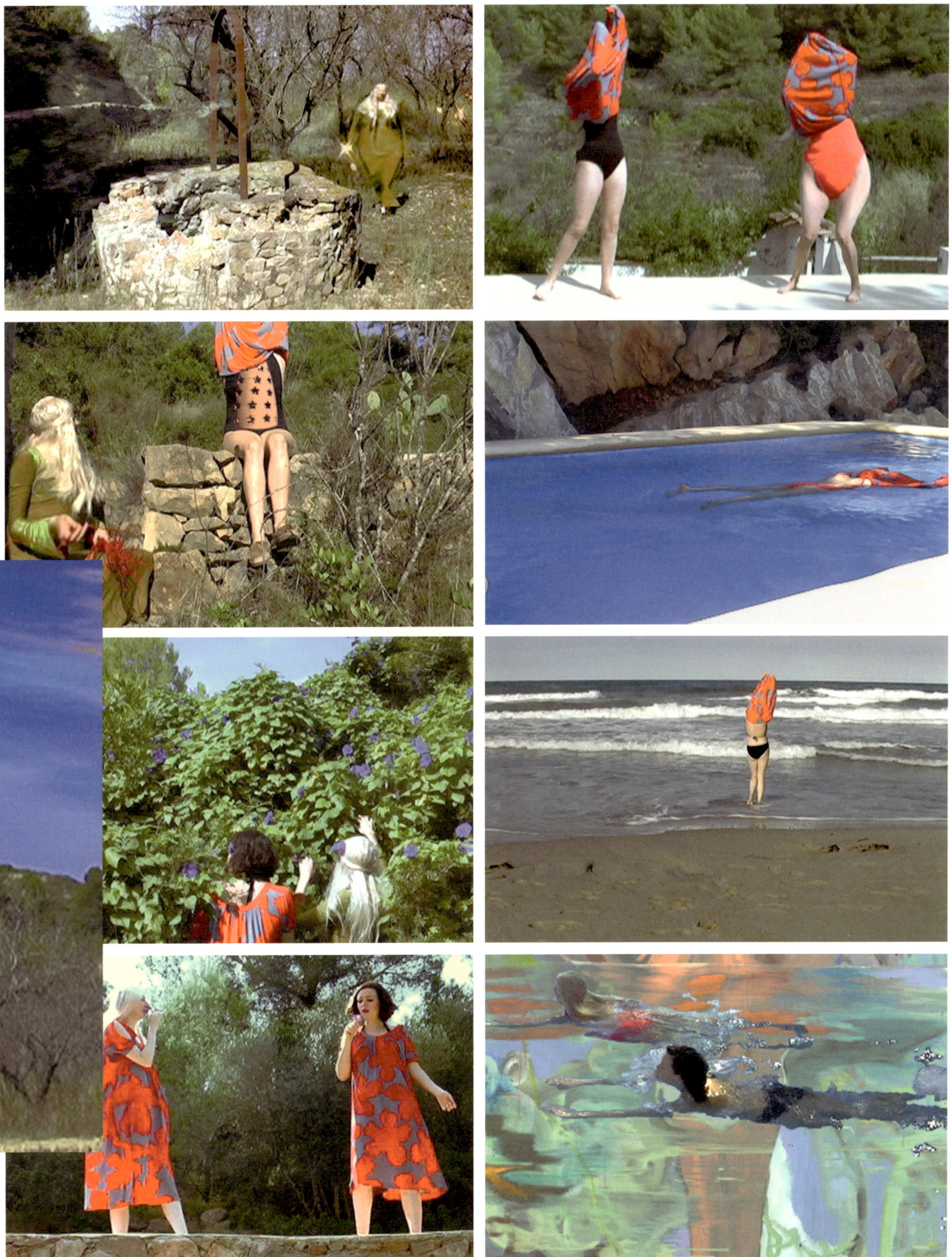

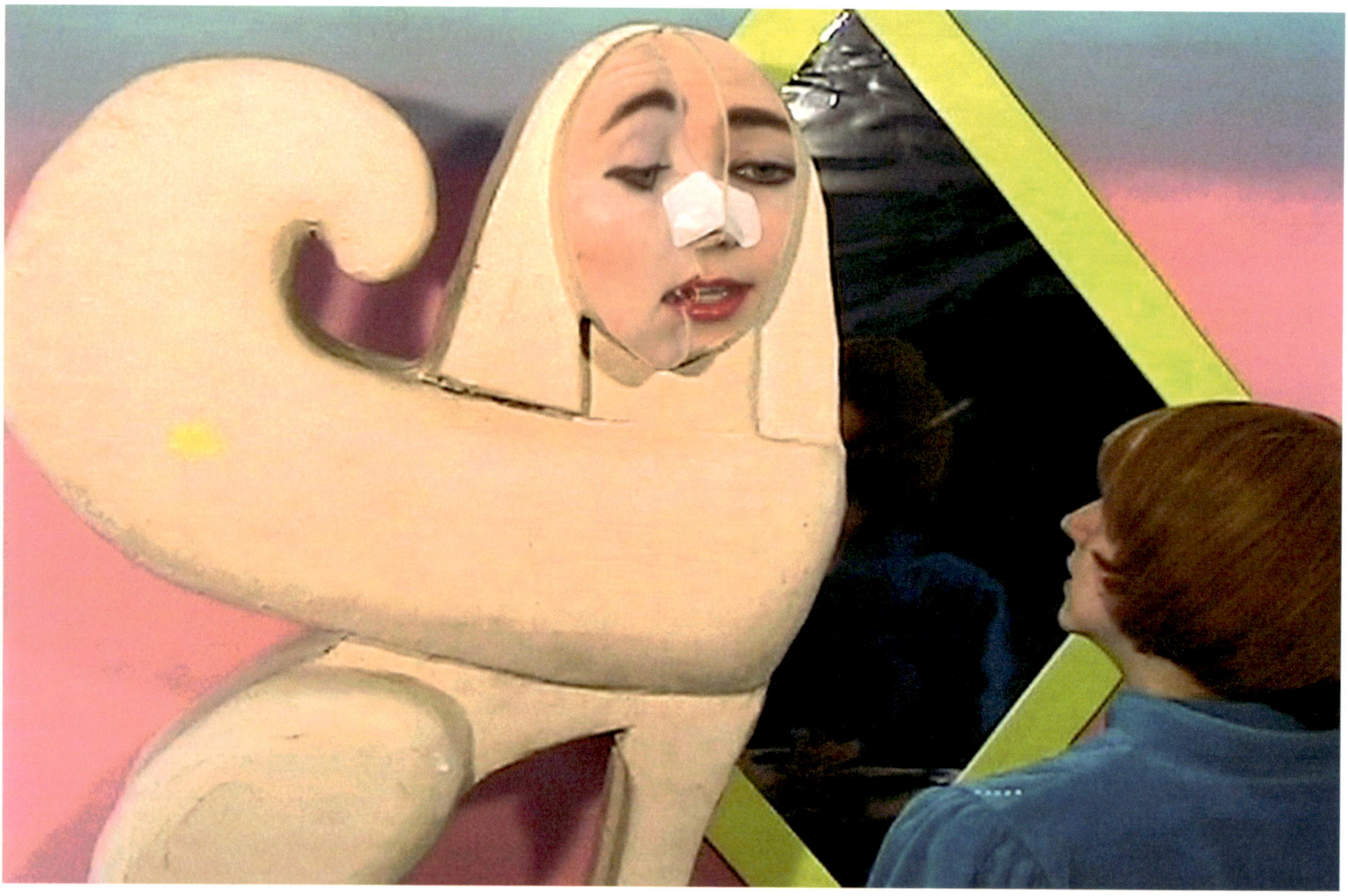

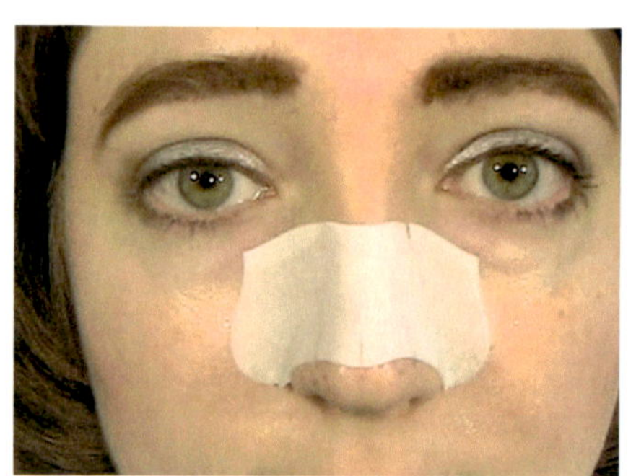

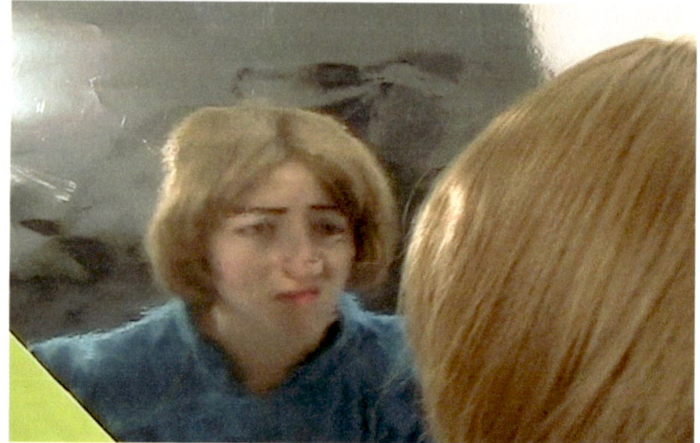

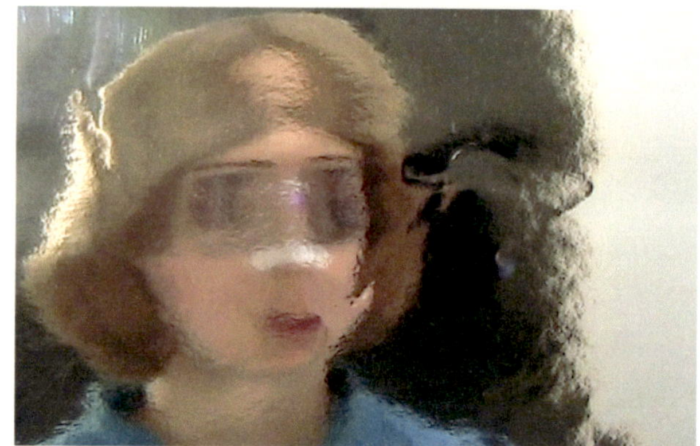

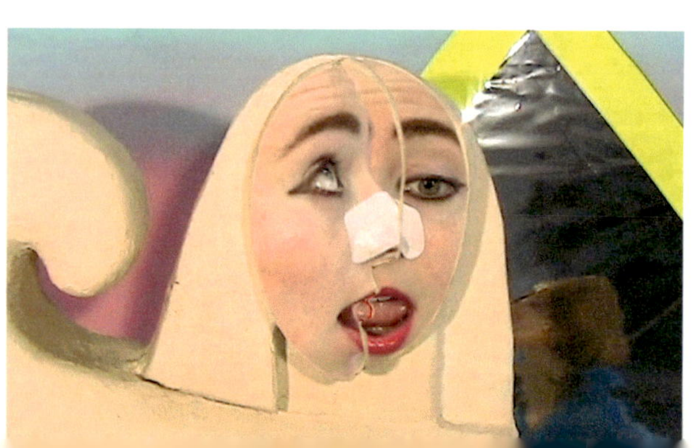

Shana Moulton
Whispering Pines 7
2006

Now That I'm a Woman, Everything Is Strange

Thomas Beard *

* —Thomas Beard is a founder and director of Light Industry, a venue for film and electronic art in Brooklyn, New York. Previously he was Program Director of Ocularis, a programmer at Cinematexas, and a programming consultant for the Internationale Kurzfilmtage Oberhausen. He has organized screenings and exhibitions at Art in General, Aurora Picture Show, Pacific Film Archive, and the Museum of Modern Art, New York and has written for *Film Comment*, *Rhizome*, and *Triple Canopy*. Most recently he edited an issue of *Cinematograph* devoted to live cinema, soon to be published by San Francisco Cinematheque.

Whispering Pines 1, the first episode in an ongoing cycle of videos by Shana Moulton, is a brief but bewildering emblem of the prevailing ideas and preoccupations that have come to characterize the artist's recent work. In it we are introduced to Cynthia (the sullen star of the series, played by Moulton) on a trip to the grocery store, but just as crucially we are introduced to her outfit: a house dress in muted pastels, augmented with a circular cushion sewn into the garment around her rear end. As she shops, glumly eying cans of organic kidney beans and massaging her awkward prosthetic, supermarket muzak is overlaid with what may be an internal monologue until all noises devolve into a slurping drone. Then the gravitational pull of the butt donut draws the camera's gaze toward it, and the plush appendage transmogrifies into a screen (or is it a portal?) where, agog, we watch a mechanical parrot—complete with LED eyeballs—enter a room of miniature dimensions. It is a potentially unremarkable scenario made transcendently bizarre by Moulton's intervention. To Be Continued… Indeed!

The second installment of *Whispering Pines* marks Cynthia's return home, and it is this domestic setting that allows Moulton's aesthetic interests to be more fully realized. The living room is a perceptual contradiction, austere yet visually hyperactive. An otherwise spartan interior, it is also populated by a handful of carefully arranged elements: a mounted orb, an encasement of plastic flowers, a bowl of glowing crystals, all of vaguely New Age provenance, all of them plugged in (their cords, umbilical, are creepily conspicuous) and methodically activated by Cynthia upon her arrival, although the sounds of their preprogrammed gurgles do little to soften her dour expression. *Whispering Pines* is a kind of melodrama, its heroine a faltering, rather than fallen, woman, and it affirms the genre's demand for a primacy of objecthood. Douglas Sirk famously noted that "you can't make films about things, you can only make films with things, with people, with light, with flowers, with mirrors, with blood," but Moulton extends this logic of artifice one step further. Even her flowers are fake.

As a serial form, however, *Whispering Pines* is not so much a soap opera as a one-woman *Twin Peaks*. À la Lynch, inexplicable

Whispering Pines 1, die erste Episode eines fortlaufenden Videoprojekts von Shana Moulton, vermittelt – so knapp wie verstörend – einen Eindruck von den Ideen und Fragestellungen, mit denen sich die Künstlerin beschäftigt. In dem Film sehen wir Cynthia (den von Moulton verkörperten Star der Serie) beim Einkauf in einem Lebensmittelgeschäft. Dabei fällt vor allem ihre merkwürdige Kostümierung ins Auge. Denn sie trägt einen Hausmantel in gedämpften Pastelltönen, in den hinten auf Gesässhöhe ein rundes Kissen eingenäht ist. Während Cynthia ihre Einkäufe erledigt, unschlüssig Dosen mit Biobohnen beäugt und ihre seltsame Po-Prothese massiert, wird die Supermarktmusik mit einer Art innerem Monolog überblendet, bis alle Geräusche zu einem schlurfenden Dröhnen verschmelzen. Dann richtet sich die Kamera – wie von magischen Kräften angezogen – auf das voluminöse Kissen. Das Plüsch-Ungetüm wiederum verwandelt sich in einen Bildschirm (oder vielleicht ein Portal?), auf dem ein mechanischer Papagei – mitsamt LED-Augen – in einem Miniaturzimmer erscheint. Erst durch Moultons Intervention erhält diese auf den ersten Blick nicht eben spektakuläre Szene ihre bizarr-transzendente Dimension. Fortsetzung folgt ... Und so ist es in der Tat!

In der zweiten Episode kommt Cynthia wieder nach Haus, in ein häusliches Ambiente, das es Moulton gestattet, ihre ästhetischen Interessen besonders wirksam zur Geltung zu bringen. Das Wohnzimmer ist ein perzeptueller Widerspruch in sich – ebenso schlicht wie visuell überladen. Die sonst sehr spartanische Einrichtung wird durch eine Handvoll sorgfältig arrangierter Elemente belebt: eine Kugel auf einem Gestell, ein Arrangement mit Plastikblumen, eine Schale mit glühenden Kristallen – alles mit einem diffusen New-Age-Touch. Diese Utensilien (deren Verkabelung an gruselige Nabelschnüre erinnert) sind allesamt elektrifiziert und werden von Cynthia nach ihrer Heimkehr methodisch aktiviert. Doch vermag auch der vorprogrammierte Gurgel-Sound des Eso-Schnickschnacks die Depressionen der jungen Frau offensichtlich kaum zu lindern. *Whispering Pines* ist eine Art Melodram, und die Protagonistin ist nicht etwa eine gefallene, sondern eine unsicher durchs Leben taumelnde Frau. Auch der genretypische Vorrang der Objekte ist unübersehbar. Von Douglas Sirk stammt der berühmte Ausspruch: «Man kann keine Filme über, sondern lediglich mit Dingen machen – mit Leuten, mit Licht, mit Blumen,

images reappear in variously altered states; the robo-bird of the project's first chapter becomes, literally, a puzzle (jigsaw) later on. One could even say that all the physical artifacts in Moulton's work—from oblong, rainbow-hued dreamcatchers to diamond-shaped, push-button wall lights—lead a double life, as objects in space and as two-dimensional video scraps, ready to be animated or otherwise repurposed. Equally Lynchian is the way a subtle sense of unease seeps through little pockets of the narrative: Cynthia is suddenly wearing a fluorescent neck brace for reasons unknown, her cat goes missing. She worries about little lost Kneefers in her diary, later making a remark in its pages about a wooden towel rack, which could apply to all of the wonderfully strange and densely layered *Whispering Pines*, "I really like its texture, but I can't understand what it is trying to say."

However, even while it flirts with something more sinister, the tone overall is a humorous one. Like Michael's Smith's recurring everyman "Mike," or Wynne Greenwood's Tracy + the Plastics, Moulton's Cynthia belongs to a significant vein within the history of video art, one where performers have constructed elaborate, straight-faced alter-egos that serve as conduits for their deadpan wit. There's something undeniably droll about the compositional excess achieved in the aggregation of items like neon sand art or 3D Magic Eye posters. Of course it would also be a mistake to think of *Whispering Pines* as simply poking fun or laughing at the ridiculousness of those products and their quasi-psychedelic ilk.

A major achievement of Moulton's saga is the way she chooses as its constituent elements those things which are aesthetically disreputable, aggressively unhip. She approaches objects rarely, if ever, given serious thought, and forces us to look at them in new and surprising ways. In 2008, at the alternative space Participant, Inc. in New York, Moulton performed in front of a projection that at one point featured a seemingly endless array of logos, culled from the Internet, of various organizations or merchandise related to the rubric of "women's health"—Centers for Women's Health, Women's Health Expos, Women's Wellness Expos, Oil of Olay—each predicated on an almost identical visual trope of curvy, line drawn figures, frequently in motion (so robust is the

mit Spiegeln, mit Blut.» Moulton treibt die Logik der Künstlichkeit noch einen Schritt weiter. Nicht einmal ihre Blumen sind echt.

Trotz des seriellen Formats ist *Whispering Pines* nicht etwa eine Seifenoper, sondern eine Ein-Frau-Variante von *Twin Peaks*. Wie bei Lynch tauchen auch hier immer wieder dieselben unerklärlichen Bilder in ganz unterschiedlichen Kontexten auf. So erweist sich etwa der Robo-Vogel aus der ersten Episode der Serie im weiteren Verlauf buchstäblich als ein Puzzle. Man könnte sogar behaupten, dass die einzelnen physischen Objekte in Moultons Werk – ob die in den Farben des Regenbogens gehaltenen länglichen Traumfänger oder die diamantförmigen Wandlampen – ein Doppelleben führen: mal als konkrete Gegenstände im Raum, mal als 2-D-Video-Verschnitte, die sich animieren oder auch anderweitig verwenden lassen. An Lynch erinnert auch die bisweilen unheimliche Atmosphäre in den einzelnen Episoden. So trägt Cynthia in einem der Videos aus völlig unerfindlichen Gründen plötzlich eine fluoreszierende Halskrause, oder aber ihre Katze ist unauffindbar. Sie ist besorgt über das Verschwinden des kleinen Kneefers, so notiert sie in ihrem Tagebuch, ihn verloren haben. Weiter notiert sie darin etwas über eine hölzerne Handtuchstange, was sie ihrer ebenso seltsamen wie vielschichtigen Videoserie *Whispering Pines* genauso gut als Generalmotto hätte voranstellen können: «Ich mag zwar die Textur, nur verstehe ich nicht, was sie mir sagen will.»

Obwohl stets ein Element des Unheimlichen spürbar bleibt, ist für humoristische Effekte reichlich gesorgt. Wie Michael Smiths stets wiederkehrendes Motiv des Jedermann «Mike» oder Wynne Greenwoods Tracy + the Plastics steht auch Moultons Cynthia für eine bestimmte Richtung der Videokunst. Diese Künstler haben hochartifizielle Figuren mit starren Gesichtszügen entwickelt, die es ihnen gestatten, ihren trockenen Witz zu artikulieren. Die kompositorischen Exzesse, die sich durch die Anhäufung von Neon-Sand-Art-Elementen und 3-D-Magic-Eye-Bildern erzielen lassen, sind gewiss ausgesprochen drollig. Wer jedoch annimmt, *Whispering Pines* wolle lediglich die Lächerlichkeit solcher Erzeugnisse und ihrer quasi psychedelischen Anmutungen aufs Korn nehmen, liegt gleichwohl falsch.

Moultons Arbeiten sind aber auch dafür bekannt, dass die Künstlerin gerne auf ästhetisch verpönte, definitiv uncoole Requisiten zurückgreift. Sie verwendet Dinge, auf die nur selten ernsthafte Gedanken

stick woman's health that she is often caught leaping about). The practice of appropriating and reconfiguring images that depict socially constructed gender norms or ideals has long been a prominent concern within feminist art (Martha Rosler's transformations, via collage, of nudie mag centerfolds into walls of bare flesh are a particularly famous example), but Moulton raises a different set of questions by way of playful repetition. Whether this corporate icon of the wavy lady is insidious or innocuous, one can't help but wonder what its ubiquity says about the culture whose focus groups approved it.

Similarly plumbed in *Whispering Pines* are the depths of New Ageism's signs, symbols, and patterns. Cynthia, suffering as usual from some malady of living, visits Healing Hands near the Sierra National Forest, and what she finds is a triumph of mis-en-scène. Innumerable sculptural permutations of a single hand, palm held upward, are on view—an open-palmed hand chair, hand chandelier, hand-shaped lotion bottle. Moulton's room functions as a perverse hieroglyph. Whereas occult traditions of knowledge, stemming from medieval conflations of science and magic, were based upon purportedly ancient, precise, and exacting semiotic systems (systems, it's worth noting, that would be creatively deployed by artists and filmmakers like Kenneth Anger, Harry Smith, and Derek Jarman, among others), New Age practices hold a more tenuous link to the past. A philosophical pastiche, its pervasive themes are often severed from history, and so Moulton's construction presents a formal situation that suggests itself as translatable, yet whose ultimate meaning is fascinatingly unmoored.

And though its presence is oblique, one might also discover within *Whispering Pines* the political implications of a New Age ethos, which are cunningly critiqued. "I am more than my physical body," intones a soothing voice—"sound medicine" emitted through conch shell headphones at Healing Hands—"I am endless, limitless, unbounded, unrestrained, and unrestricted. I am free to access the infinite, open to my true dynamic nature, constantly changing, shifting, continually adapting, evolving, perpetually expanding and transcending. I am more than my physical body [...] My awareness is capable of transcending the physical, capable of

verschwendet werden, und zwingt uns so, diese Sachen mit neuen Augen zu betrachten. So ist sie zum Beispiel 2008 in dem alternativen New Yorker Kulturtreff Participant Inc. in einer Performance vor der Projektion einer schier endlosen Abfolge von Logos aufgetreten, die sie im Internet zusammengeklaubt hatte. Die Logos verwiesen allesamt auf Einrichtungen, Veranstaltungen oder Firmen, die mit dem Thema «Gesundheit der Frau» zu tun hatten; sie bestanden ausnahmslos aus den weitgehend identischen «Umrisslinien» üppig gebauter Frauen. (Etliche der so dargestellten Damen waren offenbar gesundheitlich sogar so fit, dass sie fröhlich herumhüpften.) Feministische Künstlerinnen greifen schon seit langem auf Abbilder gesellschaftlich konstruierter Gender-Normen oder -Ideale zurück, um sie anders als gewohnt zu arrangieren oder sie ganz neu zu kontextualisieren (ein besonders berühmtes Beispiel dafür sind Martha Roslers Collagen, auf denen Playmates sich in wahre Fleischberge verwandeln). Moulton geht das Thema jedoch ganz anders an, und zwar in Form von verspielten Wiederholungen. Unabhängig davon, ob die als Werbe-Ikone instrumentalisierte Frau mit dem welligen Haar nun bedrohlich oder harmlos ist, bleibt die Frage, was ihre Allgegenwart über eine Kultur aussagt, deren Fokusgruppen genau eine solche Darstellung befürworten.

Ausgelotet wird in Moultons *Whispering Pines* aber auch das Zeichen- und Symbolarsenal der New-Age-Bewegung. So sucht die wie üblich am Dasein leidende Cynthia beispielsweise in der vierten Episode den Eso-Retreat Healing Hands in Kalifornien auf. Was sie dort vorfindet, ist ein Triumph der Inszenierung: Der Zuschauer bekommt zahllose skulpturale Varianten einer mit der Innenfläche nach oben gerichteten Hand zu sehen – eine geöffnete Hand als Sessel, einen Handkandelaber, eine handförmige Lotion-Flasche. Dabei fungiert Moultons Zimmer als perverse Hieroglyphe. Während die aus der mittelalterlichen Verschmelzung von Wissenschaft und Magie hervorgegangenen okkulten Traditionen sich auf ebenso alte wie exakte semiotische Systeme beriefen (Systeme, die sich etwa Künstler und Filmemacher wie Kenneth Anger, Harry Smith und Derek Jarman kreativ zunutze gemacht haben), sind die New-Age-Praktiken lediglich durch einen äusserst dünnen Faden mit der Vergangenheit verbunden. Die abgedroschenen Wahrheiten dieses vulgärphilosophischen

transcending any limits imposed by my waking physical reality. I have had many experiences that proved this to me, beyond the shadow of a doubt."

Though apparently the anodyne byproduct of a mishmash of West Coast hippiedom and Eastern religion, the contents of the meditation tape are by no means outside of ideology. While the mini-mantras are supposed to be empowering, they in fact point to the very heart of the anxieties that riddle *Whispering Pines*. Cynthia inhabits a world that is constantly in danger of material and corporeal collapse—ersatz video screens emerge out of prosthetic orifices, her joints ache, her pores blacken, she vomits chroma key at a rave gone bad, and even disappears completely. Leaving the broader world of human relations free of culpability, New Age thinking is a potentially conservative ideology of personal responsibility as expressed in a belief in the ultimate supremacy of one's own psyche *"You Can* Change *the Way You Feel"* reads the chapter heading of *The Feeling Good Handbook,* Cynthia's bedside tome—yet, in a manner reminiscent of Julianne Moore in *Safe,* she *can't* change the way she feels. Like Todd Haynes's film, *Whispering Pines* is a careful study in ontological disquiet, but Moulton's terminally doleful persona is also the stuff of great physical comedy—exaggerated gestures, a gawky cadence—and the boundaries between the comic and the tragic are left to dissolve and reconstitute themselves with increasing regularity.

With her latest videos and performances, Moulton has fashioned a singular body of work, though it might also be fruitful to consider her practice in a broader, generational context. Alongside contemporaries such as Cory Arcangel, Paper Rad, and Michael Robinson, to name only a handful, her project has helped further establish appropriation as a definitive mode of the early 21st century, and the means by which it departs from earlier models of assemblage are central to what make the impulse so compelling. To be sure, important precursors to those trends can be found in boomer artists like Dara Birnbaum, Matt Mullican, Cindy Sherman, and Laurie Simmons, who, being part of the first generation to grow up with television, drew on a vocabulary of Pop forms (game shows, comic books, B-movies, doll houses) in their work that reshaped and

Pasticcio haben sich meist völlig von der Vergangenheit abgekoppelt. Und so konfrontiert uns Moulton mit einer Situation, deren Elemente sich zwar als übersetzbar darstellen, deren Sinngehalt jedoch letzten Endes völlig «ungeerdet» in der Schwebe bleibt.

Die *Whispering Pines* lassen sich deshalb auch als – zumindest indirekte – Kritik an den politischen Implikationen des New-Age-Ethos deuten. «Ich bin mehr als mein physischer Körper», intoniert eine sanfte Stimme – «Sound Medicine», die in Healing Hands aus Muschelschalenkopfhörern erklingt –, «ich bin endlos, grenzenlos, ungebunden, ungehemmt, ohne Fesseln. Es steht mir frei, in das Unendliche einzutreten, mich für mein wahres dynamisches Wesen zu öffnen, mich unablässig zu verändern, mich permanent anzupassen, mich zu entwickeln, mich selbst immer grösser und weiter zu machen, über mich selbst hinauszuwachsen. Ich bin mehr als mein physischer Körper ... Mein Bewusstsein vermag die Grenzen der materiellen Welt hinter sich zu lassen, alle Grenzen zu überschreiten, in die mich das Wachbewusstsein der Alltagswelt einschliesst. Dies haben mich zahllose Erfahrungen gelehrt. Und nun ist von meinen Zweifeln nicht mal ein Schatten geblieben.»

Mag diese Meditationslitanei auch nur ein fader Aufguss aus kalifornischer Hippie-Philosophie und fernöstlicher Religion sein: Ihre ideologischen Implikationen sind gleichwohl unverkennbar. Mögen die Mini-Mantras auch vorgeblich den Zweck haben, die Protagonistin stark zu machen, weisen sie in Wahrheit doch direkt ins Herz jener Ängste, von denen Cynthia in *Whispering Pines* so massiv geplagt wird. In Cynthias Welt droht ständig der materielle oder körperliche Kollaps – prothetische Körperöffnungen verwandeln sich unversehens in Video-Bildflächen, die Gelenke der Protagonistin schmerzen, ihre Poren verfärben sich schwarz, nach einem misslungenen Rave erbricht sie Chroma Key, ja sie verschwindet sogar vollständig. Da die gesellschaftlichen Verhältnisse aus New-Age-Sicht irrelevant sind, verkündet dieses Denken eine potenziell konservative Ideologie, die jede Verantwortung dem Einzelnen aufbürdet. Auch der Glaube an den Supremat der individuellen Psyche ist Ausdruck dieser Haltung. Die Überschrift des Kapitels, das Cynthia in dem *Feeling Good Handbook* auf ihrem Nachttisch aufgeschlagen hat, lautet denn auch: *You Can* Change *the Way You Feel*. Dabei kann sie an ihrer Art zu

frequently subverted the mass-mediated world around them. So what's changed? In short, the archive has exploded. The notion of a coherent mass culture has been eroding for years, replaced instead by an ever-expanding field of subculture and market niche, all of which circulates in new ways via networked systems. Our lives are distributed differently, and to intervene as an artist now, to rummage through the dustbins of recent history, points toward something new.

empfinden ebenso wenig etwas ändern wie Julianne Moore in Todd Haynes' Film *Safe*. Wie Haynes' Film befasst sich auch *Whispering Pines* sehr einfühlsam mit der ontologischen Verunsicherung der weiblichen Hauptfigur. Gleichzeitig liefert Moultons unheilbar trübsinnige Protagonistin mit ihren übertriebenen Gesten und ihren ungelenken Bewegungen aber auch immer wieder grandiose Slapstick-Einlagen – bringt die Grenzen zwischen Komik und Tragik zum Verschwinden, bevor sie sich von neuem Geltung verschaffen.

Mit ihren neueren Videos und Performances hat Moulton einen einzigartigen Werkkorpus geschaffen. Dennoch lohnt es sich, ihre Arbeit auch im Kontext ihrer eigenen Generation zu würdigen. Zusammen mit ihren Altersgenossen Cory Arcangel, Paper Rad und Michael Robinson, um nur einige zu nennen, hat sie dabei geholfen, die Appropriation als die für das frühe 21. Jahrhundert typische Form des Kunstschaffens durchzusetzen. Dabei verdankt diese Kunstform ihre Überzeugungskraft vor allem der Wahl jener Mittel, durch die sie sich von früheren Verfahren der Assemblage absetzt. Natürlich hat die Bewegung wichtige Vorläufer, etwa Künstler/innen wie Dara Birnbaum, Matt Mullican, Cindy Sherman und Laurie Simmons, die als Angehörige der ersten mit dem Fernsehen aufgewachsenen Generation häufig auf ein Vokabular der Pop-Formen (Game-Shows, Comic-Hefte, B-Movies, Barbie-Puppen) zurückgriffen, um diese neu zu arrangieren und die von den Massenmedien bestimmte Weltsicht zu untergraben. Was hat sich also geändert? Kurz gesagt: Das Archiv ist buchstäblich explodiert. Von einer kohärenten Massenkultur kann schon seit Jahren immer weniger die Rede sein. Stattdessen gibt es heute ein unüberschaubares Konglomerat von Subkulturen und Marktnischen, die allesamt in vernetzten Systemen präsent sind. Unser Leben ist heute vielfach aufgesplittert, und wer da als Künstler interveniert, die Müllkübel der jüngeren Vergangenheit durchwühlt, stösst damit zugleich etwas völlig Neues an.

N — FOR NERD

The *New Oxford American Dictionary* defines the "nerd" as "a foolish or contemptible person who lacks social skills"—but also as "an intelligent, single-minded expert in a particular technical discipline" without any broad-based appeal. The term, whose exact origins are unknown, first emerged in the 1950s; in the last few decades in particular, it has become a firmly established colloquialism in the context of the electronic revolution. In recent years, "nerdism" has increasingly acquired a political dimension as well. This dimension manifests itself in a rejection of society, a refusal to submit to the tastes of the masses, and a choice to engage with seemingly worthless things instead. (→ LOW TECH) This attitude of general rejection and self-marginalization is reflected in the piecemeal assembly of personal constructions of reality, and in the formation of temporary communities that seal themselves off against outsiders. (→ OUR OWN COMMUNITY)

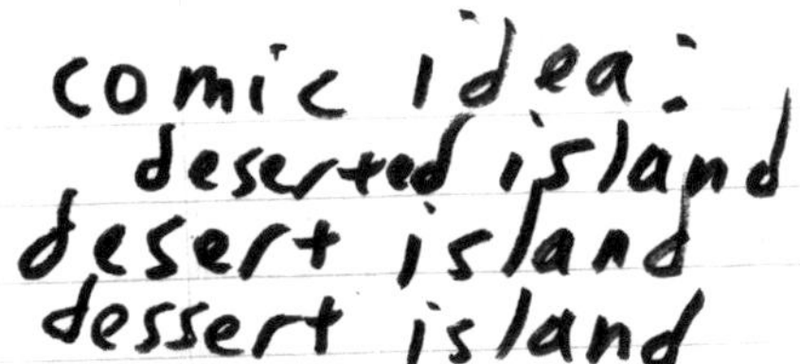

Im *New Oxford American Dictionary* wird «nerd» einerseits als verrückte, verachtenswerte Person beschrieben, der jegliche soziale Kompetenz fehlt – andererseits als «Experte» auf einem spezifischen Gebiet, das keinerlei Massentauglichkeit aufweist. Die Entstehung des Begriffs, dessen genauer Ursprung unbekannt ist, kann in die 1950er Jahre datiert werden und festigte sich gerade in den letzten Jahrzehnten im Sprachgebrauch im Zusammenhang mit der Computer-Revolution. In den letzten Jahren kam dem «nerdism» verstärkt auch eine politische Dimension zu. Diese manifestiert sich in einer Verweigerung gegenüber der Gesellschaft bzw. wenn es darum geht, sich dem Massengeschmack unterzuordnen, um sich im Gegenzug dazu mit scheinbar wertlosen Dingen zu beschäftigen. (→ LOW TECH) Diese Verweigerungshaltung und Selbstmarginalisierung widerspiegelt sich im Zusammenfinden eigener Realitätskonstrukte und in der Bildung von abgeriegelten temporären Gemeinschaften. (→ OUR OWN COMMUNITY)

O — FOR OUR OWN COMMUNITY

Around the turn of the millennium, sociologists found that globalization, the Internet revolution, and the permanent availability of communication it entailed, spurred a tendency that can be described as a withdrawal from civil society and the public—a desire to hunker down in private domesticity (a neo-Biedermeier). (→ SHANA MOULTON) Observers coined the term "cocooning" to describe this form of social behavior. While it seems in one way to be a means of removing the body from the reach of biopolitics, the concept's reactionary aspects merit critical scrutiny. (→ BIOPOLITICS) (→ XMAS AND BUY, BUY, BUY) The term "our own community" seeks to describe a less hermetic attitude that instead emphasizes the idea of a self-organized temporary community whose existence is not dependent on outside support. (→ RYAN TRECARTIN & LIZZIE FITCH) Perhaps we might also use the concept of a "gang" of youngsters resisting an establishment. (→ BIOPOLITICS) (→ NERD) The phenomenon described here can also be related to the "wild zone," a concept popularized by Gilles Deleuze. "Wild zone" describes a space that does not function in accordance with the principles of socially regulated urban spaces and is impervious to functionalization and economic exploitation—a "zone" in which anything can happen.[48] (→ PAPER RAD)

48—We might also describe this as a "control of currents," a concept related to that of the "society of control", which describes a comparable set of issues but

Im Zuge der Globalisierung, der Internetrevolution und dem damit einhergehenden permanenten Kommunikationspotenzial wurde um die Jahrtausendwende in der Soziologie eine Tendenz festgestellt, die sich als Rückzug aus der Zivilgesellschaft und Öffentlichkeit beschreiben lässt – als Verpuppung im eigenen häuslichen Privatleben (Neo-Biedermeier). (→ SHANA MOULTON) Dieses Sozialverhalten wurde unter dem Stichwort «Cocooning» zusammengefasst. Einerseits scheint dieses Verhalten eine Möglichkeit zu sein, den Körper biopolitischen Zugriffen zu entziehen – andererseits muss der Begriff unter seinem reaktionären Potenzial kritisch betrachtet werden. (→ BIOPOLITICS) (→ XMAS AND BUY, BUY, BUY) Unter dem Terminus «our own community» soll versucht werden, eine weniger hermetische Haltung zu beschreiben, um dafür die Idee einer eigenen, temporär existierenden Gemeinschaft in den Vordergrund zu stellen, die in ihrem Daseinsmoment nicht auf ein Aussen angewiesen ist. (→ RYAN TRECARTIN & LIZZIE FITCH) Vielleicht liesse sich auch mit der Bezeichnung «Jugendbande» operieren, die sich einem Establishment widersetzt. (→ BIOPOLITICS) (→ NERD) Das genannte Phänomen kann auch mit «Wild Zone», einem Begriff, den Gilles Deleuze prominent machte, in Zusammenhang gebracht werden. «Wild Zone» beschreibt dabei einen Raum, der nicht nach dem Prinzip gesellschaftlich geregelter, urbaner Räume funktioniert, sondern ausserhalb einer funktionalisierten Nutzbarkeit steht – eine «Zone», in der alles passieren kann.[49] (→ PAPER RAD)

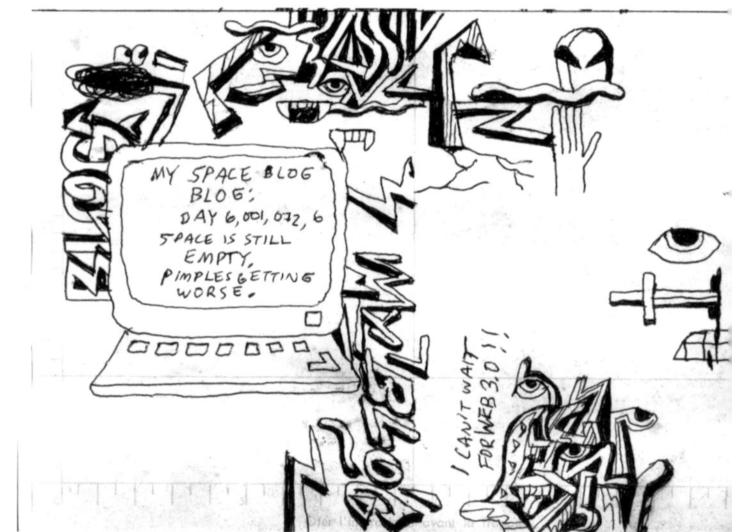

P — FOR PAPER RAD

"what is paper rad?
hmmmm, the never ending story,
for the general public i would say, just focus on our projects,
our concerts, if we are on tour, our books, videos, and website,
don't worry about members, friends or any larger social and/
or cultural relevance.
if you are trying to write an article, a school paper, or telling
your mom or dad, or boss, basically you are screwed, you can
say words like 3 member art collective, but remember that you
are lying and are just trying to translate what we are trying to
do into america-speak again, just explain a comic or joke you
saw on the website or in a book, i think that will work out better, and as for the details, good luck!
if you are an art collector, policeman, or ad agency, we are

---

is more academically accepted than the term "wild zone." Cf. Gilles Deleuze, "Postscript on the Societies of Control," *October* 59, Winter 1992, 3–7 (French original: Gilles Deleuze, "Post-scriptum sur les sociétés de contrôle", *L'autre journal* 1, May 1990.

49—So könnte man dies etwa auch als «Kontrolle der Ströme» umschreiben – ein Ausdruck, der im Zusammenhang mit dem Begriff der «Kontrollgesellschaft» steht, der eine vergleichbare Problematik skizziert, dabei aber wissenschaftlich arrivierter ist als der Terminus «Wild Zone». Vgl. Gilles Deleuze, «Postscriptum über die Kontrollgesellschaft», in: ders., *Unterhandlungen. 1972–1990*, Frankfurt 1993 (Erstveröffentlichung in Französisch: Gilles Deleuze, «Post-scriptum sur les sociétés de contrôle», in: *L'autre journal*, No. 1, Paris, Mai 1990).

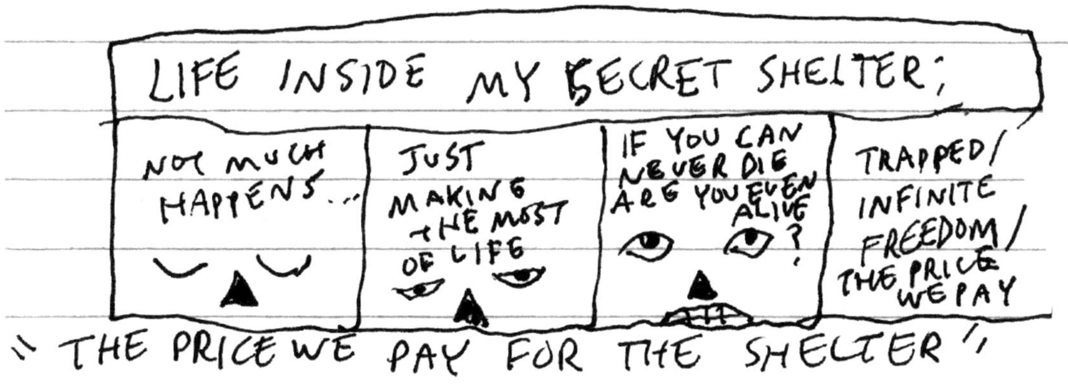

no company, its individuals making things, you like the name paper rad? great, you don't like it, even better, run with it, ask me who i am, maybe i'll tell you, you know, there is no secret, if you want to know every detail about us, then live your life, and the details will come to you, like, do you think i have to explain what paper rad is to my best friends? no, i don't, they come over and see it, and they know the details, naturally, they know what my haircut is, its no secret, its just not the fucking point.
actually my best friends have no idea what paper rad is, in fact the other day paper rad had a 4 hour argument about what paper rad is? so yah..."[50]

The label Paper Rad, founded in 2000 by Jessica Ciocci, Jacob Ciocci, and Ben Jones, employs a great variety of media, including video, drawing, and wall painting, and works in different genres such as fashion and photography. Both individually and collectively, Paper Rad forms a holistic multimedia endeavor. (→OUR OWN COMMUNITY) (→JUNK-STORE AESTHETICS) Paper Rad operates not only in the space of art, but also infiltrates cyberspace. (→YOUTUBE) Paper Rad has also repeatedly collaborated with other artists. (→CORY ARCANGEL) The videos—many of them by Jacob Ciocci—often cut movie material recorded from TV with hand-drawn comic strips and animation gimmicks into fast-paced, hallucinatory, altitude-tracking shots that can be read as a comment on today's mediated world. (→EXPERIMENTAL FILM / VIDEO) (→LOW TECH) Jessica Ciocci's mandala-like rainbow-

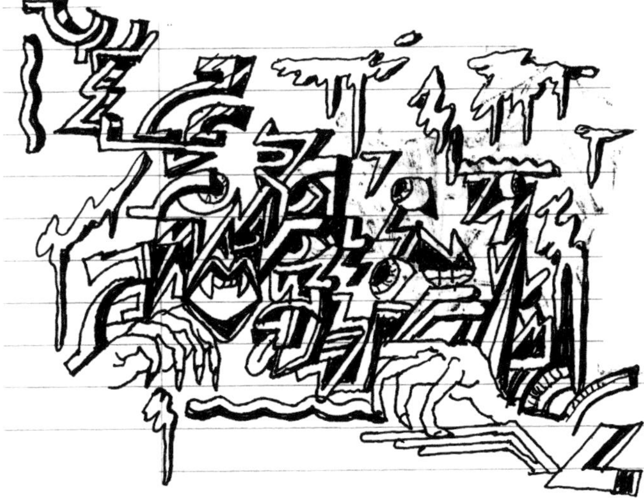

colored neo-geometrical drawings, mixing "excess" with "monotony," are direct reflections on contemporary consumerism and youth culture. (→XMAS AND BUY, BUY, BUY) (→KARMA AND OTHER NEW AGE STUFF) Paper Rad's complex installations in space frequently blend individual works with pieces produced in collective collaboration, forming a seductive yet deceptive "carpet": beneath it lurk the abysses of a world infested with consumption and media representation.

Das Label Paper Rad, das im Jahr 2000 von Jessica Ciocci, Jacob Ciocci und Ben Jones gegründet wurde, verwendet die verschiedensten Medien wie Video, Zeichnung, Wandmalerei sowie Kunstsparten wie Mode und Fotografie. Paper Rad setzt sich — sowohl kollektiv als auch individuell — zu einem multimedialen Gesamtunternehmen zusammen. (→OUR OWN COMMUNITY) (→JUNK-STORE AESTHETICS) Paper Rad ist nicht nur im Kunstraum tätig, sondern infiltriert auch den Cyberspace. (→YOUTUBE) Ebenso arbeitet Paper Rad immer wieder mit anderen Künstlern zusammen. (→CORY ARCANGEL) In den Videos — viele stammen von Jacob Ciocci — werden oft TV-Film-Mitschnitte mit selber gezeichneten Comics und Animationstricks zu schnell geschnittenen halluzinatorischen Höllenfahrten montiert, die als Kommentar auf die heutige Medienwelt gelesen werden können. (→EXPERIMENTAL FILM / VIDEO) (→LOW TECH) Die Mandala-artigen, regenbogenfarbigen Neo-Geo-Zeichnungen von Jessica Ciocci reflektieren in ihrer Mischung aus «Überschuss» und «Monotonie» unmittelbar die heutige Konsum- und Jugendkultur. (→XMAS AND BUY, BUY, BUY) (→KARMA AND OTHER NEW AGE STUFF) In Paper Rads komplexen Rauminszenierungen verschmelzen immer wieder individuelle Arbeiten mit solchen, die kollektiv entstanden sind, und bilden einen verführerischen, aber auch trügerischen «Teppich», hinter dem die Abgründe einer konsum- und medienverseuchten Welt liegen.

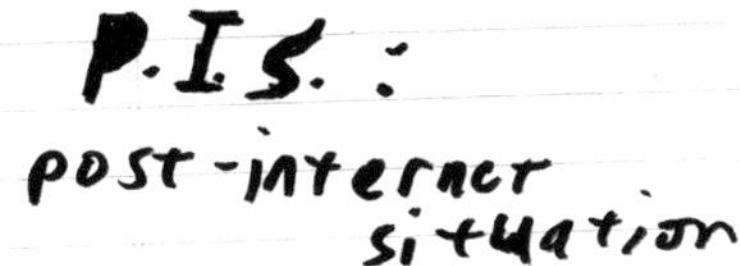

PAPER RAD Founding members are: JESSICA CIOCCI Born 1976 in Lexington, Kentucky. Lives and works in Providence. JACOB CIOCCI Born 1977 in Lexington, Kentucky. Lives and works in Pittsburgh. BEN JONES Born 1977 in Pittsburgh, Pennsylvania. Lives and works in Providence. EDUCATION JESSICA CIOCCI BA in psychology and art, Wellesley College JACOB CIOCCI BA in computer science and art, Oberlin College; MFA Carnegie Mellon University BEN JONES BFA Massachusetts College of Art SOLO & GROUP EXHIBITIONS (SELECTION SINCE 2002) — 2009 *Faking It*, Space Gallery, Pittsburgh (Jacob Ciocci, group); *In That Land of Black and Gold*, Heaven Gallery, Chicago (Jacob Ciocci, group); *The New Dark Age*, Deitch Projects, New York (Ben Jones, solo) — 2008 *Pre-Drive: After Technology*, Mattress Factory, Pittsburg (Jessica Ciocci & Jacob Ciocci, group); *Montage: Unmonumental Online*, New Museum, New York (Jessica Ciocci, group); *Macronauts*, Athens Biennial (Paper Rad, group) — 2007 *Tha Click: Beige and Paper Rad*, Event Gallery, London (Paper Rad, group); *Playback*, Musée d'Art Moderne de la Ville de Paris (Paper Rad, group); *Ocularis at 10*, Museum of Modern Art, New York (Paper Rad, group) — 2006 *P.E.A.C.E.*, Foxy Production, New York (Jessica Ciocci, solo); *Inspiration Superhighway*, Foxy Production, New York (Jacob Ciocci, solo); *The Game*, Green on Red Gallery, Dublin (Paper Rad, solo); *Panic Room*, Deste Foundation Centre for Contemporary Art, Athens (Paper Rad, group) — 2005 *Shit*, Printed Matter, New York (Paper Rad, solo); *Mixtape Clubhouse*, Space1026, Philadelphia (Paper Rad, solo); *D.I.Why?*, Foxy Production, New York (Ben Jones, solo) *SuperMarioMovie*, Deitch Projects, New York (Paper Rad in collaboration with Cory Arcangel, solo) — 2004 *3D*, Foxy Production, New York (Paper Rad, solo); *Troll Haven*, 3 Rivers Arts Festival, Pittsburgh (Paper Rad, solo); Liverpool Biennial (Paper Rad, group) — 2003 *New Counter-Media-Culture Collectives*, Contemporary Art Museum, Honolulu (Paper Rad, group); *Blinky 2*, Tate Britain, London (Paper Rad, group); *Radical Entertainment*, Institute of Contemporary Art, London (Paper Rad, group) — 2002 *Paper Rad: 10, Canada: 0*, Bathroom Gallery, Halifax (Paper Rad, solo); *Unknown Pleasures*, Daniel Reich Gallery, New York (Paper Rad, group). — 2001 *Somerville Comix Festival*, Washington Street Arts Center, Somerville (Paper Rad, group); *Boston CyberArts Festival*, Massachusetts College of Art, Boston (Paper Rad, group; *Picture Start Film Series*, Columbus Theater, Providence (Paper Rad, group) — Numerous screenings, performances, lectures, publications and more artistic activities by all members worldwide.

50—See www.paperrad.org

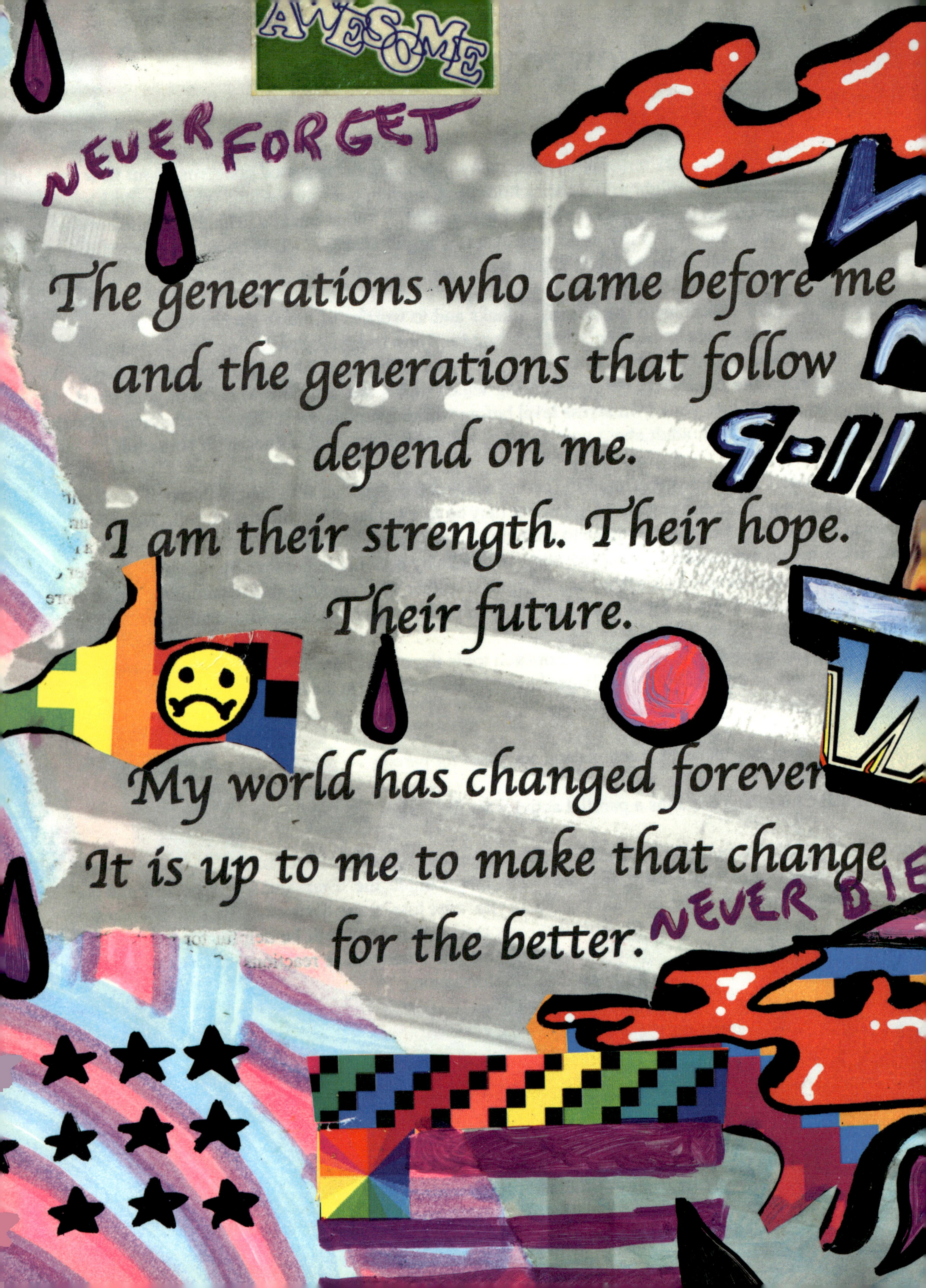

AWESOME
NEVER FORGET
9-11
The generations who came before me
and the generations that follow
depend on me.
I am their strength. Their hope.
Their future.
My world has changed forever
It is up to me to make that change
for the better. NEVER DIE

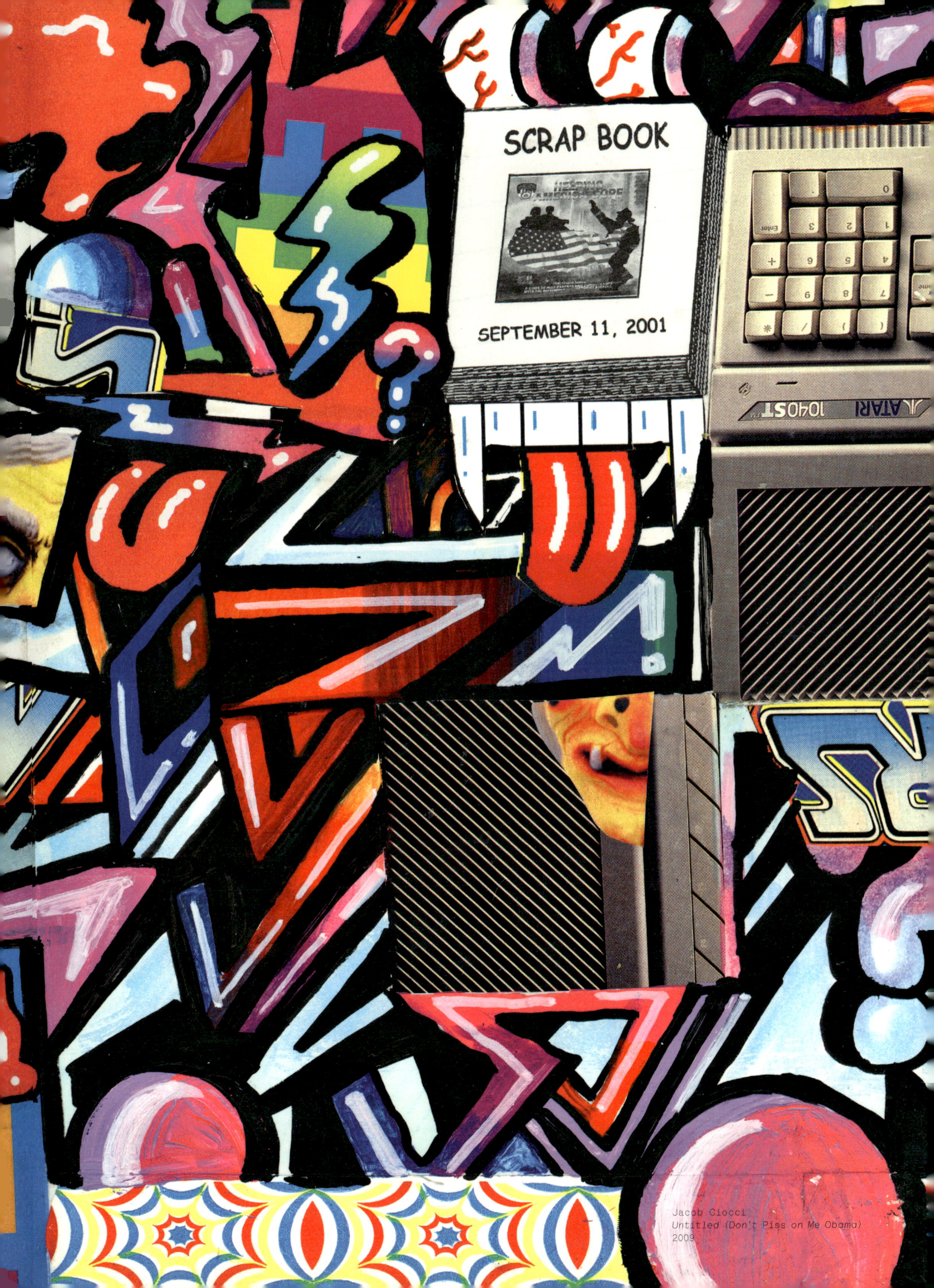

Jacob Ciocci
Untitled (Don't Piss on Me Obama)
2009

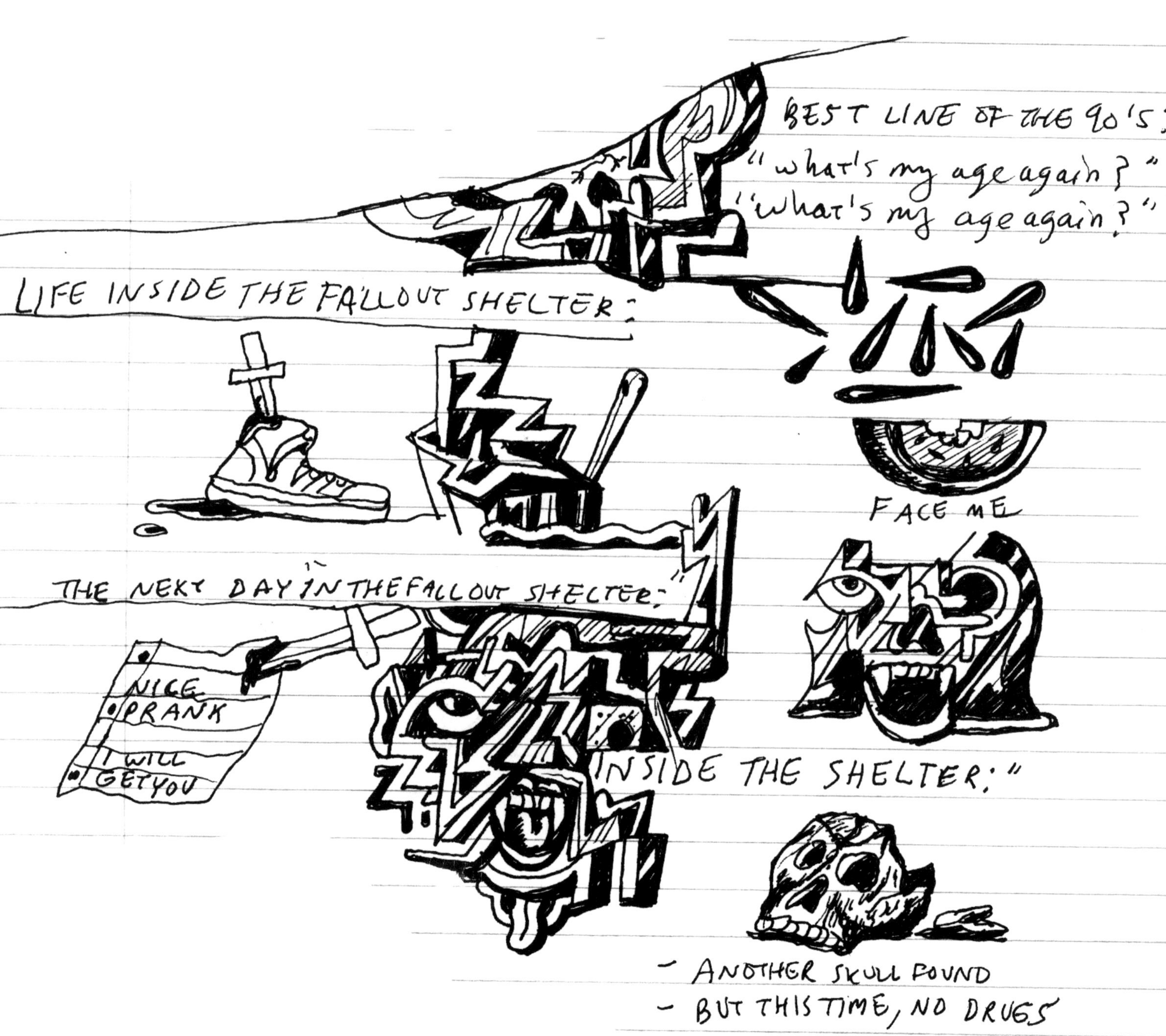
BEST LINE OF THE 90'S:
"what's my age again?"
"what's my age again?"

LIFE INSIDE THE FALLOUT SHELTER:

FACE ME

THE NEXT DAY IN THE FALLOUT SHELTER:

NICE
PRANK

I WILL
GET YOU

INSIDE THE SHELTER:"

- ANOTHER SKULL FOUND
- BUT THIS TIME, NO DRUGS

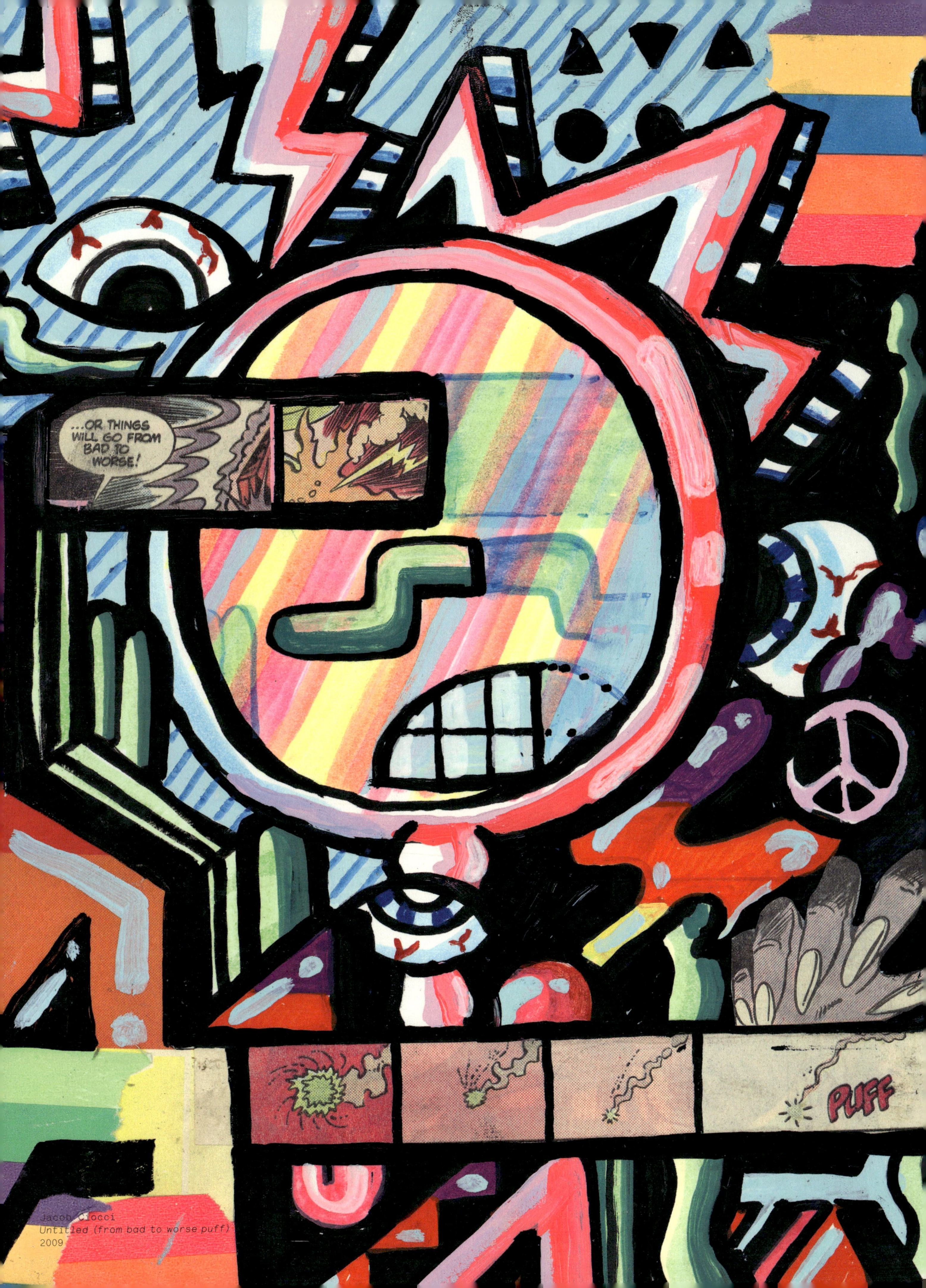
...OR THINGS WILL GO FROM BAD TO WORSE!
PUFF
Jacob Ciocci
Untitled (from bad to worse puff)
2009

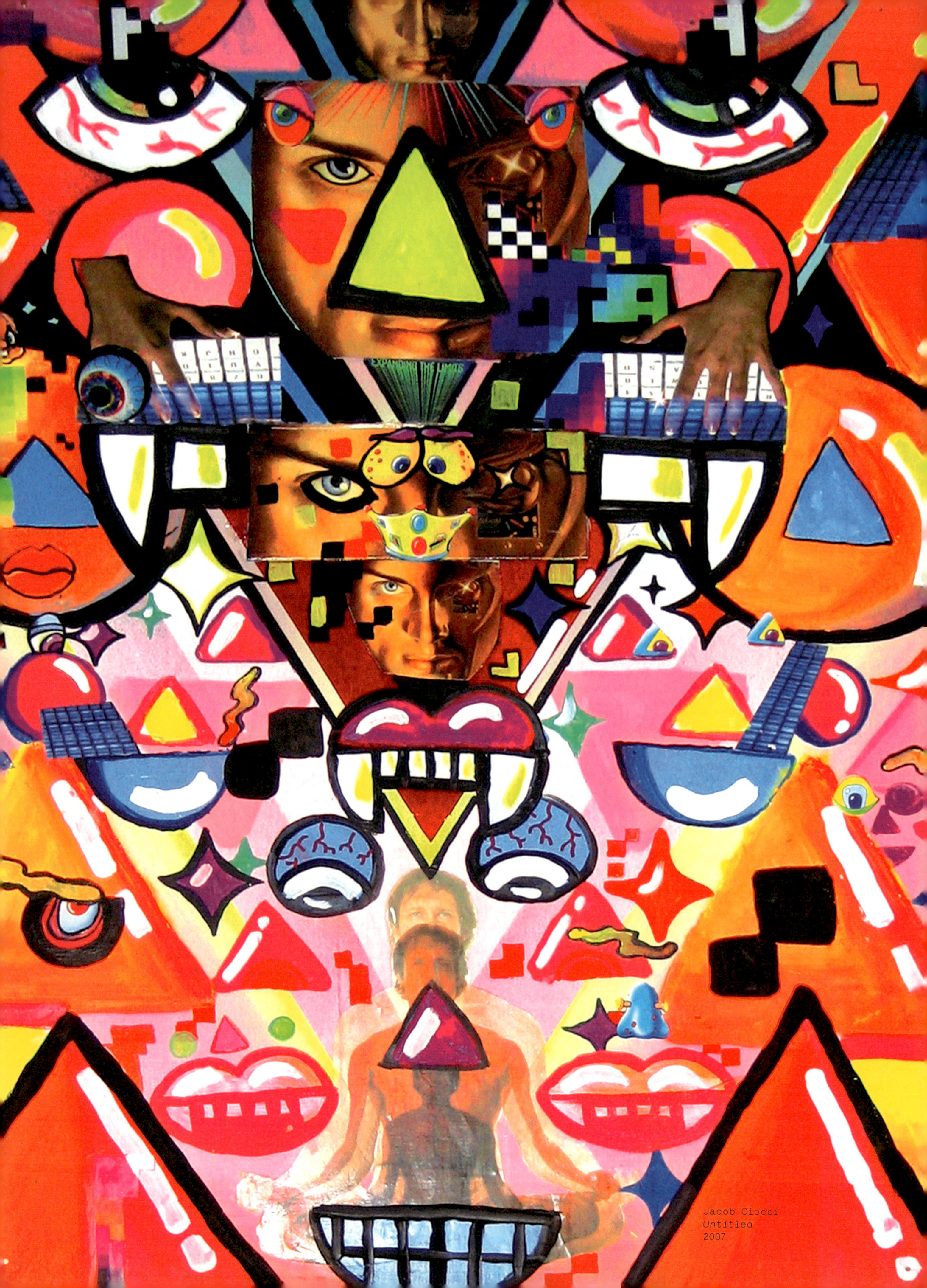

Jacob Ciocci
Untitled
2007

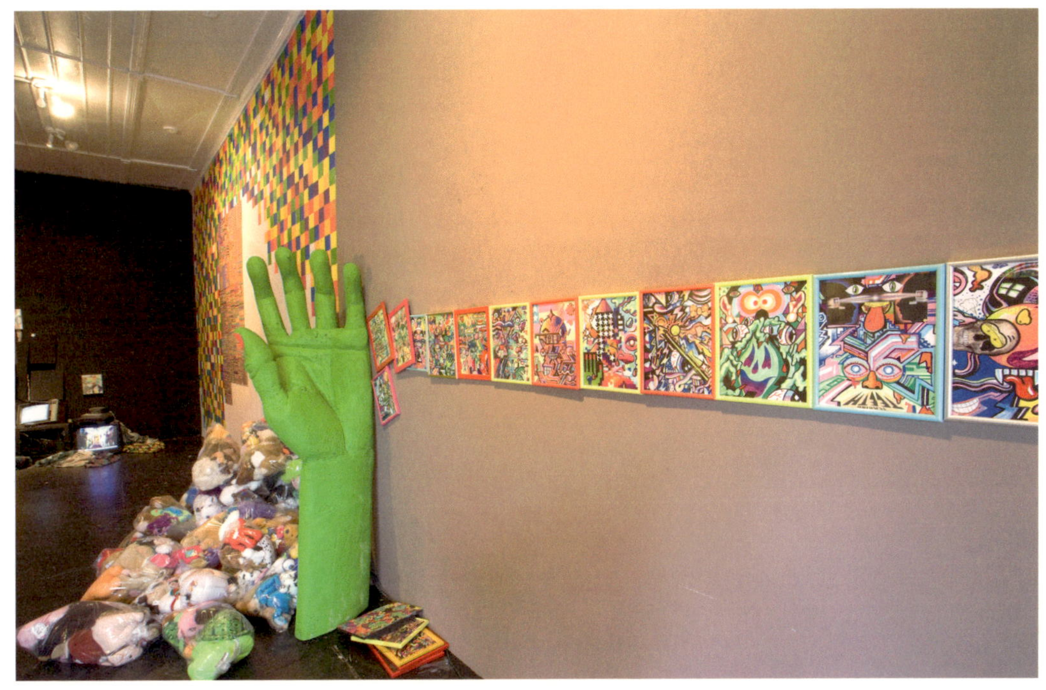

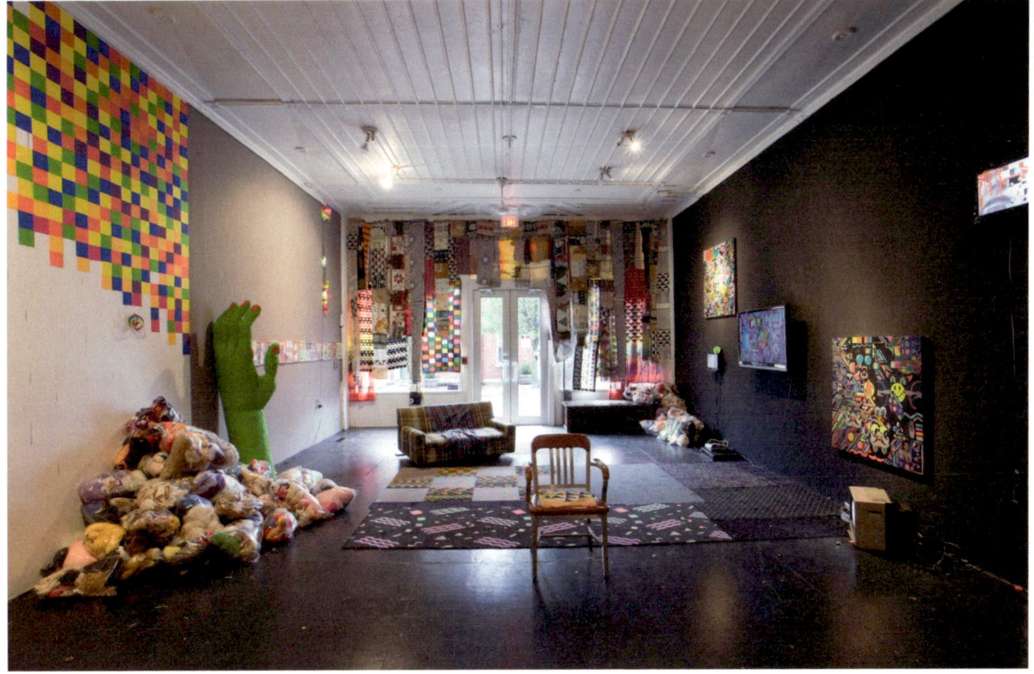

Exhibition view: The Mattress Factory Art Museum
Predrive: After Technology - Jessica Ciocci & Jacob Ciocci

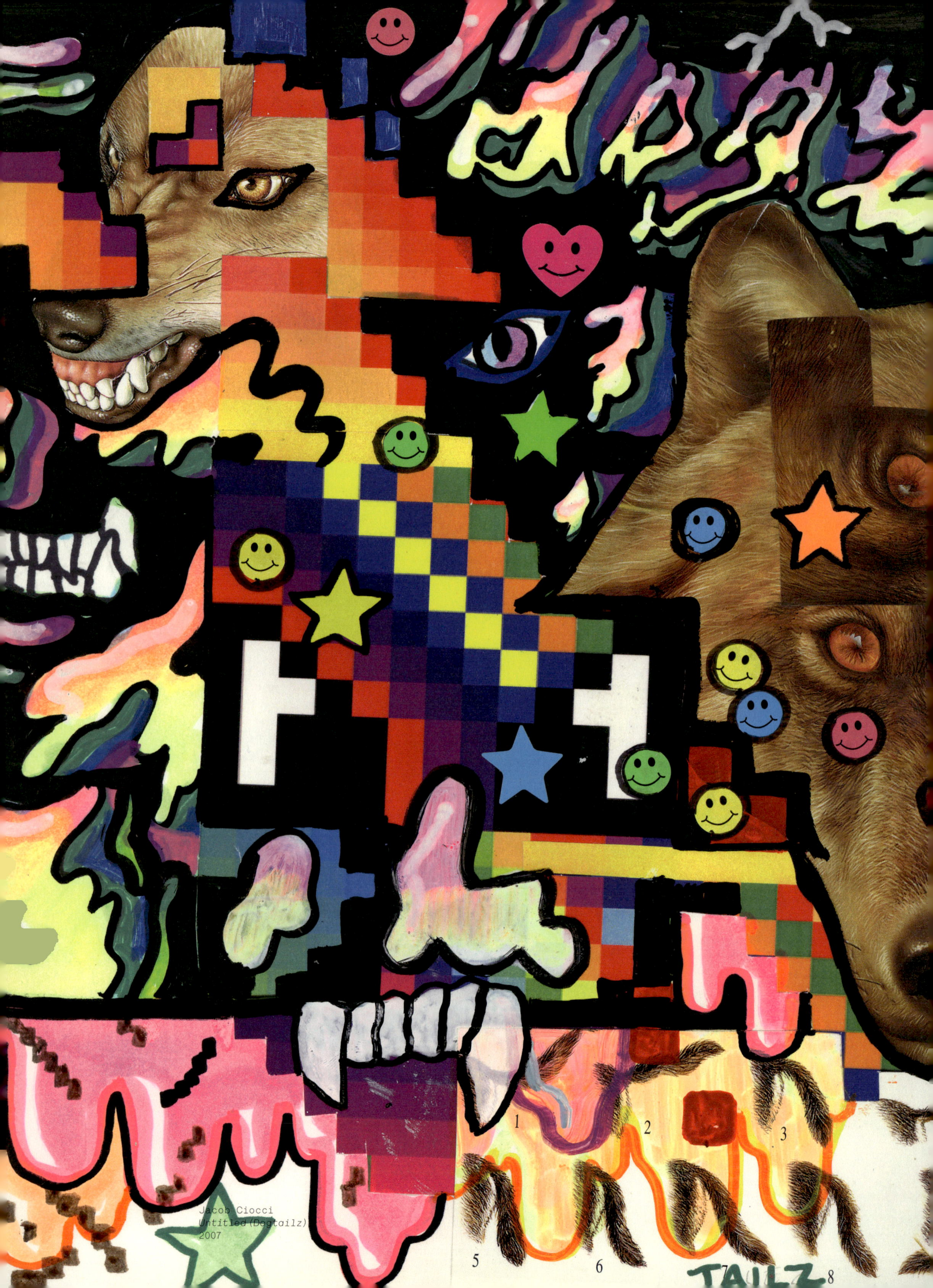

Jacob Ciocci
Untitled (Dogtailz)
2007
TAILZ

ELEVEN EVOCATIONS
(FOR PAPER RAD)

Ed Halter *

* —Ed Halter is a critic, curator and a founder and director of Light Industry, a venue for film and electronic art in Brooklyn, New York. His writing has appeared in *Artforum, The Believer, Cinema Scope, Rhizome, Triple Canopy, The Village Voice* and elsewhere, and his book *From Sun Tzu to Xbox: War and Video Games* was published in 2006. From 1995 to 2005, he programmed and oversaw the New York Underground Film Festival, and has organized screenings and exhibitions for the Brooklyn Academy of Music, Cinematexas, Eyebeam, the Flaherty Film Seminar, the Museum of Modern Art, and San Francisco Cinematheque. He teaches criticism and history in the Film and Electronic Arts department at Bard College.

1 \

The popular dissemination of magical worlds has ultimately shifted from folk tales to children's television. Paper Rad takes back this process from commercial channels, creating their own ever-shifting cosmos populated by robots, spaceships, monsters, talking animals, giants and wizards.

Like H. P. Lovecraft or J.R.R. Tolkein, Paper Rad have created their own mythos, a set of characters that jointly share a fantasy world. Like Warner Brothers or Disney, Paper Rad circulate their creations across media—websites, comics, animated videos, sculptures, screen prints—thereby establishing themselves as the creators of both an imaginary alternative universe and an audio-visual brand.

2 \

Some of the recurring personages from the Paper Rad multiverse:

Alfe: His name is pronounced "alf-ay" not "alf." He is tall, gruff and usually brown, with a long cucumber-shaped nose, double-lidded eyes and a broad, neckless head bearing two hump-like protuberances. Reminiscent of the red-haired monster found in Bugs Bunny cartoons, sometimes named "Gossamer." Often found with Roba, a human-insectoid whose streamlined design recalls robots from Japanese TV anime, and Horus (a.k.a. Horace), a pop-eyed humanoid. In the DVD *Trash Talking*, Horus fears that global thermonuclear war has begun, due to the fact that he and his roommates Alfe and Roba have not left the house in several days.

The Narrator: A squat, sarcastic character who resembles a blue cloud with stubby limbs, yellow snout and fat black eyebrows (or are they eyes?). In the video *P-Unit Mixtape 2005*, he sits in the back of a limo, administering absurd put-downs to other artists.

Nameless pig-lady hybrids, often dancing, loosely based on the Muppets' Miss Piggy. In Jessica Ciocci's 2007 cartoon book *Pig Tales* (published in a flip-over compilation with Paper Rad's *Cartoon Workshop*), one such porcine dame crafts a hair-do by spinning a beehive from cotton candy.

Tux Dog, a dapper canine based on a drawing first made by Ben Jones at the age of ten, inspired by his father's "love of Beckmann's self portrait mixed with the child's own artistic influences at the time, Bill the Cat and Garfield," according to Paper Rad's currently offline website tuxdog.org. Launched in 2004, the site promoted Tux Dog as a copyright-free, open source character, available for use by anyone.

3 \

Other characters in Paper Rad's works are pilfered from mass media, copyright be damned: Gumby, Garfield the Cat, Bart Simpson, Mario, the brush-haired Troll dolls. Along with their own creations mentioned above, any of these creatures can appear as protagonists in narrative sequences, or as decorative elements in elaborate tableaux.

All three members of Paper Rad grew up in New Age households. As a result, their work contains numerous icons commonly seen in related merchandise: peace signs, unicorns, clouds, pyramids, crystals, rainbows, yin-yang symbols, mystic gurus.

Jacob Ciocci: "Corporate companies make this garbage and then send it out into the world, and then culture makes sense of it and uses it productively."

4 \

Cartooning refutes the false dichotomy between representation and abstraction in art. To paraphrase Werner Heisenberg ("Abstraction in Modern Science," 1960), abstraction means the singling out of a limited number of features of an object while disregarding all other properties. Thus Paper Rad's Tux Dog consists of a combination of just a few circles and curved lines—an abstracted if vernacular form, evoking children's drawing, primitive symbols and approaching hieroglyphics. Consequently, these constituent elements may then be reconfigured into impossible shapes that can only be found in the realm of fantasy.

1 \

Die magischen Welten des alten Volksmärchens sind inzwischen ins Kinderfernsehen abgewandert. Paper Rad holen diese Elemente aus den kommerziellen Kanälen zurück und kreieren damit einen ständig bewegten Kosmos, der von Robotern, Raumschiffen und Monstern, von sprechenden Tieren, Riesen und Zauberern bevölkert wird.

Genau wie H. P. Lovecraft und J. R. R. Tolkien haben Paper Rad einen eigenen Mythos geschaffen – ein Ensemble von Figuren, die gemeinsam eine Fantasy-Welt bewohnen. Und nicht anders als die Warner Brothers oder Disney bringen Paper Rad ihre Kreationen über die Medien in Umlauf – Webseiten, Comics, Animationsfilme, Skulpturen, Rasterdrucke. So haben sie sich nicht nur als Erzeuger eines alternativen Universums der Imagination etabliert, sondern zugleich als audiovisuelles Markenprodukt.

2 \

Um nur ein paar Standardfiguren aus dem Paper-Rad-Multiversum zu nennen, als da wären:

Alfe: Der Name wird nicht etwa «Alf» ausgesprochen, sondern «Al-fay». Dieser Alfe ist gross gewachsen, schroff im Auftreten und meist braun dargestellt. Er hat eine lange gurkenförmige Nase, doppellidrige Augen und einen breiten, halslosen Kopf mit zwei Höckern. Die Figur erinnert an das – mitunter als «Gossamer» bezeichnete – rothaarige Monster aus den *Bugs Bunny*-Cartoons. Alfe wird häufig von Roba begleitet, einem insektenartigen Humanoiden, dessen stromlinienförmiges Design an die Roboter in japanischen TV-Animationsfilmen angelehnt scheint. Hinzu kommt Horus (alias Horace), ein glupschäugiger Humanoide. Auf der DVD *Trash Talking* ist Horus von der Idee besessen, dass auf der Welt ein Atomkrieg ausgebrochen sei, da er selbst und seine Mitbewohner Alfe und Roba das Haus schon seit Tagen nicht mehr verlassen haben.

Der Erzähler (The Narrator): ein gedrungener sarkastischer Typ, der an eine blaue Wolke mit Stummelgliedern erinnert – mit einer gelben Schnauze und dicken schwarzen Augenbrauen (oder sollen das etwa Augen sein?). Im Video *P-Unit-Mixtape 2005* sitzt er hinten in einer Limousine und zieht über andere Künstler her.

Namenlose – häufig tanzende – Pig-Lady-Hybriden, die vage von Miss Piggy aus der *Muppet Show* inspiriert sind. In Jessica Cioccis Cartoon-Buch *Pig Tales* (die auch im Paper-Rad-eigenen *Cartoon Workshop* als Flipover-Kompilation erschienen sind) bastelt sich eine solche Schweinedame aus Zuckerwatte eine hoch aufgetürmte Beehive-Frisur.

Tux Dog ist ein echt eleganter Hund und verdankt seine Existenz einer Zeichnung, die Ben Jones schon mit zehn Jahren gemacht hat. Jones hatte sich damals durch «ein [von seinem Vater verehrtes] Selbstbildnis von Max Beckmann» inspirieren lassen, aber auch durch Comicfiguren à la Bill the Cat und Garfield, schliesslich war er ja noch ein Kind. So ist jedenfalls auf der zurzeit offline geschalteten Paper-Rad-Webseite tuxdog.org. nachzulesen. Auf der 2004 eingerichteten Internetseite wurde Tux Dog als Copyright-freie Opensource-Figur eingeführt, auf die jeder nach Lust und Laune zugreifen kann.

3 \

Andere Figuren haben Paper Rad unter Missachtung des Copyright in den Massenmedien stibitzt, zum Beispiel Gumby, Garfield the Cat, Bart Simpson, Mario oder die bürstenhaarigen Troll Dolls. Zusammen mit den Paper-Rad-eigenen Kreationen tauchen diese Figuren in narrativen Sequenzen ebenso auf wie als dekorative Elemente in ausgetüftelten Tableaus.

Alle drei Paper-Rad-Mitglieder sind in New-Age-Familien aufgewachsen. Das erklärt auch, weshalb in ihren Arbeiten so viele Artikel anzutreffen sind, die sich in dieser Szene grosser Beliebtheit erfreuen: Friedensembleme, Einhörner, Wolken, Pyramiden, Kristalle, Regenbögen, Yin-Yang-Symbole, mystische Gurus.

Jacob Ciocci: «Es gibt nun mal Firmen, die solchen Müll produzieren und dann in die Welt hinausschicken. Schliesslich nimmt sich die Kultur dieser Sachen an und macht was Vernünftiges daraus.»

4 \

Der Cartoon ist der – oft ziemlich zappelige – Beweis dafür, dass es völlig falsch ist, von einer Dichotomie zwischen figürlicher Darstellung und Abstraktion in der Kunst zu sprechen. Denn wie schon Werner

5 \

In 2003 the *New York Times* critic Holland Cotter employed the term "collectives"—more common-ly associated with the art of the 1960s—to describe recent ensembles of American artists who are "identified by a group name, like rock bands," whose art "is often a multitasking mix of painting, sculpture, printmaking, design, digital art, video, zine production and musical performances." Cotter cited Paper Rad as part of this new generation of collectives, along with Forcefield, Radical Software Group and others, arguing that "what they do, or rather the way they do it, outside the centralized, market-determining power structures of the mainstream art world, could turn out to have political consequences for the way art develops."

Jones, however, later stated "I don't know anything about 60s art collectives. What we're doing is just common sense." Paper Rad's DIY ethos favors creative systems that are relatively low-cost, auto-sustaining and non-corporate. Overseeing your own alternative economic and distributive practices is a way of creating a parallel art world, based on and interwoven with existing struc-tures for bands, music labels and small publications.

6 \

Two live extrusions/social recombinations of Paper Rad:

Extreme Animals: Noise-techno-pop band consisting of Jacob Ciocci and David Wightman. Music by Extreme Animals appears on the tape *PjVidz #1*. Their frenetic, spasmodic live perfor-mances include nods to the day-glo aesthetics and high-speed beats per minute of rave.

Doo Man Group: Permutation of Paper Rad in which the three members perform with card-board instruments. Related to Jones's live percussion outfit Dr. Doo and the enigmatic character of the same name, who appears in the cartoon book *Paper Rad, BJ and Da Dogs* and elsewhere as an uncanny smiley face drawn on a monitor screen.

7 \

One of the main attributes writers have employed when describing Paper Rad's work, "Fun" is an important but complicated concept for Americans: we consider fun essential to every individual's well-being, yet denounce it as frivolous when found in "higher" creative forms like art, literature and music. The simultaneous complexity and exuberance of Paper Rad's work sharply counters this unnatural division.

8 \

Layering is a frequent graphic strategy for Paper Rad: intermeshing multiple levels of Flash car-toons, animated gifs, and VHS footage on top of one another, flattening their various depths into impossible dimensions of optical-illusion collage, risking total overstimulation. This strategy par-allels the practice of historical layering that occurs in their work, in which fictional characters from various decades appear in the same space (Gumby meets Bart Simpson), and vernacular styles from different stages of life cohere—toddlers' scribblings, children's art, school-kids' hand-written notes, stoner doodles—all these moments bleeding into one.

Jessica Ciocci: "I feel like it is the same kind of energy as when you are a kid and drawing. It's just about sharing something awesome with people."

9 \

A copy of *PjVidz #1: Color Vision* that I purchased at an Extreme Animals show in 2003 is a VHS tape, wrapped in a laser-printed paper sleeve, with no title on the tape itself. Rather, it's a generic black tape with the words "—Sprite Commerical / --Barq's Got Bite" hand-written in bubbly letters with a pink Sharpie. It's meant to masquerade as just another tape of random TV snippets that you might find lying next to your VCR. It takes the mixtape as its form, stringing together early Flash animations, music videos for Extreme Animals and clips of weird television: a coherent chaos.

Heisenberg (in: *Die Abstraktion in der modernen Naturwissenschaft,* 1960) gesagt hat, werden im Prozess der Abstraktion einzelne Merkmale eines Objekts zu Lasten aller übrigen Eigenschaften isoliert betrachtet. Zum Beispiel besteht Paper Rads Tux Dog lediglich aus einer Kombination weniger Kreise und geschwungener Linien. Wir haben es hier also mit einer zugleich abstrahierenden und «volksnahen» Vorgehensweise zu tun, die an Kinderzeichnungen erinnert, an primitive Symbole oder Hieroglyphen. Aus diesen Grundelementen entstehen dann ganz neue Formen und Figuren, wie sie nur im Reich der Fantasie anzutreffen sind.

5 \

Im Jahr 2003 hat der *New York Times*-Kritiker Holland Cotter neuere amerikanische Künstlergruppen als «Kollektive» bezeichnet – also mit einem Begriff, der eigentlich vor allem mit der Kunst der 1960er Jahre assoziiert wird. Gemeint waren mit dieser Bezeichnung amerikanische Künstler, die wie etwa die diversen Rockbands unter einem «Gruppennamen» auftreten und in ihrem Schaffen häufig auf «Mischformen aus Malerei, Skulptur, Druckgrafik, Design, Digitalkunst, Video, Zine-Produktion und Musikdarbietung» zurückgreifen. Dabei nannte Cotter unter anderem Paper Rad, aber auch Forcefield und die Radical Software Group als typische Vertreter dieser neuen Richtung. Er behauptete sogar: «Was [diese Leute] ausserhalb der zentralisierten marktbeherrschenden Machtstrukturen der Mainstream-Kunst machen, aber auch wie sie arbeiten, könnte einmal politische Folgen für die weitere Entwicklung der Kunst haben.»

Ben Jones hat später allerdings festgestellt: «Von den Kunstkollektiven der 60er Jahre habe ich keine Ahnung. Was wir heute tun, ist einfach nur vernünftig.» Paper Rads Do-it-yourself-Ethos favorisiert relativ kostengünstige, selbsttragende und von der Unterhaltungsindustrie unabhängige kreative Systeme. Der Gruppe geht es vor allem darum, ihre ökonomische Situation und Vertriebspraxis selbst zu kontrollieren. So möchte sie eine parallele Kunstszene etablieren, die sich auf bereits existierende alternative – kleinformatige – Strukturen im Musikgeschäft und Verlagswesen stützt und mit diesen kooperiert.

6 \

Zwei Live-Ableger / Neuformierungen von Paper Rad:

Extreme Animals: Diese Noise-Techno-Pop-Band besteht aus Jacob Ciocci und David Wightman. Die Musik der Extreme Animals ist auch auf dem Tape *PjVidz #1* zu hören. Bei ihren wilden, spasmodischen Live-Auftritten taktet die Band Highspeed-Beats mit Day-glo-Animationen.

Doo Man Group: eine Mutation von Paper Rad, in der die drei Mitglieder mit Pappmaché-Instrumenten auftreten. Das Ganze ist inspiriert durch Jones' Live-Percussion-Outfit Dr. Doo und die enigmatische Figur gleichen Namens, die in dem Cartoon-Buch *Paper Rad, BJ and Da Dogs* und auch anderswo vorkommt: ein unheimliches Smiley-Face, das vorne auf einen Monitor gezeichnet ist.

7 \

Eines der Hauptattribute, mit dem Paper Rads Arbeit häufig in Verbindung gebracht wird, lautet: «Fun». Für Amerikaner ist dieser Begriff ebenso wichtig wie kompliziert. Für das persönliche Wohlbefinden ist «Fun» zwar absolut unverzichtbar, in der sogenannten Hochkultur dagegen – ob nun Kunst, Literatur oder Musik – ist uns das Konzept nicht mehr ganz geheuer. Die mit Überschwang gepaarte Komplexität, durch die sich Paper Rads Schaffen auszeichnet, grenzt sich von dieser unnatürlichen Unterscheidung jedoch scharf ab.

8 \

Eine der beliebtesten grafischen Strategien von Paper Rad ist das *Layering* (Bildschichtung). Dabei werden Flash-Cartoons, animierte GIFs und VHS-Material so häufig übereinander gelegt, bis sich ihre unterschiedlichen Tiefenwirkungen zu einer eigentlich unmöglichen optisch-illusionistischen Collage verflachen und es zu einer völligen Überforderung für den Betrachter kommen kann. Diese Strategie geht mit der ebenfalls Paper-Rad-typischen Praxis einher, diverse historische Ebenen übereinanderzuschichten, etwa Figuren aus ganz unterschiedlichen Dekaden miteinander agieren zu lassen (z. B. Gumby

P-Unit Mixtape 2005, their follow-up to *PjVidz #1*, retained mixtape format, now inflected with a running Wu-Tang Clan theme of ominous bling.

Trash Talking, a 2006 DVD released by Load Records, begins with a ridiculously long sequence with The Narrator, who trundles through a graffiti-strewn neighborhood to a midi version of the Bee Gee's song "Jive Talkin," then gives a long talk about CD-ROM technology, before allowing the viewer to access the menu.

Problem Solvers, a DVD released in 2008, takes the form of an episodic animated TV show for kids—"like how we remember from our childhood," as its opening titles state.

10 \

Some of the materials Paper Rad has worked with: Flash animation, VHS video, cardboard, clothing, paper, acrylic, pencil, audio recordings, live performance, spray paint, vegan chocolate. The sculpture *Extreme Animals #1* embeds small video panels within a roboticized conglomeration of stuffed animals that rotate and twist spasmodically, furry 3–D versions of the animated gifs found in Paper Rad videos like *Welcome to My Home Page*, a 10-year-old's bedroom gone wild.

11 \

Reminiscent of Op Art and psychedelia, the use of repeating patterns and strobing colors attests to the group's desire to create visual forms with the same visceral rhythms as music. Jessica Ciocci's solo work includes a series of "grid drawings" that create reticulated patterns of color, as if obsessively executed on graph paper, that connect to similar reverberating structures found elsewhere in Paper Rad's work.

In her essay "Grids," published in the journal *October* in 1979, art historian Rosalind Krauss identifies the grid as "an emblem of modernity [...] the form that is ubiquitous in the art of our century, while appearing nowhere, nowhere at all, in the art of the last one." She writes that "the relationships in the aesthetic field are shown by the grid to be in a world apart and, with respect to natural objects, to be both prior and final. The grid declares the space of art to be at once autonomous and autotelic." In short, "the grid functions to declare the modernity of modern art."

If the modernist grid, as seen in the paintings of Mondrian or Agnes Martin, provides a marker of art's release from representation and, thereby, the mind's triumph over nature, then Jessica Ciocci's 21st century hand-made color grids express something else—a living grid, perhaps: a formal system that, while based on a cool mathematical geometry, pulses with an individual spark, vibrates with prismatic life.

mit Bart Simpson), und für verschiedene Altersstufen typische Stile – Babygekritzel, Kindermalereien, handschriftliche Notizen von Schulkindern, Kiffer-Gedudel – miteinander zu verschmelzen.

Jessica Ciocci: «Für mich fühlt sich das genauso an wie damals als Kind, wenn man was gezeichnet hat: Man will anderen einfach was total Beeindruckendes mitteilen.»

9 \

Eine Kopie von *PjVidz #1: Color Vision,* die ich 2003 bei einem Extreme-Animals-Auftritt gekauft habe, ist nichts weiter als ein VHS-Band in einer bedruckten Papierhülle. Auf der Kassette selbst ist kein Titel vermerkt. Einfach die übliche schwarze Kassette. Darauf steht mit einem pinkfarbenen Sharpie-Stift in Bubble-Letters: «Sprite Commercial / –Barq's Got Bite». Die Kassette soll vermutlich aussehen wie irgendein Videoband mit irgendwelchen TV-Mitschnitten, das zufällig neben deinem Videogerät liegt. Die Kassette ist wie ein Mixtape aufgebaut – eine Aneinanderreihung früher Flash-Animationen, älterer Musikvideos der Extreme Animals und verrückter Fernsehclips: also das komplette Chaos.

Auch das *P-Unit Mixtape 2005,* der Nachfolger von *PjVidz #1,* ist ein Mixtape, diesmal jedoch mit einem Wu-Tang-Clan-Thema unterlegt und mit reichlich Bling-Bling.

Trash Talking, eine DVD, die 2006 bei Load Records erschienen ist, zeigt in einer lächerlich langen Eröffnungssequenz den Erzähler (The Narrator), der sich – begleitet von einer Midi-Version des Bee-Gees-Songs *Jive Talkin* – durch eine mit Graffiti zugepflasterte Nachbarschaft bewegt. Dann hält er einen langen Vortrag über die CD-ROM-Technik, bevor der Zuschauer schliesslich das Menü aktivieren darf.

Die DVD *Problem Solvers,* die 2008 herauskam, besteht aus mehreren animierten Episoden im Stil des Fernsehens für Kinder – Geschichten, «wie wir sie noch aus unserer Kindheit kennen» – heisst es im Vorspann.

10 \

Hier einige der Materialien und Verfahren, mit denen Paper Rad bisher arbeiteten: Flash-Animation, VHS-Video, Pappmaché, Klamotten, Papier, Acryl, Filzstift, Audioaufnahmen, Live-Performance, Sprayfarben, veganische Schokolade. In der Skulptur *Extreme Animals #1* sind kleine Monitore in eine Ansammlung ausgestopfter – roboterartiger – Tiere eingelassen, die rotieren und wild zucken. In Videos wie *Welcome to My Home Page,* in dem das völlig chaotische Schlafzimmer einer Zehnjährigen zu sehen ist, arbeitete das Kollektiv auch mit pelzigen 3-D-Versionen animierter GIFs.

11 \

Die Verwendung ständig wiederkehrender Muster und farbiger Strobo-Effekte, die an Op Art oder Psychedelia erinnern, zeugen von dem Wunsch der Gruppe, visuelle Formen zu kreieren, die – wie Musik – unmittelbar körperlich spürbar sind. So hat Jessica Ciocci etwa eine Serie von «Rasterzeichnungen» geschaffen, die wie netzartige Farbmuster wirken, die auf Karopapier ungestüm ausgeführt sind. Die Arbeiten erinnern an jene wiederkehrenden Strukturen, die sich auch sonst bei Paper Rad häufig finden.

In dem Essay *Grids,* der 1979 in der Zeitschrift *October* erschien, hat die Kunsthistorikerin Rosalind Krauss das Raster einmal «als Inbegriff der Moderne» bezeichnet, als «*die* Form, die in der Kunst unseres Jahrhunderts allgegenwärtig ist, während sie in der Kunst des vergangenen Säkulums absolut nirgendwo vorkommt». Weiter schreibt sie, dass «das Raster die Beziehungen innerhalb des ästhetischen Feldes als einer ganz eigenen Welt zugehörig ausweist – einer Welt, die zugleich diesseits und jenseits der Naturobjekte Geltung besitzt. Das Raster erklärt den Raum der Kunst zugleich für autonom und für selbstgenügsam.» Kurz: «Das Raster hat den Zweck, für die moderne Kunst den Status der Modernität einzufordern.»

Das Raster der Moderne, wie es uns auf den Gemälden eines Mondrian oder einer Agnes Martin begegnet, markiert die Abnabelung der Kunst von der Abbildung – und damit zugleich den Triumph des «Geistes» über die Natur. Jessica Cioccis Anfang des 21. Jahrhunderts von Hand kolorierte Farbraster dagegen drücken etwas anderes aus. Man könnte sie vielleicht sogar als lebendige Raster bezeichnen, als ein System der Formen, das – auf der Basis einer kühlen mathematischen Geometrie – von einem ganz persönlichen Funken durchpulst wird und ein vibrierendes prismatisches Leben entfaltet.

Q — FOR QUOTES

To alcohol! The cause of... and solution to... all of life's problems!
Homer Simpson [51]

Auf den Alkohol! Die Ursache und die Lösung aller Probleme!
Homer Simpson [52]

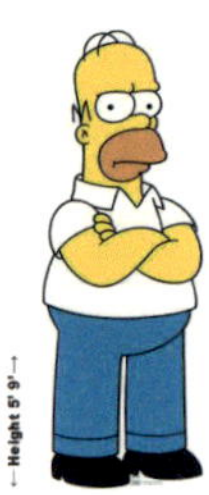
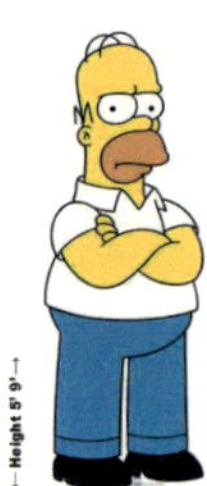
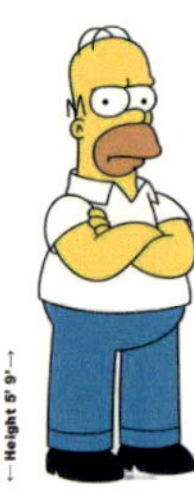

R — FOR RHIZOME

The 'rhizome' is a central concept in the philosophy of Gilles Deleuze and Félix Guattari; it is derived from the term for the root networks of plants (rhizomes). In Deleuze and Guattari, it serves as a metaphor for a post-modern or post-structuralist model for the organization of knowledge and the description of the world. The rhizomatic model supplants the old image of the world, whose emblem is the tree, as a metaphor for hierarchical structures.[53]

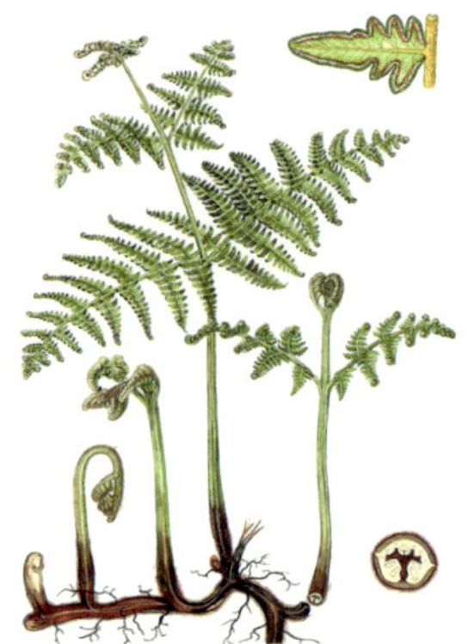

Das ‹Rhizom› ist ein zentraler Begriff der Philosophie von Gilles Deleuze und Félix Guattari und leitet sich ab von der Bezeichnung für Wurzelgeflechte (Rhizome) von Pflanzen. Deleuze und Guattari dient er als Metapher für ein postmodernes beziehungsweise poststrukturalistisches Modell der Wissensorganisation und Weltbeschreibung. Das Modell des Rhizoms ersetzt das alte Bild der Welt, das durch die Baum-Metapher mit seinen hierarchischen Strukturen versinnbildlicht wird.[54]

S — FOR SPECTACULAR, SPECTACULAR EXCESS

In his seminal essay *The Cinema of Attractions*, Tom Gunning pointed out that the early "cinema of attractions" is marked, among other things, by the display of its technological range and by a diegesis tending toward openness. This tendency is not without contemporary successors; paradigmatic examples are the films of "New Hollywood."[55] Movies such as *Jaws* or *Star Wars* have been part of the academic canon for a long time; their "aesthetic of overwhelmment" has long been outdone by the rapid cuts and the special effects of more recent works. The idea of overwhelmment—a total satisfaction of the spectator's eye—as an aesthetic feature separates the spectacle from the filmic excess.[56] Drawing on Grindon's distinction between "excess" and "spectacle," we can describe the filmic excess as containing an aspect of reflection, a self-reflective component. On the one hand, excess (like spectacle) complicates the reception and interpretation of a movie, which can no longer be described as a semiotic system or text. On the other hand, it tempts the critic to focus his examination on the film's excessive elements and to lose sight of its narration. (→ SHANA MOULTON) (→ RYAN TRECARTIN & LIZZIE FITCH) The discourse around the interrelation between excess and narration is fragile—not least because the former is located on the visual plain of order while the latter is anchored at the level of content and structure. There is a general consensus that these two entities cannot simply be separated. But opinions differ regarding the question of how they affect one another: is excess nothing but a willful cosmetic intervention, a confusion of the senses that blocks the plot in order to conceal potential weaknesses in the narration, or does it succeed, by virtue of its reflectivity, in adding new levels of meaning?

Bereits in seinem grundlegenden Essay *Das Kino der Attraktionen* wies Tom Gunning darauf hin, dass das frühe «Kino der Attraktionen» sich unter anderem durch die Zurschaustellung der technischen Möglichkeiten und seiner zur Offenheit tendierenden Diegese auszeichnet. Diese Tendenz hat heute noch ihre Aktualität, wie etwa Werke von «New Hollywood» beispielhaft verdeutlichen.[57] Filme wie *Der weisse Hai* oder *Star Wars* haben heute Eingang in den akademischen Filmkanon gefunden und wurden in ihrer «Überwältigungsästhetik» beispielsweise durch hohe Schnittfrequenzen oder Special Effects seit langem von Werken neueren Datums überboten. Die Idee der Überwältigung im Sinne einer völligen Befriedigung des Auges als ästhetisches Merkmal grenzt das Spektakel vom filmischen Exzess ab.[58] In Anlehnung an Leger Grindons Unterscheidung von «Exzess» und «Spektakel» wird dem filmischen Exzess zusätzlich ein Moment der Reflexion, eine selbstreflexive Komponente zugeschrieben.[59] Der Exzess (wie auch das Spektakel) erschwert einerseits die Rezeption und Deutung des Films, da dieser nicht mehr als Zeichensystem oder Text beschrieben werden kann. Andererseits verführt er dazu, nur noch die exzessiven Elemente des Films zu untersuchen und dabei die Narration aus den Augen zu verlieren. (→ SHANA MOULTON) (→ RYAN TRECARTIN & LIZZIE FITCH) Der Diskurs um das Verhältnis von Exzess und Narration ist fragil – schon alleine dadurch, dass Ersteres der visuellen Ordnungsebene zuzuordnen, Letzteres in der inhaltlich-strukturellen Ebene verankert ist. Es besteht ein allgemeiner Konsens darüber, dass die Entitäten nicht einfach voneinander zu trennen sind. Allerdings gehen die Meinungen bei der Frage über ihr gegenseitiges Einwirken auseinander: Ist der Exzess bloss ein kosmetischer Eigeneingriff, eine handlungsblockierende Sinnesverwirrung, um allfällige Schwächen der Narration zu kaschieren, oder schafft er es, in seiner Reflexivität weitere Bedeutungsebenen hinzuzufügen?

51—From the episode "Homer vs. the Eighteenth Amendment," *The Simpsons*, season 8, episode 18.

52—Zitat aus der Folge «Homer vs. the Eighteenth Amendment», aus: *The Simpsons*, 18. Episode der 8. Staffel.

53—Gilles Deleuze, Félix Guattari, *A Thousand Plateaus. Capitalism and Schizophrenia*, Brian Massumi (trans.), Minneapolis 1987. (French original: Gilles Deleuze, Félix Guattari, *Mille Plateaux*, Paris 1980).

54—Gilles Deleuze, Félix Guattari, *Tausend Plateaus: Kapitalismus und Schizophrenie*, Berlin 1992 (Erstveröffentlichung in Französisch: Gilles Deleuze, Félix Guattari, *Mille Plateaux*, Paris 1980).

55—Cf. Tom Gunning, "The Cinema of Attraction: Early Film, its Spectator and the Avant-garde," *Wide Angle* 8, 1986.

56—A basic definition of filmic excess has been offered by Kristin Thompson; see her "The Concept of Cinematic Excess," in: *Film Theory and Criticism: Introductory Readings*, Jean-Louis Baudry et al. (eds.), New York 1999, 487–498. (First in: Kristin Thompson, *Eisenstein's "Ivan the Terrible": A Neoformalist Analysis*, Princeton 1981).

57—Vgl. Tom Gunning, «Das Kino der Attraktionen. Der frühe Film, seine Zuschauer und die Avantgarde», in: *Meteor. Texte zum Laufbild*, Nr. 4, Wien 1996, S. 25–34 (Erstveröffentlichung in Englisch: Tom Gunning, «The Cinema of Attraction: Early Film, its Spectator and the Avant-garde», in: *Wide Angle*, Vol. 8, Baltimore 1986).

58—Als Grundlage für die Definition des filmischen Exzesses kann das Konzept von Kristin Thompson verwendet werden, vgl. Kristin Thompson, «The Concept of Cinematic Excess», in: *Film Theory and Criticism: Introductory Readings*, hrsg. von Jean-Louis Baudry et al., New York 1999, S. 487–498 (Erstveröffentlichung in: Kristin Thompson, *Eisenstein's «Ivan the Terrible»: A Neoformalist Analysis*, Princeton 1981).

59—Vgl. Leger Grindon, «The Role of Spectacle and Excess in the Critique of Illusion», in: *Post Script*, Nr. 2, S. 35–42, 1994.

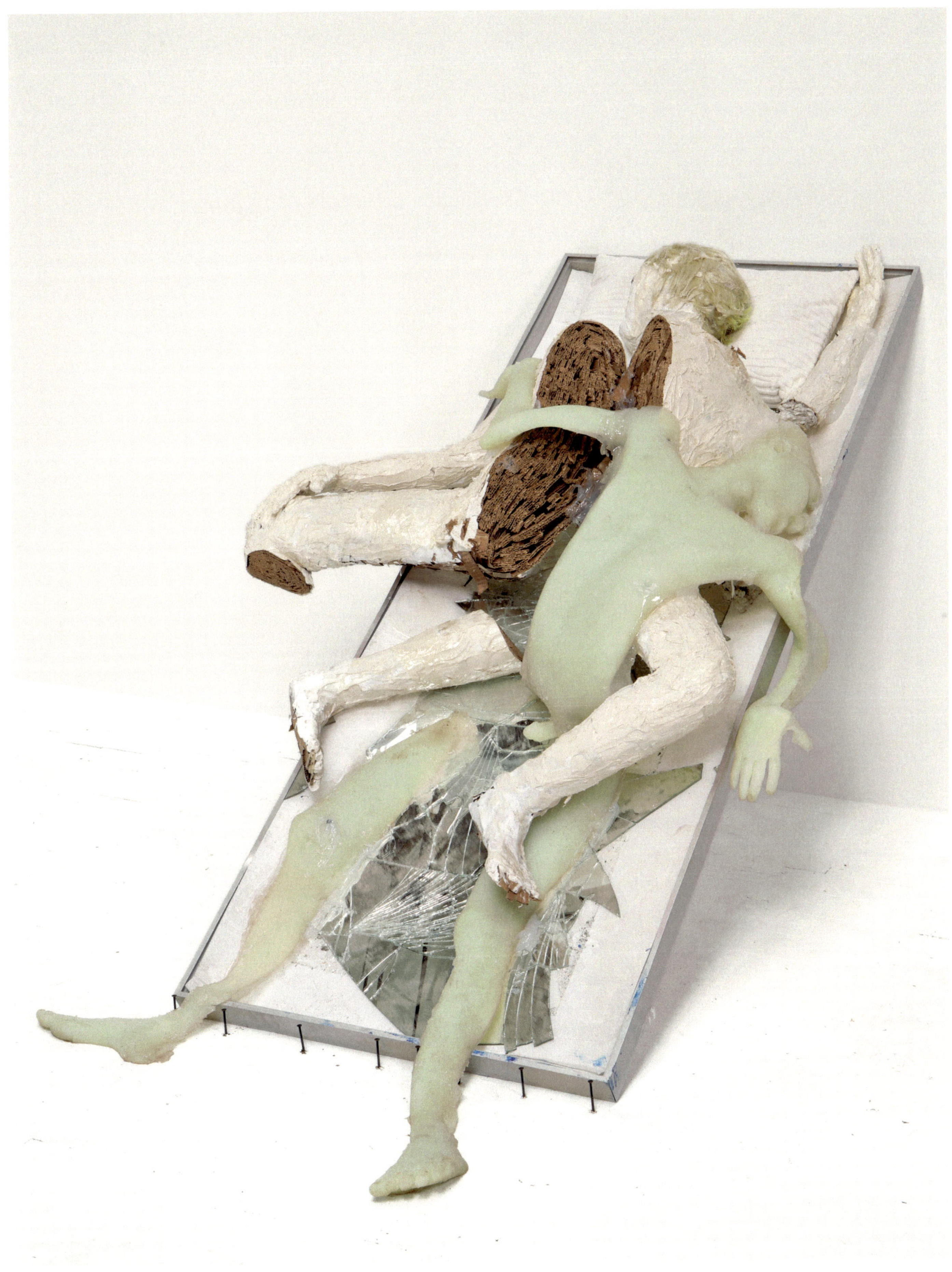

Ryan Trecartin & Lizzie Fitch
2 Companies, 1 Bed
2008

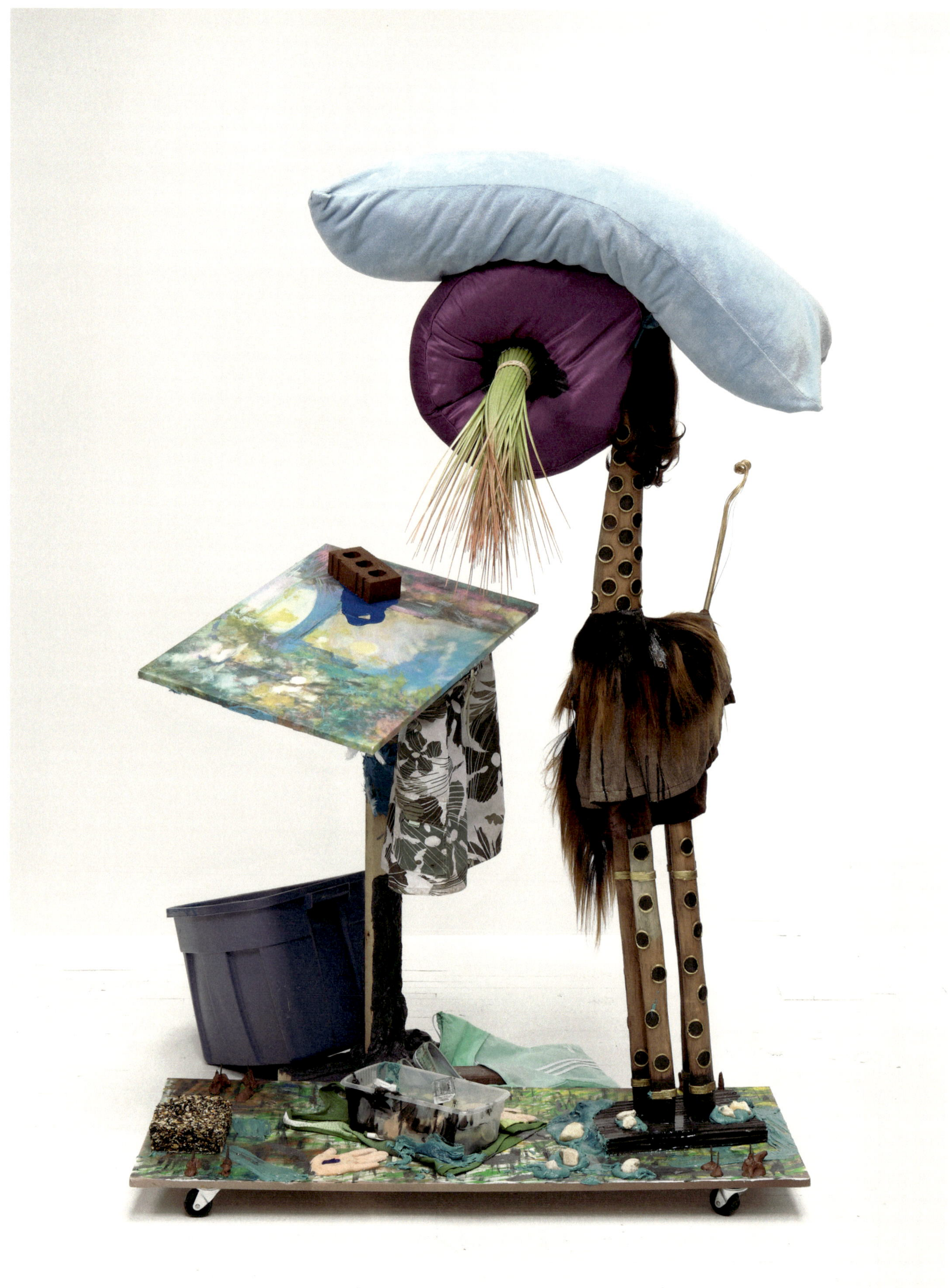

Ryan Trecartin & Lizzie Fitch
Import Landscape Exploit
2008

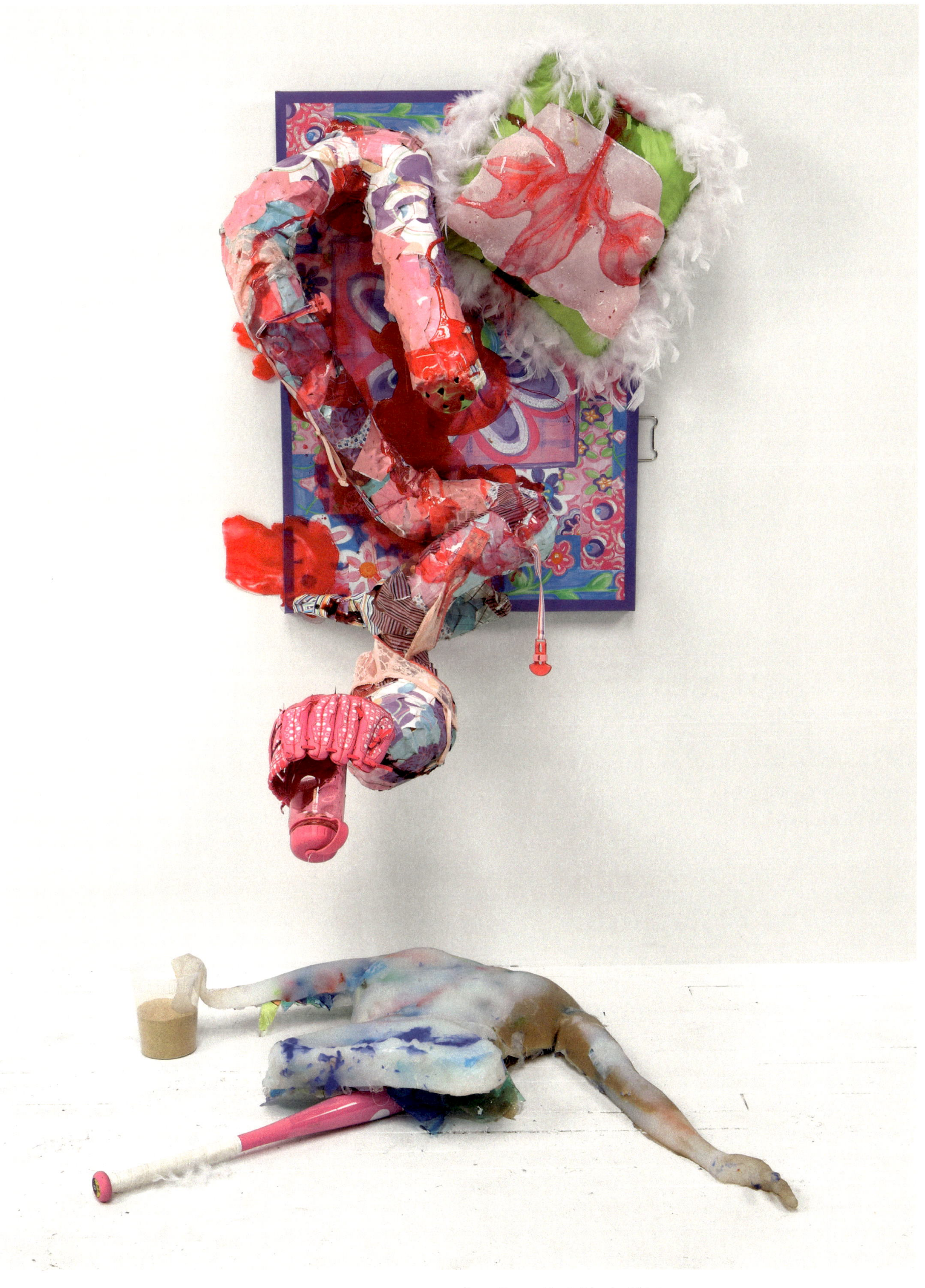

Ryan Trecartin & Lizzie Fitch
Early Catcher
2008

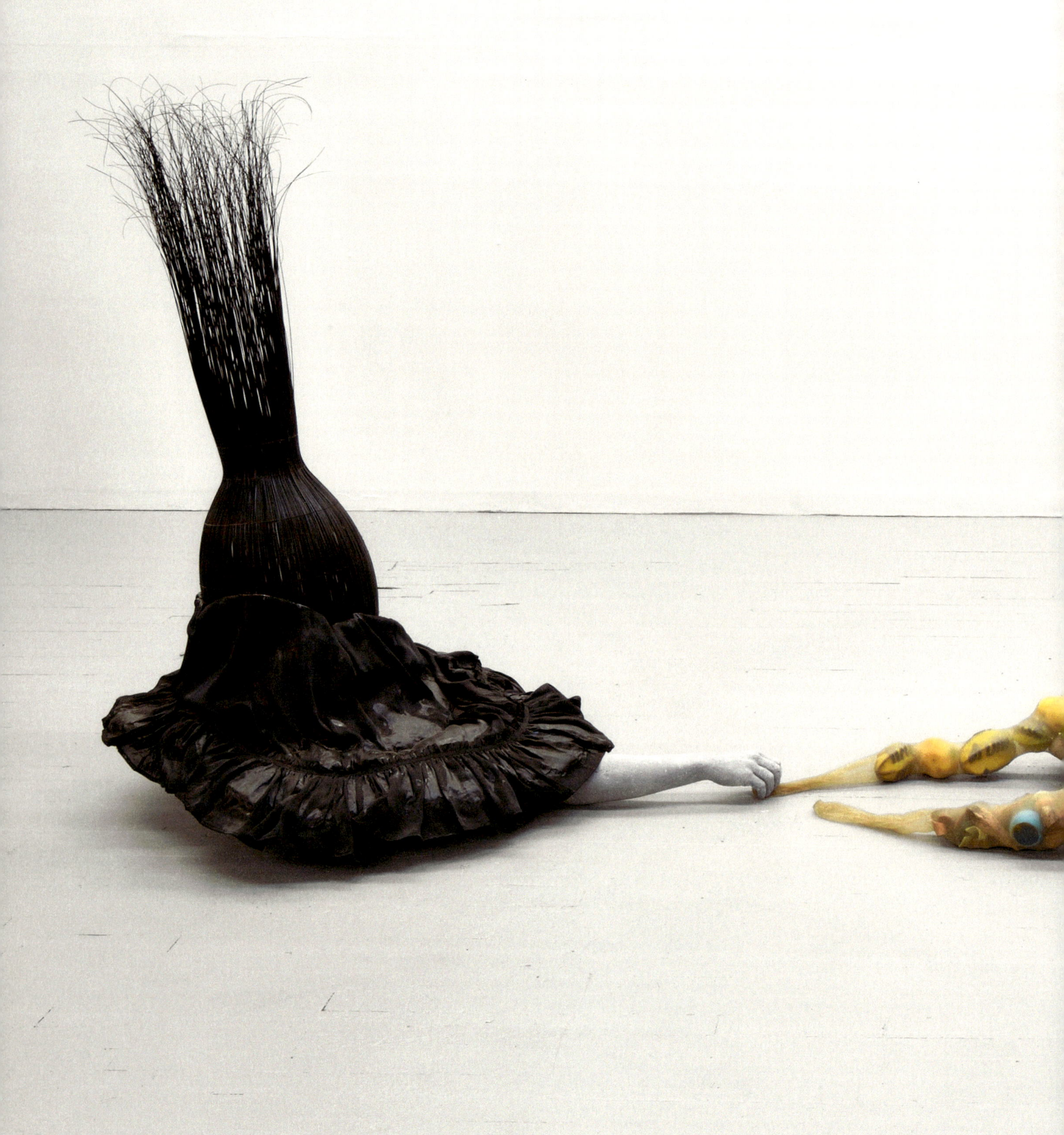

Ryan Trecartin & Lizzie Fitch
Choice Shopping
2006

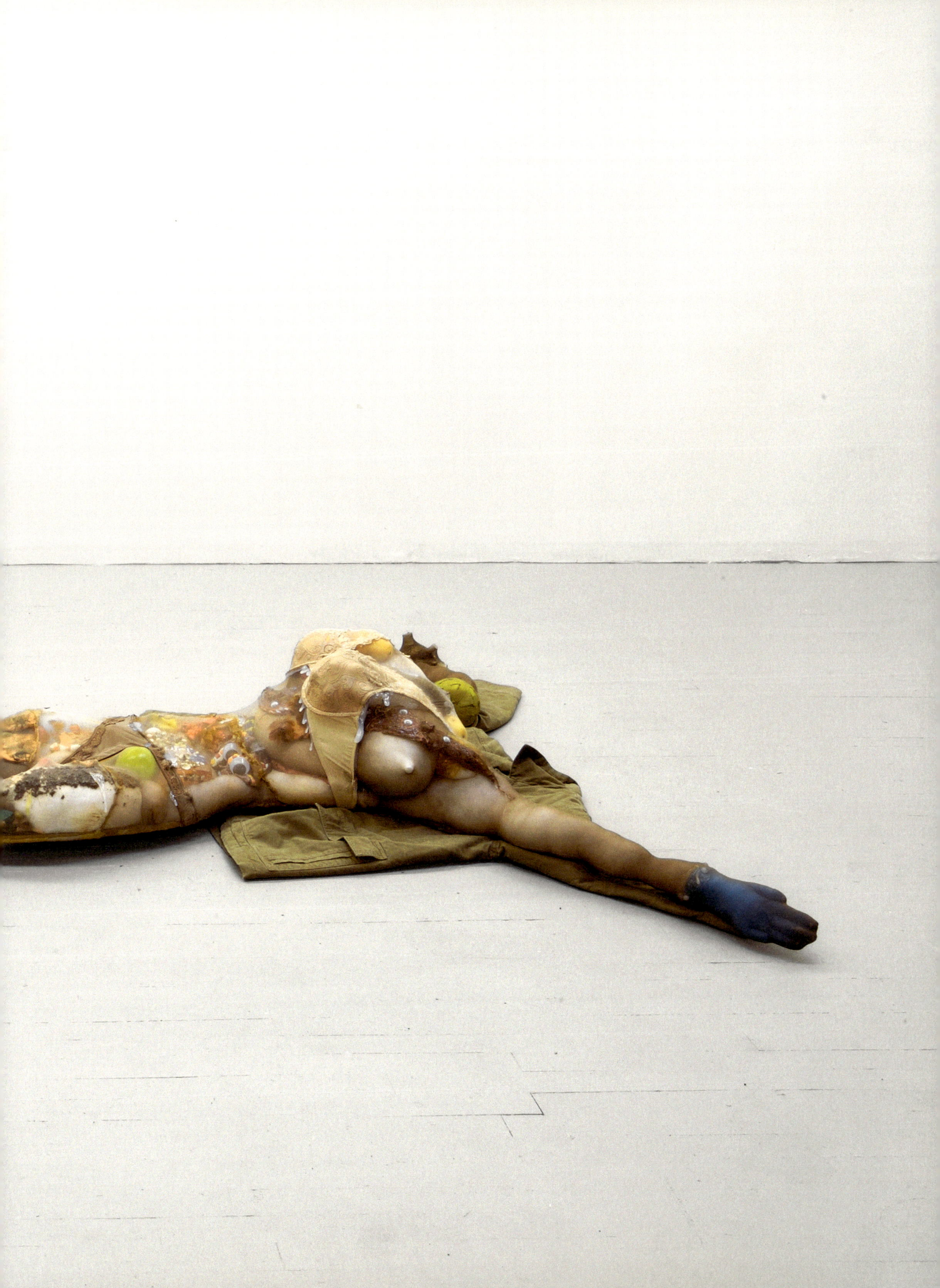

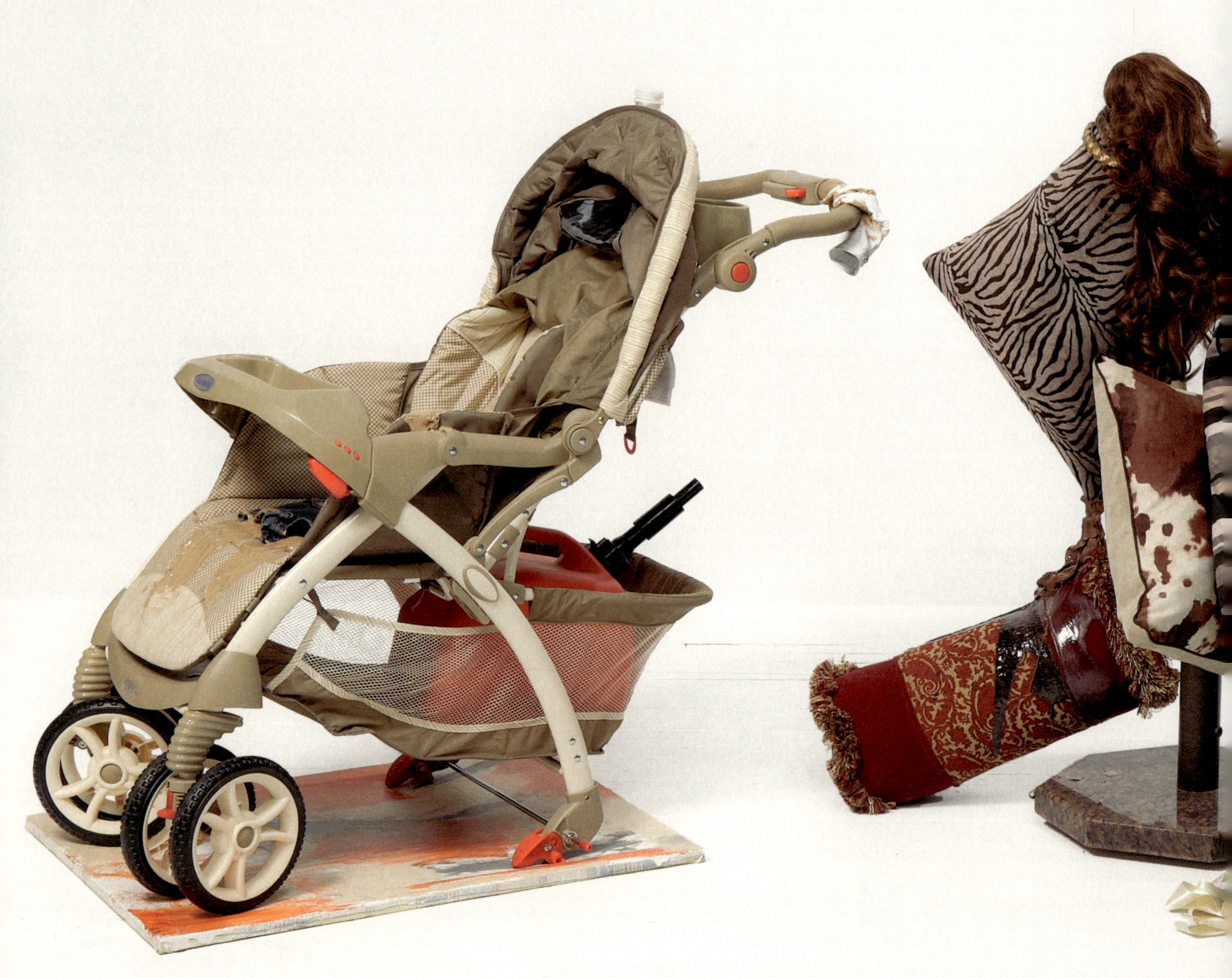

Ryan Trecartin & Lizzie Fitch
Agenda Pusher
2008

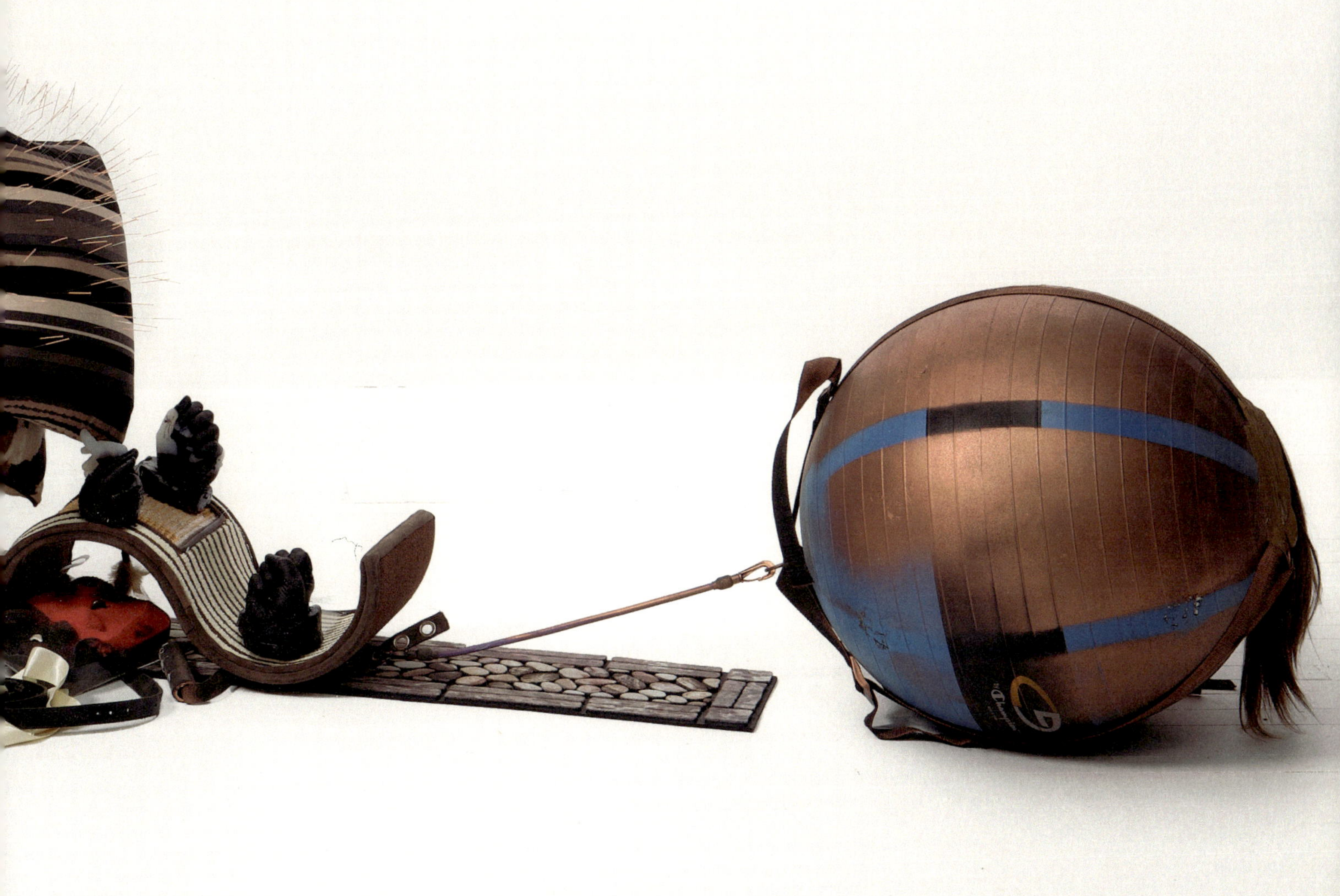

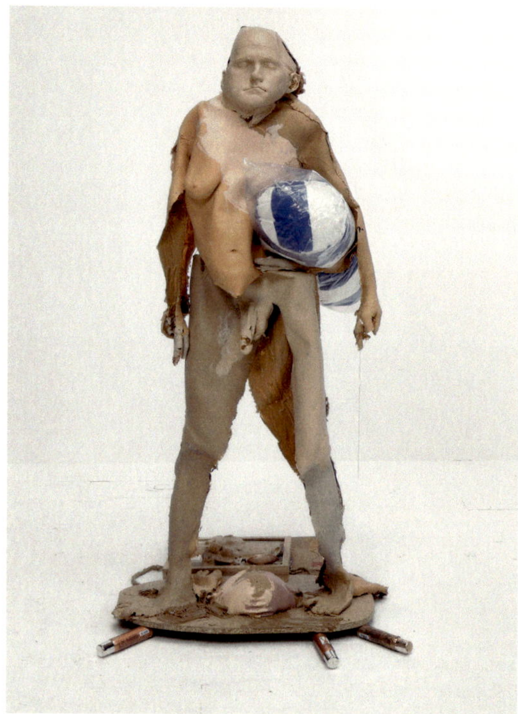 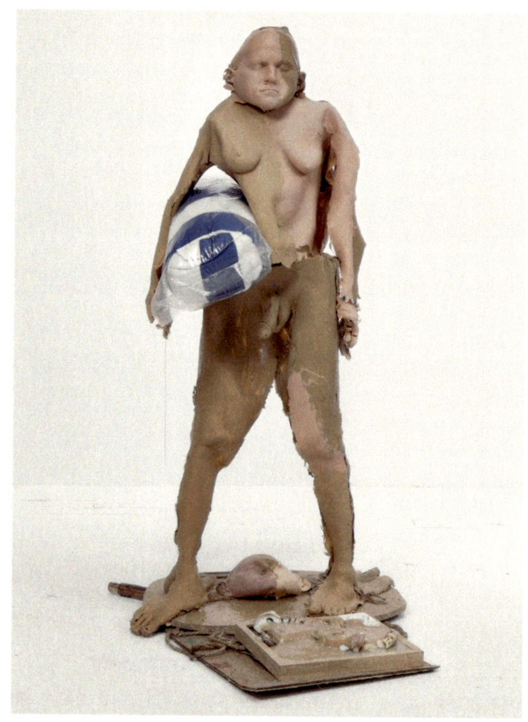

At first glance, Ryan Trecartin and Lizzie Fitch's sculptures are marked on the one hand by their fragility and the small scale of their components, and on the other by their bluntly colorful narration and their formal playfulness. For instance, in the sculpture *Choice Shopping* (2006), a character with a pumpkin-like head extends a hand toward an anthropomorphic stocking figure reminiscent of Hans Bellmer's dolls, barely touching it. Upon closer inspection, we see that this affectionate gesture determines the form of the stocking figure, because it alone keeps the stocking under tension. At a second glance, we recognize that the body proper of the stocking figure is composed of a variety of consumer goods. The gesture of affection for consumption becomes the agency that defines the body. (→ XMAS AND BUY, BUY, BUY) In making their sculptures, Trecartin and Fitch draw on a variety of techniques, prominent among them paper-mâché, and frequently collaborate with other artists. (→ OUR OWN COMMUNITY) Paper-mâché is not only a simple and inexpensive way to create a sculptural body, but it also recalls childhood experiences of using it to make masks and costumes. (→ CARNIVALESQUE) (→ D(O)I(T)Y(OURSELF) AND BRICOLAGE) The sculptures often also serve as props and settings in Trecartin's films.

In his often feature-length videos, Ryan Trecartin creates dream-like narratives, in which role-playing games and video manipulations repeatedly fragment classic narrative patterns—now with graphic sequences that draw on the aesthetic of music videos, now with advertising-like insertions. (→ EXPERIMENTAL FILM / VIDEO) The main narratives of Trecartin's films engage with contemporary American youth culture and its escapist flights from reality. His rapid cuts create a tension between the different formats, forms, and readings. (→ FICTION AND NARRATIVE METHODS) (→ WAR OF FORMS) Another means of guiding their reception is the variety of distribution methods the artist employs, presenting his films as clips on YouTube, but also in movie theaters, or integrating them in installations in exhibition spaces. (→ YOUTUBE) The artist himself, members of his family, and friends such as Lizzie Fitch play multiple roles. The films are strongly "over-acted," as the characters engage in exaggerated histrionics both in their gestures and their facial expressions. The actors usually wear non-naturalistic make-up and appear in eccentric costumes. In the postproduction phase, Trecartin uses audio-visual distortion to defamiliarize the entire act, inserting graphic effects, and distorting or heightening voices. (→ IDENTITY MARKETING)

Die Skulpturen von Ryan Trecartin und Lizzie Fitch zeichnen sich auf den ersten Blick einerseits durch ihre Fragilität und Kleinteiligkeit, andererseits durch ihre farbenfrohe, formverspielte und narrative Plakativität aus. In der Skulptur *Choice Shopping* (2006) streckt etwa eine Figur mit kürbishaftem Kopf ihre Hand nach einer – an Hans Bellmers Puppen erinnernde – anthropomorphe Strumpffigur aus und berührt diese knapp. Bei genauerem Hinsehen wird sichtbar, dass die Geste der Zuneigung die Form der Strumpffigur bestimmt, da nur so die Spannung des Strumpfs bestehen kann. Erst auf den zweiten Blick wird erkennbar, dass der eigentliche Körper der Strumpffigur aus verschiedensten Konsumgütern gebildet wird. Die Geste der Zuneigung hin zum Konsum wird zu einer den Körper definierenden Instanz. (→ XMAS AND BUY, BUY, BUY) Für ihre Skulpturen, die mit den unterschiedlichsten Materialien gefertigt wurden, wovon eine der wichtigsten das Pappmaché darstellt, kollaborieren Trecartin und Fitch oftmals mit weiteren Künstlern. (→ OUR OWN COMMUNITY) Die Technik des Pappmaché ist nicht nur eine einfache und kostengünstige Methode, einen skulpturalen Körper aufzubauen, sondern erinnert auch an Kindheitserfahrungen, wobei man mittels dieser Technik Masken und Kostüme bastelte. (→ CARNIVALESQUE) (→ D(O)I(T)Y(OURSELF) AND BRICOLAGE) Die Skulpturen dienen des Öfteren auch als Props und Bühnenbilder für Trecartins Filme.

In seinen Videos, die oftmals Spielfilmlänge haben, schafft Ryan Trecartin traumartige Erzählungen, in denen klassische Erzählmuster durch Rollenspiele und Videomanipulationen immer wieder aufgebrochen werden – sei es durch grafische Sequenzen, die an Musikvideos angelehnt sind, oder werbeartige «Einspieler». (→ EXPERIMENTAL FILM / VIDEO) In der Hauptnarration der Filme thematisiert Trecartin die heutige amerikanische Jugendkultur mit ihren Realitätsfluchten. Durch den schnellen Schnitt schafft

RYAN TRECARTIN Born 1981 in Webster, Texas. Lives and works in Philadelphia EDUCATION 2004 BFA, Rhode Island School of Design LIZZIE FITCH Born 1981 in Bloomington, Indiana. Lives and works in Philadelphia EDUCATION 2004 BFA, Rhode Island School of Design SOLO EXHIBITIONS — 2009 Elizabeth Dee Gallery, New York — 2007 *Big Room Now*, Crane Arts, Philadelphia GROUP EXHIBITIONS — 2009 *Solaris*, Gio Marconi, Milan — 2008 *Funny Not Funny*, Bellwether Gallery, New York; *The Left Hand of Darkness*, The Project, New York; Vestfossen Kunstlaboratorium, Vestfossen — 2007 Milan Triennial; *Between Two Deaths*, ZKM, Karlsruhe — Ryan Trecartin has shown his video/film work worldwide among others in the exhibitions *The Generational: Younger than Jesus*, New Museum, New York (2009), Whitney Biennial (2006), Hammer Museum, Los Angeles (2008) and Wexner Center for the Arts, Columbus (2008). — Numerous screenings, performances and lectures worldwide.

Trecartin ein Spannungsverhältnis zwischen den verschiedenen Formaten, Formen und Lesarten. (→FICTION AND NARRATIVE METHODS) (→WAR OF FORMS) Die Rezeption wird einerseits in der vielfältigen Distribution der Filme gesteuert, die der Künstler einerseits als Clips auf YouTube präsentiert, andererseits in Kinos zeigt oder aber in Installationen in Ausstellungsräume integriert. (→YOUTUBE) Der Künstler nimmt nebst Familienmitgliedern und Freund/innen wie Lizzie Fitch selber mehrere Rollen ein. Die Filme zeichnen sich durch ein starkes «over-acting» aus, das heisst, dass der Modus des Schauspiels sowohl in Gestik als auch Mimik stark überzeichnet ist. Zusätzlich sind die Schauspieler meist auf unnaturalistische Weise geschminkt und treten in exzentrischen Kostümen auf. In der Postproduktion verfremdet Trecartin den gesamten Akt auf der audiovisuellen Ebene; grafische Effekte werden eingebaut, Stimmen verzerrt oder erhöht. (→IDENTITY MARKETING)

U — FOR UNICORN

The unicorn—a horse-like mythical creature with a single horn on its forehead—has been a frequent motif in art and literature since the Middle Ages. An especially important source of this creature's popularity was the book *Physiologus*, created in the Near East between the 2nd and 4th centuries CE, which offers typological readings of animals, plants, and stones.[60] As a symbol of the good, of genuine inviolacy and innocence, the unicorn has sometimes been used as an attribute of the Virgin Mary, and it continues to figure (perhaps more strongly than ever) in our contemporary culture, having experienced a particular revival as a symbol during the New Age movement. (→KARMA AND OTHER NEW AGE STUFF) But by way of fantasy culture, it simultaneously became a much-cited symbol in various derivations of pop culture. (→QUOTES) One well-known example is the animated movie *The Last Unicorn* (1982), based on Peter S. Beagle's novel of the same title, which presents an epically sappy treatment of the themes of redemption and sacrifice. One song from the film, sung by the actress Mia Farrow, serves as a narrative component in Shana Moulton's video *Whispering Pines 7* (2006).[61] (→SHANA MOULTON) In the first climax of the film, the unicorn, which has been transformed into a young woman, sings a song lamenting its new state, in which it confronts the human experience of being in love. Unicorn-like beings and various fantastic creatures also appear in the comic-strip worlds of Jessica Ciocci, who uses them to frame a critique of consumerist desires. (→PAPER RAD)

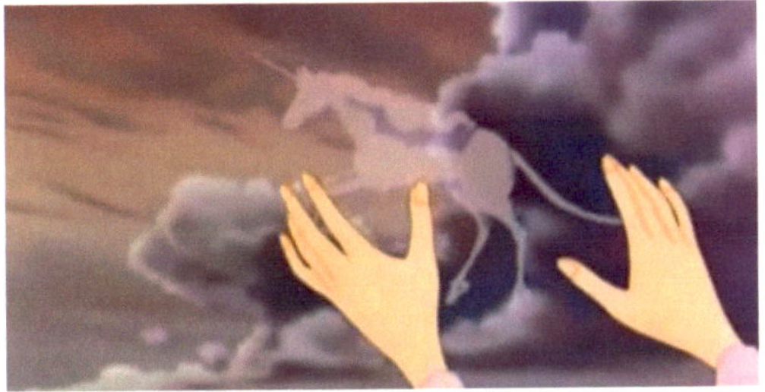

Still from *The Last Unicorn*, 1982

Das Einhorn – ein pferdeähnliches Fabeltier mit einem Horn auf der Stirn – ist seit dem Mittelalter in Kunst und Literatur ein häufig verwendetes Motiv. Besonders bekannt wurde dieses Wesen durch die Schrift *Physiologus*, die zwischen dem 2. und 4. Jahrhundert im Vorderen Orient entstand und in der Tiere, Pflanzen und Steine christlich-typologisch gedeutet werden.[62] Als Symbol für das Gute, genuin Unberührte und Unverdorbene wurde das Einhorn mitunter als Attribut der Jungfrau Maria ver-

wendet und ist auch (und gerade) heute noch in unserer Kultur vertreten. Ein Revival erlebte das Einhorn insbesondere als Symbol in der New-Age-Bewegung. (→KARMA AND OTHER NEW AGE STUFF) Gleichzeitig wurde dieses auch via Fantasy-Kultur zum viel zitierten Symbol in unterschiedlichen Derivaten der Pop-Kultur. (→QUOTES) Bekannt ist etwa der Animationsfilm *The Last Unicorn* aus dem Jahr 1982, der nach der gleichnamigen Erzählung von Peter S. Beagle verfilmt wurde und in welchem eine kitschig-epische Erlösungs- und Aufopferungsthematik aufgenommen wurde. Ein Song aus dem Film, synchronisiert von der Schauspielerin Mia Farrow, dient Shana Moulton in ihrem Video *Whispering Pines 7* (2006) als narrative Komponente.[63] (→SHANA MOULTON) Während des retardierenden Moments des Films singt das Einhorn, welches im Filmverlauf in eine junge Frau verwandelt wurde, ein Klagelied über seinen transformierten Zustand, in dem es mit der menschlichen Erfahrung des Verliebtseins konfrontiert wird. Einhorn-ähnliche Wesen und verschiedene Fantasiegestalten finden auch Eingang in die Comic-Welten von Jessica Ciocci, die anhand dieser ihre Kritik an Konsumsehnsüchten formuliert. (→PAPER RAD)

V — FOR VOID [64]

60—Cf. Jürgen Einhorn, *Spiritalis unicornis: Das Einhorn als Bedeutungsträger in Literatur und Kunst des Mittelalters*, Munich 1998.

61 See the scene "Now that I'm a Woman" from *The Last Unicorn*: http://www.youtube.com/watch?v=IlUnq2d9pMU&feature=related.

62—Vgl. Jürgen Einhorn, *Spiritalis unicornis: Das Einhorn als Bedeutungsträger in Literatur und Kunst des Mittelalters*, München 1998.

63—*Now that I'm a Woman*-Filmszene aus *The Last Unicorn*: http://www.youtube.com/watch?v=IlUnq2d9pMU&feature=related.

64—Regarding the empty exhibition, which is, as it were, the antithesis, see *Voids. A Retrospective*, John Armleder et al (ed.), Zurich 2009. Zur leeren Ausstellung, die gleichsam die Antithese bildet: *Voids. A Retrospective*, hrsg. von John Armleder et al. Zürich 2009.

W—FOR WAR OF FORMS

Documenta 12, curated by Roger Buergel and Ruth Noack, was
guided by three leitmotifs; the first was the question of a
"migration of form(s)." The show emphasized formal corre-
spondences between widely differing works in order to generate and redistribute meaning.[65] The concept of a "migration
of form(s)" promises a positive approach implying coexistence,
but we must also ask whether a war of forms is not in fact the
prevalent state of affairs today. (≠VOID)

Die Documenta 12 von Roger Buergel und Ruth Noack wurde
von drei Leitmotiven geleitet, wovon das erste Motiv die Frage
nach einer «Migration der Form(en)» stellte. Dabei standen
die formalen Korrespondenzen zwischen unterschiedlichsten
Arbeiten im Vordergrund, um auf diese Weise Bedeutungen
neu zu erzeugen und zu verteilen.[66] Während der Begriff der
«Migration der Form(en)» einen positivistischen Ansatz ver-
spricht, der ein Miteinander impliziert, muss auch gefragt werden, ob heute nicht vielmehr ein Krieg der Formen vorherrscht.
(≠VOID)

X—FOR XMAS AND BUY, BUY, BUY

Christmas is the holiday when people celebrate the birth of
Jesus and thus, according to Christian belief, the incarnation
of the second divine person, the "logos." The central holiday
is December 25, but celebrations begin at sundown on the
preceding evening, or Christmas Eve. Christmas is more commercialized than any other Christian holiday; commercialization begins long before the Advent season proper. Statistics
show that Christmas is the year's most important period of
consumerism, accounting, in some industries, for up to 20 percent of annual sales. Festivities often include an exchange
of gifts.[67]

Weihnachten ist das Fest der Geburt Jesu und damit nach christ-
lichem Glauben der Menschwerdung der zweiten göttlichen
Person, dem «Logos». Festtag ist der 25. Dezember, dessen
Feierlichkeiten mit Sonnenuntergang am Vorabend, am Heilig-
abend, beginnen. Wie bei keinem anderen Fest des Christentums
findet eine starke Kommerzialisierung statt, die lange vor der
eigentlichen Adventszeit einsetzt. Statistiken zeigen, dass Weihnachten in vielen Ländern *das* Konsumereignis des Jahres ist
und in manchen Branchen bis zu 20 Prozent des Jahresumsatzes
ausmacht. Die Festlichkeiten gehen oftmals mit einem Gaben-
tausch einher.[68]

Y—FOR YOUTUBE

Over the course of only four years, YouTube has become the
leading online video platform. Users can watch, post, and
distribute movie files of any sort. In 2007, YouTube already
accounted for a full tenth of total Internet data traffic.[69] In
November 2006, Google Inc. bought YouTube for the spectacular sum of $1.65 billion in Google stock. This platform is of
interest to artists not only as a distribution channel; the video
material others upload in turn becomes material for their

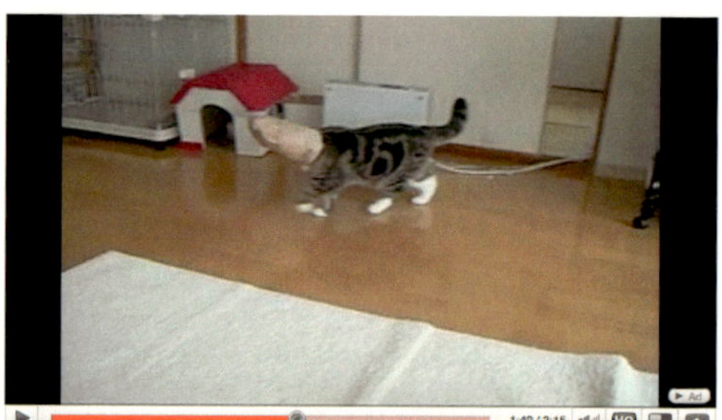

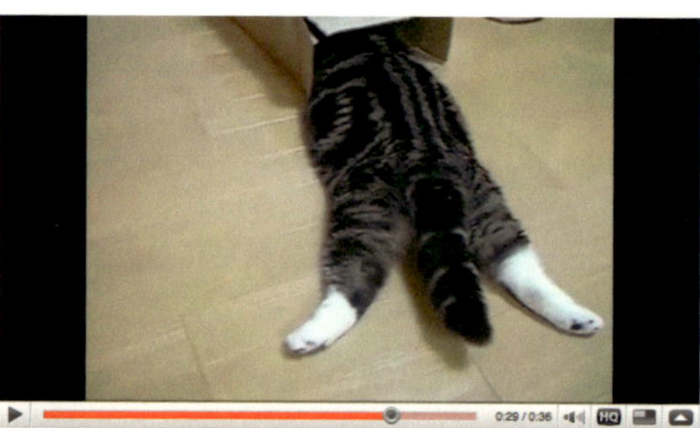

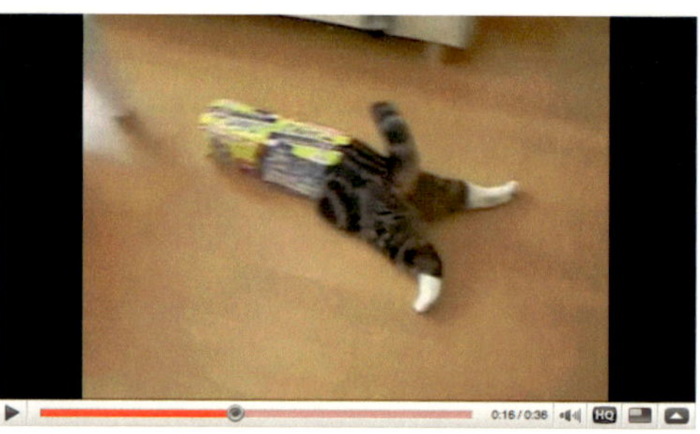

artistic work. (→CORY ARCANGEL) (→PAPER RAD) (→SHANA MOULTON)
(→RYAN TRECARTIN & LIZZIE FITCH) In this sense, YouTube must also
be seen as a site for guerrilla marketing, especially for artists.
(→BIOPOLITICS) Yet the carnivalesque aspect (→CARNIVALESQUE)
of YouTube—copyright laws are at least temporarily suspend-
ed—must also be seen critically: YouTube's terms of use stipu-
late that the company can sell or license uploaded content
without requiring the author's consent. With its aspects of the
collection, preservation, and archiving of imagery, YouTube
has also become an object of interest in studies of visual culture. Publishing and watching clips on YouTube seems to have
become a popular sport. Images of any kind (with the excep-
tion, thus YouTube, of pornographic and violent material;
although this is not entirely correct, as a search for keywords
such as "rape," "kidnapping," or "suicide" demonstrates) form
a seamless stream. Still, we may well ask whether this platform will retain its popularity, or whether another technology
will supplant it in a few years' time.

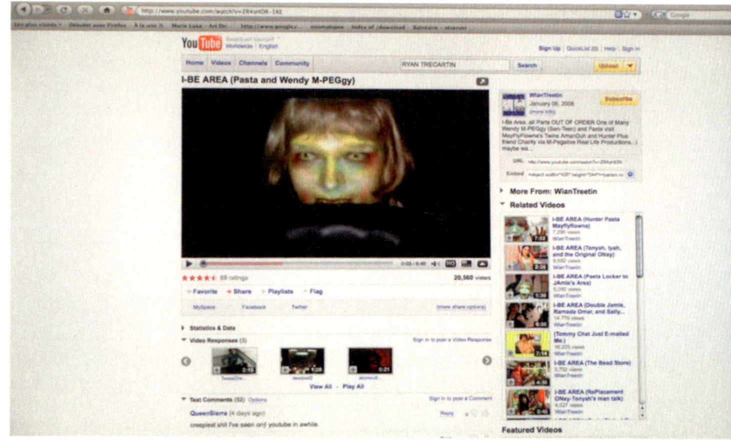

65—Cf. *Documenta Magazine No. 1, 2007, Modernity?*, Georg Schöllhammer
(ed.), Cologne 2007.

66—Vgl. *Documenta Magazine No. 1, 2007, Modernity?*, hrsg. von Georg
Schöllhammer, Köln 2007.

67—The seminal contribution to the concept of "gift exchange"—virtually all
cultures know a form of exchange of goods that serves to stabilize relationships—has been made by the sociologist Marcel Mauss. Cf. Marcel Mauss,
The Gift. The Form and Reason for Exchange in Archaic Societies, W.D. Halls
(trans.), New York 1990. (French original: Marcel Mauss, *Essai sur le don.
Forme et raison de l'échange dans les sociétés archaïques*, 1923/24.)

68—Das Konzept des «Gabentauschs» – praktisch jede Kultur kennt eine solche
Form des Warentauschs zur Stabilisierung von Beziehungen – ist ein Begriff, der
vom Soziologen Marcel Mauss stark geprägt wurde. Vgl. Marcel Mauss, *Die Gabe:
Form und Funktion des Austauschs in archaischen Gesellschaften*, Frankfurt 2001
(Erstveröffentlichung in Französisch: Marcel Mauss, *Essai sur le don. Forme et
raison de l'échange dans les sociétés archaïques*, 1923/24).

69—Current statistics continue to show an upward trend; cf. http://www.
youtube.com.

Innerhalb von nur vier Jahren hat sich YouTube zur führenden Plattform für Online-Videos entwickelt. YouTube kann zum Ansehen, Zeigen und Distribuieren von Filmdateien jeglicher Art genutzt werden. Bereits 2007 wurde ein Zehntel des gesamten Datenverkehrs von Internet-Usern via YouTube genutzt.[70] Im November 2006 wurde YouTube von Google Inc. für die spektakuläre Summe von 1,31 Milliarden Euro übernommen. YouTube ist heute für Künstler nicht nur als Distributionsplattform von Interesse, sondern das hochgeladene Videomaterial fremder Personen fliesst wiederum in die künstlerische Produktion ein. (→ CORY ARCANGEL) (→ PAPER RAD) (→ SHANA MOULTON) (→ RYAN TRECARTIN & LIZZIE FITCH) So ist YouTube auch als Guerilla-Marketing-Ort zu verstehen, insbesondere für Künstler. (→ BIOPOLITICS) Das karnevaleske Moment (→ CARNIVALESQUE) im Sinne eines zumindest momentanen Aushebelns von Urheberrechtsbestimmungen, muss jedoch auch kritisch betrachtet werden: In den Geschäftsbedingungen von YouTube ist reglementiert, dass hochgeladene Inhalte weiterverkauft oder lizenziert werden können, ohne den Autor vorher um Zustimmung fragen zu müssen. Auch für die Bildwissenschaft ist das Phänomen YouTube mit seinen Aspekten des Sammelns, Bewahrens und Archivierens von Bildern ins Interessenfeld gerückt. Die Aktivitäten auf der Plattform scheinen sich geradezu zu einem Volkssport entwickelt zu haben. Bilder jeglicher Art (ausgenommen sind laut YouTube Pornografie- und Gewaltvideos, was jedoch auch nur begrenzt stimmt, man suche beispielsweise nach Schlagwörtern wie «Vergewaltigung», «Entführung» oder «Selbstmord») fügen sich reibungslos aneinander. Die Frage ist jedoch berechtigt, ob diese Plattform in einigen Jahren immer noch derart populär sein oder bereits von einer anderen Technologie abgelöst wird.

Z — FOR ZAK MCKRACKEN AND THE ALIEN MINDBENDERS

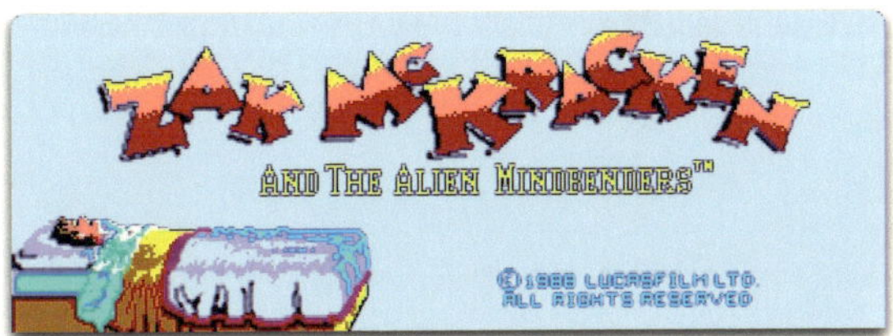

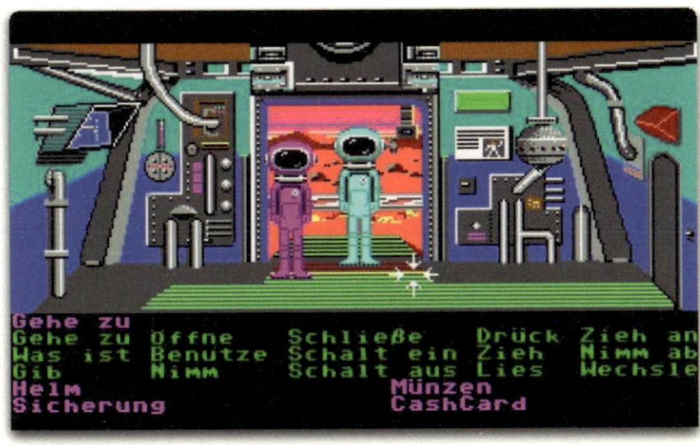

Zak McKracken and the Alien Mindbenders is a computer game in the point-and-click adventure genre, published by Lucasfilm Games in 1988. The player slips into the role of the "nerd" and journalist Zak McKracken, travelling across the globe to save the world from an invasion of enemy aliens. (→ NERD) The screen is divided into three sections for the game's fictional world, an inventory of verbs of action, and a list of props the player has collected, creating not only a large radius of possible action but also a virtually exponential number of combina-

tions. In *Zak McKracken and the Alien Mindbenders* and a generation of similar games, this ternary combinatorics (in the sense of "use" [verb of action] "key" [collected prop] and "door" [fictional world]) opens up a form of interactive complexity. For the first time in a computer game, this gives rise to an ongoing and interesting fiction (→ FICTION AND NARRATIVE METHODS), a fiction to which critics have applied Gérard Genette's narratology with his distinction between plot, story, and narration.[71] Today, the connection between computer games, narrative, and potential cognitive changes in teenagers is a much-debated issue. One problem with computer games is the combination of linear narrative structures with non-linear gaming structures. The failure to integrate them is a typical phenomenon in older games, in which narrative elements and changes in the structure of the game remain unrelated to one another, such that the narrative structures present an unvarying appearance irrespective of the progress of the game. Changes toward a more complex gaming structure have led to rapid growth of the industry over the past 20 years; computer games are now a multi-billion dollar industry. (→ XMAS AND BUY, BUY, BUY) Moreover, video game characters, such as the plumber Mario, have found their way into the pop-cultural canon; a variety of contemporary cultural products quote and reuse them. (→ CORY ARCANGEL) (→ PAPER RAD) (→ QUOTES)

Zak McKracken and the Alien Mindbenders ist ein 1988 erschienenes Computerspiel der Firma Lucasfilm, das dem Genre des Point-and-Click-Adventure angehört. Der Spieler übernimmt die Rolle des «nerd»-Journalisten Zak McKracken und reist kreuz und quer durch die Welt, um diese vor einer Invasion feindlich gesinnter Ausserirdischen zu retten. (→ NERD) Die Dreiteilung des Bildschirms in Spielraum, Inventar von Aktionsverben und einer Liste von gesammelten Spielgegenständen ermöglicht dem Spieler nicht nur einen grossen Aktionsradius, sondern gleichsam eine exponentiell hohe Anzahl von Kombinationen. *Zak McKracken and the Alien Mindbenders* gehört zu einer Generation von Computerspielen, die durch diese Dreierkombinatorik (im Sinne von: «benutze» [Aktionsverb] «Schlüssel» [gesammelter Gegenstand] mit «Tür» [Spielraum]) eine Form komplexer Interaktivität eröffnet. Dadurch entsteht auch eine fortlaufende Fiktion (→ FICTION AND NARRATIVE METHODS), wobei Gérard Genettes Erzähltheorie mit seiner Unterscheidung in Geschichte, Erzählung und Narration anwendbar wird.[72] Gerade der Zusammenhang von Computerspielen, Narration und möglichen kognitiven Veränderungen bei Jugendlichen ist heute ein viel diskutiertes Thema. Ein Problem der Computerspiele liegt in der Kombination linearer Erzählstrukturen mit den nonlinearen Spielstrukturen. Das Misslingen einer Integration ist ein typisches Phänomen in älteren Spielen, in denen Erzählelemente und Veränderungen in der Spielstruktur noch nicht aufeinander bezogen werden können, sodass sich die Erzählstrukturen immer in gleicher Weise präsentieren – unabhängig vom Fortschritt des Spiels. Solche Veränderungen Richtung grösserer Komplexität der Spielstruktur liess diese Industrie in den letzten 20 Jahren zu einem Multimilliardensektor anwachsen. (→ XMAS AND BUY, BUY, BUY) Ebenso haben sich Spielfiguren wie der Klempner Mario in einen populärkulturellen Kanon vorgearbeitet und werden heute in verschiedenen Kulturerzeugnissen zitiert und verwendet. (→ CORY ARCANGEL) (→ PAPER RAD) (→ QUOTES)

70—Die laufenden Statistiken zeigen im Moment immer noch einen Aufwärtstrend. Vgl. http://www.youtube.com.

71—Cf. Karin Wenz, "Computerspiele: Hybride Formen zwischen Spiel und Erzählung," http://www.netzliteratur.net/wenz/wenz_computerspiele.htm (4/17/2009).
72—Vgl. Karin Wenz, «Computerspiele: Hybride Formen zwischen Spiel und Erzählung», Internet 17. 04. 2009: http://www.netzliteratur.net/wenz/wenz_computerspiele.htm.

LIST OF WORKS

pp. 3–5, 92
CORY ARCANGEL
*a couple thousand short films
about Glenn Gould*
2007
Dual-channel projection from a digital
source (02:09 min, color, sound)
Commissioned by the Film and Video
Umbrella
Courtesy of the artist and Team
Gallery, New York
Installation view / Photo:
The Northern Gallery of
Contemporary Art, Sunderland, UK

p. 23
PAPER RAD
P-Unit Mixtape 2005
2005
Single-channel projection (21:08 min,
color, sound)
Courtesy of the artists and Electronic
Arts Intermix, New York

pp. 24/64/65/92
JACOB CIOCCI
Untitled (from the *Doodles* Series)
2009
Pencil on Paper (Dimensions variable)
Courtesy of the artist

p. 25
PAPER RAD
P-Unit Mixtape 2005
2005

pp. 27–32
JESSICA CIOCCI
Untitled (Grid Drawings)
2009
Marker on paper (21 x 28 cm)
Courtesy of the artist

pp. 43–45
SHANA MOULTON
Whispering Pines 4
2007
Single-channel projection
(10:53 min, color, sound)
Courtesy of the artist, Broadway
1602, New York and Electronic Arts
Intermix, New York

p. 47
SHANA MOULTON
Whispering Pines 8
2006
Single-channel projection (07:34 min,
color, sound)
Courtesy of the artist, Broadway
1602, New York and Electronic Arts
Intermix, New York

pp. 48–49
SHANA MOULTON
Sand Saga
2008
Single-channel projection (10:32 min,
color, sound)
Courtesy of the artist, Broadway
1602, New York and Electronic Arts
Intermix, New York

pp. 50–51
SHANA MOULTON
(in collaboration with Lucy Stein)
Exstasi Exstano
2008
Single-channel projection
(06:47 min, color, sound)
Courtesy of the artists and Broadway
1602, New York

p. 52
SHANA MOULTON
Whispering Pines 7
2006
Single-channel projection
(04:43 min, color, sound)
Courtesy of the artist, Broadway
1602, New York and Electronic Arts
Intermix, New York

pp. 66–67
JACOB CIOCCI
Untitled (Don't Piss on Me Obama)
2009
Acrylic and collage on Paper
(21.59 x 35.56 cm)
Courtesy of the artist

p. 68
JACOB CIOCCI
Untitled (inside the fall out shelter)
2009
Pencil on Paper (21.59 x 27.94 cm)
Courtesy of the artist

p. 69
JACOB CIOCCI
Untitled (from bad to worse puff)
2009
Acrylic and collage on paper
(21.59 x 27.94 cm)
Courtesy of the artist

p. 70
JACOB CIOCCI
Untitled
2007
Acrylic and collage on wood
(60.96 x 121.92 cm)
Courtesy of the artist

p. 71
Exhibition view: The Mattress Factory
Art Museum, Pittsburgh
*Predrive: After Technology – Jessica
Ciocci & Jacob Ciocci (Paper Rad)*
November 14 – April 5, 2009
Photo: The Mattress Factory Art
Museum. Pittsburgh

p. 72
JACOB CIOCCI
Untitled (Dogtailz)
2007
Acrylic and collage on Paper
(21.59 x 27.94 cm)
Courtesy of the artist

p. 81
RYAN TRECARTIN & LIZZIE FITCH
2 Companies, 1 Bed
2008
Acrylic paint, mirror, pillow,
cardboard, screws, ink, wig,
caulk, contact cement, plastic and
dragonskin
119.4 x 86.4 x 195.6 cm
Goetz Collection, Munich
Photo: Aaron Igler

p. 82
RYAN TRECARTIN & LIZZIE FITCH
Import Landscape Exploit
2008
Pier 1 giraffe, hair, hair extensions,
plastic, skirt, plastic grass,
decorative straw, pillows, Plasty-
paste, rocks, Quick copper, acrylic
paint, Ikea canvas, wood, wheels,
Tupperware, natural kitty litter,
corn, foam, paper mache, swimming
trunks, feathers, bric, Ikea painting,
woven cornucopia, birdseed, jersey,
condoms, caulk, sponge, shoes and
sports bag
213.4 x 167.6 x 121.9 cm
Courtesy of the artists and Elizabeth
Dee Gallery, New York
Photo: Aaron Igler

p. 83
RYAN TRECARTIN & LIZZIE FITCH
Early Catcher
2008
Cardboard, printed paper, acrylic
medium, plastic, contact cement,
caulk, bra, baby toy, Dragonskin,
Target painting for girl's bedroom,
seashells, Nalgene water bottle,
baseball mitt, Wiffle ball, pillow
feathers, baseball bat, plastic cup,
sand and plastic shreds
160 x 114.3 cm
Goetz Collection, Munich
Photo: Aaron Igler

pp. 84–85
RYAN TRECARTIN & LIZZIE FITCH
Choice Shopping
2006
Mixed media
259.1 x 198.1 x 114.3 cm
Goetz Collection, Munich
Photo: Aaron Igler

pp. 86–87
RYAN TRECARTIN & LIZZIE FITCH
Agenda Pusher
2008
Baby carriage, rubber, baby shorts,
breast cancer golf glove, Alternative
Energy drink, gasoline tank, acrylic
painting on plaid canvas, Dragonskin,
cat scratch toy, plastic, ribbon, belt,
doormat, wood, exercise ball, hair,
acupuncture needles, fly (insect),
earring, headband, Quick copper,
flagpole stand, thread, pillows, rock
and sand
121.9 x 304.8 x 91.4 cm
Courtesy of the artists and Elizabeth
Dee Gallery, New York
Photo: Aaron Igler

p. 88
RYAN TRECARTIN & LIZZIE FITCH
The Edge, Skinny
2008
Wood, epoxy, thread, rubber, plastic
packaged Ikea pillow, ankle bracelet,
rock and sheep brain vacuum-packed
in formaldehyde
165.1 x 91.4 x 91.4 cm
Goetz Collection, Munich
Photo: Aaron Igler

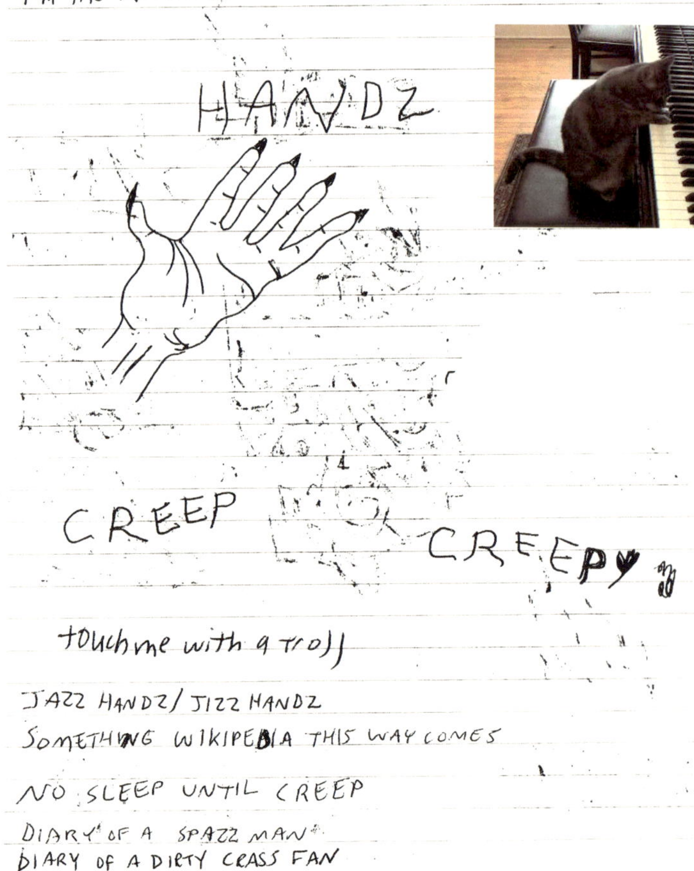

IMPRINT

This book was published on the occasion of the exhibition
DETERIORATION, THEY SAID—CORY ARCANGEL, JESSICA CIOCCI
& JACOB CIOCCI / PAPER RAD, SHANA MOULTON, RYAN TRECARTIN
& LIZZIE FITCH at the migros museum für gegenwartskunst Zürich,
August 29–November 8, 2009.

MUSEUM

DIRECTOR
Heike Munder

CURATOR OF THE EXHIBITION
Raphael Gygax

EXHIBITIONS
COORDINATOR &
REGISTRAR
Judith Welter

ADMINISTRATIVE
MANAGEMENT
Catherine Reymond

ADMINISTRATION
Rosmarie Battaglia

INTERN
Franz Krähenbühl

TECHNICAL MANAGER
EXHIBITIONS
Monika Schori

TECHNICAL MANAGER
COLLECTION
Roland Bösiger

TECHNICAL SUPPORT
Gabi Deutsch
Joël Frattini
Athene Galiciadis
Muriel Gutherz
Basil Kobert

RECEPTION
Céline Beyeler
Valentin Magaro
Christa Michel
Pablo Müller
Katharina Rippstein
Simone Schardt
Mareike Spalteholz

PUBLICATION

PUBLISHED BY
migros museum für
gegenwartskunst
& JRP|Ringier

EDITORS
Raphael Gygax,
Heike Munder

EDITORIAL COORDINATION
Raphael Gygax

TRANSLATION FROM GERMAN
Gerrit Jackson
(Text: Raphael Gygax)

TRANSLATION FROM ENGLISH
Christian Quatmann
(Texts: Thomas Beard,
Ed Halter)

COPY EDITING
& PROOFREADING, GERMAN
Doris Senn

COPY EDITING
& PROOFREADING, ENGLISH
Rowena Smith

CONCEPT & GRAPHIC DESIGN
Marie Lusa

LITHOGRAPHY
Georg Sidler,
Schwyz

PRODUCTION
Odermatt AG,
Dallenwil

The migros museum für gegenwartskunst would like to thank:
Cory Arcangel, Jessica Ciocci, Jacob Ciocci, Lizzie Fitch, Ben Jones,
Shana Moulton, Ryan Trecartin; Broadway 1602, New York,
Elizabeth Dee Gallery, New York, Team Gallery, New York; Leif
Djuhruus, Copenhagen, Goetz Collection, Munich, Enrico Mambretti,
Torino; Film and Video Umbrella, London.

migros museum für
gegenwartskunst
Limmatstrasse 270
CH–8005 Zurich
T +41 (0) 44 277 20 50
F +41 (0) 44 277 62 86
info@migrosmuseum.ch
www.migrosmuseum.ch

migrosmuseum
FÜR GEGENWARTSKUNST
ZÜRICH

The migros museum für
gegenwartskunst is an
institution of the Migros
Culture Percentage.
www.kulturprozent.ch

JRP|Ringier
Letzigraben 134
CH–8047 Zurich
T +41 (0) 43 311 27 50
F +41 (0) 43 311 27 51
info@jrp-ringier.com
www.jrp-ringier.com

jrp|ringier

JRP|Ringier books are
available internationally at
selected bookstores and from
the following distribution
partners:

SWITZERLAND

Buch 2000, AVA
Verlagsauslieferung AG
Centralweg 16
CH–8910 Affoltern a. A.
buch2000@ava.ch
www.ava.ch

FRANCE

Les Presses du réel
35 rue Colson
F–21000 Dijon
info@lespressesdureel.com
www.lespressesdureel.com

GERMANY AND AUSTRIA

Vice Versa Vertrieb
Immanuelkirchstrasse 12
D–10405 Berlin
info@vice-versa-vertrieb.de
www.vice-versa-vertrieb.de

UNITED KINGDOM AND OTHER
EUROPEAN COUNTRIES

Cornerhouse Publications
70 Oxford Street
UK–Manchester M1 5NH
publications@cornerhouse.org
www.cornerhouse.org/books

USA, CANADA, ASIA, AND AUSTRALIA

D. A. P. / Distributed Art
Publishers
155 Sixth Avenue, 2nd Floor
USA–New York, NY 10013
dap@dapinc.com
www.artbook.com

For a list of our partner
bookshops or for any general
questions, please contact
JRP|Ringier directly at
info@jrp-ringier.com,
or visit our homepage
www.jrp-ringier.com
for further information
about our program.